The Sword and the Mask

The Sword and the Mask

Building an Antifragile Approach to Spiritual Warfare

Jon C. Furgeson

WIPF & STOCK · Eugene, Oregon

THE SWORD AND THE MASK
Building an Antifragile Approach to Spiritual Warfare

Copyright © 2022 Jon C. Furgeson. All rights reserved. Except for brief quotations in critical publications or reviews, no part of this book may be reproduced in any manner without prior written permission from the publisher. Write: Permissions, Wipf and Stock Publishers, 199 W. 8th Ave., Suite 3, Eugene, OR 97401.

Wipf & Stock
An Imprint of Wipf and Stock Publishers
199 W. 8th Ave., Suite 3
Eugene, OR 97401

www.wipfandstock.com

PAPERBACK ISBN: 978-1-6667-3652-6
HARDCOVER ISBN: 978-1-6667-9490-8
EBOOK ISBN: 978-1-6667-9491-5

JULY 1, 2022 9:34 AM

Scripture quotations are from the *ESV® Bible (The Holy Bible, English Standard Version®)*, Copyright © 2001 by Crossway, a publishing ministry of Good News Publishers. Used by permission. All rights reserved.

To Alice, Ian, and Aidan, masks of God through whom God's blessings are daily manifest in my life.

Contents

Acknowledgements | ix

Abbreviations | x

1. Defining Spiritual Warfare | 1
2. The Spiritual Salad Bar and the Excluded Middle: Secular and Ecclesial Messiness Regarding the Supernatural in the Post-Enlightened West | 18
3. The Social Approach to Spiritual Warfare and Walter Wink | 33
4. The Pneumatic Approach and C. Peter Wagner | 52
5. The Bifurcated Approach and Lutheran Voices | 69
6. The Antifragile Approach: A Confessional Lutheran Approach to Spiritual Warfare | 108
7. Further Implications of an Antifragile Approach to Spiritual Warfare | 191

Bibliography | 203

Acknowledgements

THIS WORK HAS BEEN long in gestation and those who have encouraged me along the way have been invaluable. I want to express loving thankfulness to my parents, Mel and Donna, and my family, Alice, Ian, and Aidan, for all of their support, encouragement, and patience with their respective son, husband, and father as he navigated this project.

Thanks also goes to Leopoldo Sánchez, Robert Kolb, Thomas Egger, Beth Hoeltke, and the many others at Concordia Seminary who gave encouragement and provided many valuable insights through writing and in conversation.

Thanks also needs to be given to the congregation members of Peace Lutheran Church in St. Louis, Missouri for being constant (and flexible) in their support and encouragement of their pastor in his doctoral efforts. To all of the pastors, friends, and others who have long encouraged me on this project, thanks for your interest and support.

Thanks must also be given to the fallen powers discussed in this book who, like for Luther, have provided the crucible by which God has increased my faith, and, finally, all thanks and praise to God, who takes fragile sinners, like me, and turns us into antifragile saints.

Abbreviations

Ap	Apology of the Augsburg Confession
BDB	Francis Brown, S. R. Driver, and Charles A. Briggs. *Hebrew and English Lexicon of the Old Testament*. Oxford: Clarendon, 1907.
CA	*Confessio Augustana* (Augsburg Confession)
Ep	Epitome of the Formula of Concord
FC	Formula of Concord
LC	Large Catechism
LW	*Luther's Works*, American ed. 55 vols. Philadelphia: Fortress; St. Louis: Concordia, 1955–86.
LSB	Committee on Worship of The Lutheran Church—Missouri Synod. *Lutheran Service Book*. St. Louis: Concordia, 2006.
SA	Smalcald Articles
SC	Small Catechism
SD	Solid Declaration of the Formula of Concord
WA	*Luthers Werke: Kritische Gesamtausgabe*. 65 vols. Weimar: H. Böhlau, 1883–1993.

I

Defining Spiritual Warfare

Four Usual Approaches and a New Definition

When we hear the term *spiritual warfare*, we tend to think of powers which seek to defy God's will and of the Christian in conflict with those evil powers. Spiritual warfare is a term used to reference various views on the antagonistic interaction of those powers with God and his creation, particularly those powers we call *demonic*. Western churches, especially in North America, have increased their attention to this topic over the last sixty years, during which time many articles, studies, and books have been written on it. Yet, most authors who speak of such warfare simply assume it is understood or self-evident and never actually define it.[1] Others avoid the term[2] by using other emphases, such as speaking of

---

1. Some examples include: Arnold, *3 Crucial Questions about Spiritual Warfare*; Beilby and Eddy, *Understanding Spiritual Warfare*; Penn-Lewis and Roberts, *War on the Saints*; Barnhouse, *The Invisible War*; Wagner, *Confronting the Powers*; Alves, *Becoming a Prayer Warrior*; Prince, *Spiritual Warfare*; Arthur, *Lord, is it Warfare?*; and Larson, *Larson's Book of Spiritual Warfare*.

2. There is a debate about whether "warfare" language is even appropriate for the church. A sampling of the spectrum of criticism includes projection of the demonic onto other groups, as in Alon and Omer, *The Psychology of Demonization*; claims against the existence of evil, Cole, *The Myth of Evil*; and the new atheist claim of violence and its origination in religion, such as Harris, *The End of Faith*. In rebuttal, see Wright, *Jesus and the Victory of God*, 450–51; Durst, "Fighting the Good Fight"; and Neufeld, *Killing Enmity*.

the nature of *Powers*,[3] biblical demonology,[4] or deliverance ministry,[5] but very few, regardless of the title they choose, find succinct terminology to describe the whole of the situation they discuss.

Across the writings of the many authors on the subject, most acknowledge a few general factors: spiritual warfare concerns a type of force for evil, often called demonic, which is doing harm in some way. A battleground exists where that evil contests against good. God is involved in some way against the demonic and its actions. Christians are caught in this war, either as victims or soldiers. Beyond these generic descriptions, differences emerge in the details of what these terms mean and how they relate to one another.

For example, a closer look at the differences reveals that the *spiritual* component of this battle is understood in a variety of ways. It may mean strictly the supernatural angels and demons[6] or it can mean the battleground is primarily on a spiritual level, primarily concerning the temptation to sin rather than any overt conflict.[7] It can mean something very technical, like the impersonal interiority of cultural power structures playing out to the health or harm of others within a given sphere of influence.[8]

This wide array of viewpoints emerges from the contrasting theological and hermeneutical perspectives which underlie each paradigm. Issues such as God's saving interaction with his creation and his sovereign authority, biblical inerrancy and inspiration, modern and postmodern philosophical influences, and how much humanity takes center place all have influences on the major approaches to spiritual warfare in the

---

3. Definition can remain elusive even with such alternate strategies. Walter Wink opens the first of his *Powers Trilogy* by admitting, "The reader of this work will search in vain for a definition of power." Wink, *Naming the Powers*, 3. See also: Schlier, *Principalities*; Berkhof, *Christ and the Powers*; and Dawn, *Powers, Weakness, and the Tabernacling of God*.

4. One issue with the term demonology is that it only accounts for the demonic itself, when there are other factors at play. See, for example, Unger, *Biblical Demonology*; and Cook, "Devils and Manticores," 165–84.

5. Deliverance ministry is primarily focused on the removal of demons from individuals. Examples include: Basham, *Deliver Us From Evil*; Finlay, *Demons!*, 122–25; Larson, *Larson's Book of Spiritual Warfare*, 407–64; and MacNutt, *Deliverance from Evil Spirits*.

6. This view is addressed in chapter 4.

7. This perspective is examined in chapter 5.

8. For more on this perspective, see chapter 3.

West. Yet from this disparity emerges a concern for the interrelationship of four parties: God, the visible church, the demonic, and the world. The ways in which these parties are understood and how they interact mark the different contemporary Western approaches to spiritual warfare.

I have categorized these differing views into four main approaches. The first is a *dismissive approach*, wherein the idea of the supernatural outside of God, including intermediary beings such as angels and demons, are relegated to myth. Here, concepts of personal demonic beings are either ignored or demythologized in an attempt to uncover truths about human evil and the church. The second is a *social approach*. Emerging from the dismissive paradigm, it posits the value of symbol in order to interpret biblical supernatural references. It applies these symbols to determine directions for the church's intervention in the face of human evil and societal oppression. The main negative structures noted in the social approach are broken corporate and governmental systems. It connects the "powers" that Paul mentions in his letters to the need for the church to properly address social ills.

The third is what I call the *pneumatic approach*. Pneumatic here means "spiritual." This view attempts to acknowledge the spiritual reality of supernatural beings and merge the physical and spiritual planes into a cohesive narrative. Coming predominantly out of a Pentecostal perspective, this approach emphasizes the faith of the individual Christian expressed in such a way as to have authority over the demonic. The focus here is on the Christian as a type of soldier fighting against demonic powers in various places and at various strengths.

The fourth is what I term the *bifurcated approach*.[9] This is the dominant approach of mainline churches in the West to spiritual warfare. While the pneumatic reality is upheld, there is an underlying bifurcation of the material and spiritual planes of existence, a dualism of separation.[10] The reality of angels and demons is recognized, but how they relate to daily life for the church and in the world, and God's interaction with all of them, lacks specificity and clarity. In other words, the pneumatic reality is not dismissed but it is relegated to esoterism. Such a stance has rendered,

---

9. I have chosen this term as opposed to the use of "classic" by some contemporary theologians like David Powlison for two reasons. First, classic is undescriptive. Second, the bifurcated view is not that of the early church but arises from twentieth-century concerns. I will address this further in chapters 2 and 5. Powlison, *Power Encounters*.

10. This concept of dualistic planes is often termed *the excluded middle* and will be further explored in chapters 2 and 5.

over time, the concepts inherent to spiritual warfare as unfamiliar (and uncomfortable) territory for most mainline Western Christians.

My goals, in looking at these four views, are first to answer the question, "what is a Western, confessional Lutheran approach to spiritual warfare?" and, second, whether or not that answer posits a new approach to the subject (it does) and, third, if that approach has answers for persons beyond confessional Lutherans (it also does). The answer also has implications for economic Trinitarian theology, pastoral care, ethics, and ecumenism. This exploration fills a void in contemporary Lutheran theology, which tends toward the bifurcated approach to this topic,[11] and adds a fresh perspective to the spiritual warfare discussion. There have been other attempts at a Western assessment of positions on spiritual warfare, but they have not moved the conversation forward, nor do they offer perspectives which could be considered for a confessional Lutheran stance.[12] While addressing the issue from a Lutheran perspective, one goal of this project is to create a viable approach to spiritual warfare which would be useful for Christians inside and outside of the Lutheran tradition.

From a review of the available materials, one might initially expect that a proper Lutheran understanding of spiritual warfare would simply be a synthesis of the constructive elements of the latter three approaches (social, pneumatic, and bifurcated), perhaps tied to God's word (the sword of the Spirit, according to Paul in Eph 6:17). However, a mere synthesis of categories around God's word is insufficient. Three concerns emerge when a synthesis is attempted. First, the social approach assumes a mythological, symbolic character in relation to all of the supernatural references in Scripture. This limits the implications of this approach to its own social agenda because it cannot encompass the larger picture of God's action when it denies the supernatural world. This hermeneutical approach to Scripture also challenges its synthesis with a confessional Lutheran approach and its traditional stance on the Bible.

Second, and more significant, where the pneumatic and bifurcated approaches do provide a rare definition of spiritual warfare, those definitions imply some level of dualism between God and the devil. Chuck Lawless and John Franklin, for example, define spiritual warfare as "the conflict of two opposing wills—namely that of God and his followers

---

11. This assertion will be examined in chapter 5.

12. For example, Coleman, "Principalities & Powers"; and M. Wagner, "Overcoming the Demonic Distortions."

Defining Spiritual Warfare

versus Satan and his followers."[13] Similarly, Gregory Boyd defines his warfare worldview:

> Stated most broadly, this worldview is that perspective on reality which centers on the conviction that the good and evil, fortunate or unfortunate, aspects of life are to be interpreted largely as the result of good and evil, friendly or hostile, spirits warring against each other and against us.[14]

Or even C. S. Lewis, describing the Christian situation in warfare terms, implies a dualism of good and evil:

> Enemy-occupied territory—that is what this world is. Christianity is the story of how the rightful king has landed, you might say landed in disguise, and is calling us all to take part in a great campaign of sabotage.[15]

In each of these quotes, there is an implication about God's sovereignty. These views imply that somehow God is not able to eradicate evil completely or is unable to control the portions of the natural and supernatural aspects of his creation which work at odds with his will. This is a type of dualism. Also, this dualism implies that Jesus has not completely won the victory and is only partially reigning. Neither of these implications or positions integrate with Lutheran doctrine.

The third major hurdle to the synthesis of the other approaches is the typical assertion of the place of Christians in spiritual warfare. This will be explored in later chapters, but a brief sketch is in order here. In the social approach, there is an impetus placed on the Christian and the corporate church to be the catalyst for all positive change in the world. In this view, spiritual warfare is summed up as God expressing a mandate for Christians to act for mercy and justice on behalf of the neighbor. In other words, the law engages the Christian and requires him to act for the other in a fight for justice. In the pneumatic approach, the Christian's role is put primarily in martial terms. The Christian is enlisted in the war against the demonic to fight against the power of evil.[16] This view is

---

13. Lawless and Franklin, *Spiritual Warfare*, 7.

14. Boyd, *God at War*, 13. Boyd's work is primarily on spiritual warfare doctrine in pursuit of theodicy. His conclusion is that God does not have foreknowledge, so can only react to evil after the fact, but cannot prevent it if he guesses the future incorrectly.

15. Lewis, *Mere Christianity*, 46.

16. As a further example, "You are in the middle of that war. Whether your heart is peace-loving or warlike makes no difference. You can't get out of it. You can only

derived, for example, from 2 Tim 2:3 which speaks of Christians as "good soldiers" for Christ. This comment and others of Paul's are taken out of their greater context and combined with Paul's discussion in Ephesians about the "whole armor of God" in an attempt to create a full metaphor for Christian life as battle and as the soldier's struggle. However, a close reading of these passages does not produce this militaristic picture. In context, the imagery Paul chooses is limited by its greater context, where we find his emphasis is not warfare or battle in any usual sense.[17]

In both the social and pneumatic approaches, there is an anthropological maximalism when addressing spiritual warfare, meaning that the Christian is ultimately found responsible for whether or not Satan and the fallen angels are halted or succeed with their schemes. This centering of success against the fallen powers on humanity is not compatible with Lutheran theology. Additionally, the soldierly metaphor as put forth merely in terms of social justice or demonic battle is inconsistent with a Lutheran understanding of humanity and of Christ's sovereignty.

A New Definition and a New Approach

The aforementioned issues render a synthesis of various approaches wrapped in Lutheran metaphors inadequate. To address these concerns, I have defined spiritual warfare in a new way that is theologically consistent with Scripture and the Lutheran Confessions: *Spiritual warfare is the powers of the fallen creation railing against the reign of Christ.*[18] The confirmation of this definition and its implications will unfold over the course of the book. However, let's unpack some of this now.

The term "fallen creation" refers to those aspects of God's creation, after the fall into sin, of which Scripture speaks as antagonistic toward God's will. As Lutherans, we see these as, first, the sinful nature in each person. The second is the world, both in terms of nature and human culture, both corrupted by sin. The third is the fallen angels, the demons.[19] Each of these powers works (individually and in tandem) to defy God's

---

choose whether to fight or to be mowed down as a civilian casualty." McCallum, *Satan and His Kingdom*, 12.

17. The image from Eph 6 will be examined in more detail in chapter 6.

18. Going forward, this definition will serve as the functional definition of spiritual warfare being used in the antifragile approach.

19. LC III.101–102 in Kolb and Wengert, *Book of Concord*, 400.

will and contains components which seek to draw the Christian away from the faith or to encourage the unbeliever to reject the Gospel. In other words, they seek to deny what Jesus Christ has accomplished and intends for humankind.

This leads to another term to unpack, the "reign of Christ." In contrast to the views above, Martin Luther argued that Christ's victory is whole. Christ ascended to heaven and took onto himself all glory and all power over creation. There is no place or being over which he is not sovereign.[20] The Christian is not needed by God for a militaristic strike against demonic entities, nor needed for God to enact justice in the world. God has complete dominion already.

Christ rules now, but it is not yet the Last Day wherein the fullness of the eschaton will be revealed. In that day, Christ will reveal himself in all glory and judge all humans. In this age, between his ascension and return, Christ provides mercy through the Gospel, a mercy on account of which the Holy Spirit saves by bringing persons to faith in Jesus. This gift of faith in the gospel brings about the regeneration of a person as God's child, making him righteous before God on account of Christ. As Philip Melanchthon observes, "Now the gospel brings not the shadow of eternal things but the eternal blessings themselves, the Holy Spirit and the righteousness by which we are righteous before God."[21]

I use the verb "rail" because the fallen powers deny the reality of both Christ's reign and the Holy Spirit's work of regenerating persons through the gospel but cannot alter these truths. They wage war against the effects of this reality. It does not necessarily follow, however, that God and, by extension, the regenerate person, are then at war in opposition to these antagonists. In other words, the fallen creation is at war against God and the church, but the reverse is not true. Instead, in this project I argue that the Christian relies on God to act in his defense when the devils directly assail him and those around him with various stratagems. At the same time, the Christian goes about doing the work to which he is daily called by God, his "vocation" in Luther's terminology. As God acts through these daily works, the schemes of fallen creation are thwarted. Moreover, God can even take the assailing work of the fallen powers and increase the faith of the Christian by them.

---

20. Ep VIII.16 in Kolb and Wengert, *Book of Concord*, 511; see also Matt 28:18 and Eph 4:10.

21. Ap VII.15 in Kolb and Wengert, *Book of Concord*, 176.

Finally, the "spiritual" descriptor of this definition of spiritual warfare serves to describe that which is being assailed, both the Holy Spirit's work and the regenerated spirit of each Christian. It is warfare against the Spirit and against the Christian's spirit. It may take the form of physical persecution, distraction, temptation, or other forms in our concretized world and daily life, but the underlying goal of the actions of the fallen powers is for humans to reject regeneration of their spirit in Christ and deny the reality of the reign of Christ brought to fruition for them through the Holy Spirit's actions.

In light of this definition, then, a proper Lutheran account of spiritual warfare recognizes that the Holy Spirit acts not only by means of word, sacrament, and prayer to preserve, and even strengthen, the regenerated Christian in faith against the warfare of the demonic, the world, and the sinful nature, but also works through the Christian by means of vocation to bring God's recreative acts upon the neighbor.

This account also offers a unifying narrative from aspects of the other approaches and invites them to consider this proposal as well. The social approach's concern is addressed by attending to the Spirit's action through individual and corporate vocation in order to address the various kinds of suffering of the neighbor. This enables the Christian to enact his identity in Christ for the aid of the neighbor, and also reinforces this identity in the Christian. The pneumatic approach's concern is dealt with by attending to the Spirit's preservative and strengthening action for the Christian, individually and corporately, particularly in word and prayer, against the demonic. This work drives the Christian to focus on the work and action of Christ in the midst of the situation, reinforcing faith and identity in Christ.

In forging new ground in spiritual warfare, this book is going to propose a new framework concerning spiritual warfare, a fifth approach. I have called this account of spiritual warfare *the antifragile approach*.[22]

This new approach advances the constructive appropriation of a receptive account of Christian spirituality, grounded in a Spirit Christology, as a fruitful eschatological framework for constructing a contemporary confessional Lutheran account of spiritual warfare. In this account, God and the visible church are not, strictly speaking, at war. The fallen

---

22. The term *antifragile* was coined by Nicolas Nassim Taleb in book of the same title. It represents the concept that an object or being not only can make it through problems unscathed (which would be robust) but actually improves due to adversity (the opposite of fragility). This concept is explored in chapter 6.

aspects of creation wage war against God and the church in an attempt to deny the reality of Christ's victorious reign and the Spirit's enactment of this reality in the regeneration of men by faith. Christians, in contrast, are called upon in the face of the fallen powers to simply embrace their new identity in Christ and enact it in the world. Throughout all of this, God's not only preserves but even strengthens Christians through the adversity of the fallen powers,

This approach is not trivial or esoteric. Rather, it accounts for a proper understanding of the fallen powers in light of the Trinitarian economy of salvation. It offers an augmentation to the understanding of the role of the church in the world and an invigoration of the doctrines of confession, baptism, the Lord's Supper, vocation, and exorcism. It provides the Christian with a proper lens through which to perceive life in Christ in the face of the human and supernatural evils that one encounters. This approach also has potential impact for ecumenical discourse between the Western confessional Lutheran churches and the churches (both Lutheran and other) of the Global South.[23]

What This Book Is Not Doing

Spiritual warfare touches on a slew of other topics that, if addressed, would make this book much too large to be useful. Here are a few of them at a glance and a brief thought on why each is not a focus of this book. These topics include theodicy, a general history of evil spirits in world religions and cultures, the state of Jewish apocalyptic literature at the time of the New Testament, occultism, the psychology of evil, and spiritual warfare views beyond the West.

Theodicy, the problem of evil, is an important topic with its own literary history and ongoing discussion. The origin of evil and its compatibility with the nature of God is worth examination. Spiritual warfare, however, is not a study of why evil exists or its origins. Rather, it is about evil as it is now and the ways in which we encounter it during this age, how the fallen angels and Christian vocation relate to the evil encountered in the world.

---

23. I will use the term "Global South" to describe the non-Western Christians of South America and Africa as well as the Indonesian and Pacific Islands and the burgeoning Christian movements of Asia. "Majority world" is another term that has been proposed for this concept.

Even though one of the fallen powers is the fallen angels, the various accounts of demonology in the general realm of religious history and culture only indirectly relate to the topic of spiritual warfare. Paul calls all religious teaching outside of Christ "the teachings of demons" (1 Tim 4:1), and for a confessional Lutheran understanding of spiritual warfare, the sacred writings of other religions are not considered normative for the Christian faith, including statements about the unseen;[24] a history *of belief in* evil spirits is not the same as a history *of* evil spirits. Jeffrey Burton Russell's catalogue of work on the history of such belief is the contemporary authority on the history of the belief in evil spirits in Western cultures.[25] Rather, our project focuses on Scripture's account of Satan and the fallen angels.

This focus also excludes Jewish apocalyptic literature. A common argument is made from a biblical-critical view that the Old Testament has very little mention of the spiritual warfare language which seems to pervade the New Testament. Such scholars point to the genre of apocalyptic Jewish literature from the intertestamental period, particularly the books of Enoch, and highlight the similarities between some of what is said there and what Jesus and the New Testament authors say regarding spiritual warfare. But they are putting the proverbial cart before the horse. For the Christian, who considers Jesus to be God the Son, Jesus' teachings validate those particular teachings of the Jewish authors in concord with his words rather than Jesus and the other authors gaining their ideas merely from the influence of contemporary Jewish thought or an amalgamation of it with Zoroastrian influences.[26]

---

24. The law, the demand upon men for righteousness, is the only aspect of true faith that is sensed by all other religions: "All men, including the philosophers, know something about the Law of God. 'The work of the Law' is written also in the hearts of the philosophers (Rom 2:15) But that is the limit of their innate religious knowledge. It follows that their religious thoughts are confined within the limits of the Law and the works of man." Pieper, *Christian Dogmatics*, 1:17; also, "The opponents single out the law (because to some extent human reason naturally understands it since reason contains the same judgment divinely written on the mind), and through the law they seek the forgiveness of sins and justification." Ap IV, 7 in Kolb and Wengert, *Book of Concord*, 121.

25. Jeffrey Burton Russell's series includes, *The Devil, Lucifer, Mephistopheles, Prince of Darkness,* and *Satan*.

26. For an overview of the debate on the relationship of Zoroastrianism to Jewish apocalyptic literature, see Boyd, *God at War*, 171–80. For a brief, yet thoughtful, discussion of Jewish apocalyptic literature and Paul's use of powers terms, see Berkhof, *Christ and the Powers*, 10–11, 16–20; and Schlier, *Principalities*, 12–14.

Another broad term associated with spiritual warfare is the occult. The term encompasses most explorations of the supernatural outside of Christianity, including ancient theologies from Egyptian, Mesopotamian, Babylonian, and Chinese cultures, which are still influential today at various levels. The term is often associated with groups that perform acts of evil towards others that have reference to supernatural entities, though it can apply to those who attempt benevolence as well. Christians, in what has been termed a "post-Christian" culture, will increasingly encounter practitioners of the occult and occultic beliefs in their myriad forms. In chapter 2, some aspects of the occult within Western culture will be assessed in terms of their influence on the common understanding of spiritual warfare and the supernatural. But a detailed analysis of what is believed and practiced concerning the unseen in areas outside of Christianity, whether in the West or the rest of the world, is left for another work.

The occult is often blamed for aberrant practices, but such beliefs are not necessary for human evil to be encountered and perpetuated. The psychology of evil is its own field of study with a long history of debate and thought. The psychological motivations of men to do evil are many and varied and it is worth exploring why some consciously accede to egregious evil actions against their fellows and whether possession and the demonic have a place in such evil. Spiritual warfare has contributions to make toward the discussion of the psychology of evil, but it is less concerned with how humans rationalize evil than how God intervenes in the midst of the depraved human condition.[27] This work will merely touch on this topic in the conclusion when discussing prudent use of exorcistic practices.

Finally, treatments of spiritual warfare outside of the West have their own interpretations reflecting their milieu. Some Global South churches, for example, being excluded from much of the influence of the

---

27. A vigorous, yet behind-the-scenes debate continues in psychology regarding the existence of demonic harassment, oppression, and possession versus various mental illnesses and how to distinguish between them. For a look at the side affirming demonic conflict, see: Peck, *People of the Lie*; Peck, *Glimpses of the Devil*; and Isaacs, "Possessive States Disorder." An account of the potential benefits of both religious and psychological help, though not asserting personal demons, is given in: Barry, "Quantitative Analysis of Reports." For a skeptical clinical perspective of deliverance ministry as opposed to clinical disorders, see: DePalatis, "Explanation of Different Responses." For a similar conclusion on a journalistic level, see: Cuneo, *American Exorcism*. For an opposing perspective to Peck, see Powlison, *Power Encounters*.

Enlightenment, bring traditional cultural perspectives on the reality of the supernatural into their comprehension of the Christian faith.[28] These traditions have some influence upon the major voices in the West, as will be noted, but a thoroughgoing survey of global southern and eastern Christian accounts of spiritual warfare is a task for different work.

A Summary of What Is Ahead

If the foregoing topics are not main features of this book, then here are the highlights of what is covered in the pages ahead. Chapter 2 explores why spiritual warfare is a significant theological challenge today for the church in the West, given its current cultural milieu. I assess why the Western church has suffered an eclipse of thought on this subject in the last two centuries (until the recent renewal of interest). To do so, the chapter will provide an overview of the increasing interest by Western culture in many forms of spiritism and its uncritical exploration of the supernatural. The chapter will then explore the roots of the theological absence of spiritual warfare (and the supernatural) as a topic in the Western church to gain an understanding of why most mainline denominations are now trying to catch up to the cultural fascination with the supernatural—a fascination that can easily enter into the lives of Christians and congregations with negative constructions of reality with non-Christian foundations.[29]

Chapters 3–5 will present constructive and critical analyses of the major contemporary paradigms of spiritual warfare. Chapter 3 provides a brief account of the *dismissive approach* and then an analysis of the *social approach*. The dismissive approach itself has, by its nature, little to say on the subject of spiritual warfare. It will only be covered in terms of its historical impact and its influence on the creation of the *social approach*. The social approach will be analyzed in greater detail, using the work of Walter Wink as the primary example of this account. This approach deemphasizes all notions of personified supernatural beings (other than God) and instead highlights both beneficial and oppressive social constructs as instances of, respectively, impersonal "angelic" and "demonic" activity on earth.

---

28. See for example, Fernando, "Screwtape Revisited," 103–32; Hiebert, "Spiritual Warfare and Worldviews"; and Jenkins, *New Faces of Christianity*, 98–157.

29. For Lutheran assessments of the assimilation of spiritism into the Western church, see Winker, *New Age Is Lying to You*, 175–87; and Bennett, *Afraid*.

To highlight its point, the social approach argues that the positive or negative interiority of a powerful social construct determines the spiritual attitude of its interior culture. This cultural spirit then determines how it enacts its exteriority, the use of its power to help or harm those who are subject to its power. The church's job in this approach is to work by proper means to change the interiority of a broken system from a demonic influence to an angelic one by calling out its illegitimate exterior acts. Among the constructive aspects of this account will be the stress Wink places upon the concrete needs of the neighbor, particularly in terms of social justice, and the church's impetus to be engaged in addressing such needs.

Chapter 4 examines the *pneumatic approach* which emerges primarily from a Pentecostal influence and is often described in terms of deliverance ministry. The primary proponent representing this view is C. Peter Wagner, whose work culminates in an account of Strategic-Level Spiritual Warfare (SLSW). Here, the personified reality of intermediary beings is highlighted with particular regard for the demonic. In reaction to a supernatural force such as the fallen angels, the Christian is called upon to act with authority against these forces in various ways, including identificational repentance,[30] prayer walking,[31] and various levels and types of exorcistic practices. One constructive highlight of this account of spiritual warfare is the attention it pays to the reality of the supernatural and the demonic as pertinent to the life of the Christian and the world. Some of the language in this approach is useful to bridge the bifurcation in much of the contemporary Western church between the material and spiritual planes.

The Western confessional Lutheran viewpoint will be addressed in connection with the *bifurcated approach* in chapter 5. A brief examination will be undertaken of some of the ways in which spiritual warfare has been addressed in mainline denominations, followed by noting its connection to the work of Lutherans in the past. Then, an assessment of contemporary Lutheran contributions will be made. These are not full accounts of spiritual warfare, but they address components of the

---

30. This is the identification of sins committed in the region's history that have gone unrepented and so unforgiven, leaving the area susceptible to demonic control. This will be examined further in chapter 4.

31. Prayer walking is the practice of walking a region and praying for persons one contacts or for the area in any way in which one feels the Spirit direct. This will be discussed further in chapter 4.

topic. Three voices in the contemporary Lutheran discussion are Gustav Wingren, John Kleinig, and Leopoldo Sánchez. Wingren's account of vocation in Luther shows how individual and corporate accounts of vocation relate to God's governance of his kingdoms and Satan's attempts to distort vocation so that persons act against God's will. Kleinig examines Luther's three facets of the Christian life, namely, *oratio* (prayer), *meditatio* (meditation on the word of God), and *tentatio* (suffering, including spiritual attacks). He writes of spiritual warfare in discussing the third facet, describing *tentatio* as our daily struggle with the sinful nature and temptation from Satan. Sánchez presents various accounts of the Trinitarian relationship between Jesus and the Holy Spirit in God's economic work, providing some perspectives on the devil's work against that of the joint mission of Jesus and the Holy Spirit in God's world. He reflects upon Luther's comment that God can bring good out of the devil's attempts at evil in an attempt to move beyond a dualistic account of the work of the Spirit against the evil spirits. He also contributes some models of life in the Spirit that help frame aspects of spiritual warfare. Finally, his insights into the church's life in the Spirit toward the world in service to neighbors are also important for a proper account of God's sanctifying work in the world.

Chapter 6 brings the threads from these assessments together to form a more robust understanding of spiritual warfare. It begins with an introduction of other resources which will be used to construct the *antifragile approach* to spiritual warfare, including works from Luther and other Lutheran works. This brief review of additional resources will be followed by an examination of the Lutheran doctrine concerning the reign of Christ in our current age. There, it will be noted that Christ truly is reigning over all things in this age but does so in a certain manner. That manner is not a reflection of a lack of authority or power against the fallen powers, nor a denial of their reality, but is the manner in which he chooses to enact his reign at this time. This distinction is important because it gives a proper foundation for understanding the Christian's nature and situation in regard to God and the fallen powers. After addressing the reign of Christ, the chapter will examine the three fallen powers which assail that reign, the unregenerate nature of the individual, the fallen world, and the fallen angels.

The section on the unregenerate natures depicts the status of man in sin and antagonistic to God and his will. When the Holy Spirit regenerates a person to have faith in Jesus Christ, they are a new creation.

The regenerate nature of the person is a saint and child of God. In that conversion, a paradox is created. The regenerate nature is immediately set upon by the unregenerate nature seeking to remove the new, imputed nature, denying that Christ has any authority over the sinful self. While the person has both natures, the Christian is still a single, whole person and still accountable for sin. Therefore, a cycle of repentance and forgiveness is a central mark of this paradoxical life, but the Christian's given identity as God's child is central. God acts for the Christian, by means of word and sacrament, to continue to grow and shape the faith of the Christian despite the work of the unregenerate nature. He also turns the Christian away from the self to act in love toward the neighbor.

The following section looks at the fallen world, examining the status of the Christian in contrast to secular cultures and societal structures. The nature of these constructs is to be set against God and his will because of communal sin; putting sinners together does not make them less sinful. The goal of the world is to remove the faith of individuals and, by extension, of Christian groups in a denial of the reign of Christ and his authority over all creation, every society, and all persons. As such structures oppose Christ's reign, they are also set against aspects of the church, which is the gathering of Christian persons. The community of the church has characteristics which contrast with the fallen world. First, the church is where God gives his gifts to his people by word and sacrament through which the Holy Spirit acts (the sword of the Spirit) to create and ongoingly build up faith in Christ in the Christian. Second, the church is the closest set of persons upon whom a Christian enacts God's love, becoming the mask of God to fellow Christians. Third, the church as community supports and encourages acts of love to the world by its members. This includes witness to Christ as well as addressing large and small social ills. These works of the church are enacted as the church lives out its communal identity as the people of God in the midst of the larger community of the world. The church, like the individual, is marked with an ongoing cycle of repentance and forgiveness. The fallen world assails the church and the individual Christian, but the persons and peoples of God are called not to fight the world, but to simply enact their identities in Christ in the midst of the world, and so be the masks of God.

The third fallen power, the fallen angels, also receive a close examination. In summary, we take an overview of references to the demonic in Scripture to construct a narrative concerning the fallen angels as they stand in this age. This is the first such assessment from a Lutheran perspective. The fallen angels are now without access to heaven on account of Christ's reign as High Priest and Mediator for his people. Satan's former job as accuser was rendered ineffective and worthless by Christ's work. The fallen angels fought against God's merciful acts in Christ and were removed from heaven. Satan knows that this removal is a part of the inaugurated eschaton, so final judgment is coming.

Therefore, Satan hates God but cannot get at God so, to spite God, he seeks to destroy what God loves in the time he has left before the coming judgment. Satan will use any method at his disposal to prevent or ruin Christian faith in a person to wrest as many persons from God by the last day as he can and to delight in motivating humanity to act contrary to God's will. He seeks for human rejection of Christ's reign out of spite for God.

The Holy Spirit acts through his sword of the word and his love enacted through his people toward one another to protect his people from the works of the fallen angels. Possession is a particular extension of the acts of the fallen angels to deny the reign of Christ. Exorcism is a response which simply calls on Jesus to bring his presence to bear on the situation.[32]

These three fallen powers are in denial of Christ's kingship for differing reasons, yet they join in a complimentary defiance of God's will. The fallen angels have no problem working in tandem with the world and unregenerate nature to rail against Christ's reign, but through the sword of the Spirit and the masks of God, God not only can preserve the Christian, but can use the antagonism to increase the faith of the person over time, using the adversity to bring strength.

In the end, this new *antifragile* approach addresses both the pneumatic and social aspects of spiritual warfare. It also maintains the sovereignty of God against the disjunction of the temporal and celestial planes of the bifurcated approach. It avoids the supernatural dualism between good and evil (God and Satan) of the pneumatic approach. It highlights instead the Trinitarian understanding of God's economy of salvation and in doing so removes the anthropological maximalism which distorts the social and pneumatic approaches when they make humans and human institutions the central agents in the battle against the demonic. It also creates a narrative of spiritual warfare which depicts its relevance

---

32. Exorcism will be considered more in chapter 7.

for daily life, reinvigorating the understanding of what it means to be a Christian in daily interaction with the self and the world.

This last section also uses our findings as a lens to reflect back upon common passages used in the literature to examine spiritual warfare. Ephesians 6:10–20 concerns Paul's account of power and the armor of God. Luke 8:26–39 relates the event of Jesus and the Gerasene demoniac. In both instances, this study finds that the theological paradigm offered by our new approach provides a more compelling and comprehensive way to understand these passages which is both consistent with their context and enhances their significance for the Christian life.

After these findings, the epilogue addresses some of the directions in which our paradigm may be beneficial for further discussion. This includes, first, implications for pastoral care, including the practice of exorcism. Second, its ramifications for ethics and the third use of the law. Third, its potential uses for ecumenical dialogue, particularly with the churches of the Global South.

2

The Spiritual Salad Bar and the Excluded Middle

Secular and Ecclesial Messiness Regarding the Supernatural in the Post-Enlightened West

Secular Supernatural Confusion

The previous chapter offered a definition of spiritual warfare as fallen creation railing against the reign of Christ. The fallen creation includes two components that have natural correspondences, that is, a person can apprehend them and observe them through the senses and direct interaction. First, the sinful nature can be seen acting out through each person's life. Each person can see his/her own wrong behavior and that of other individuals. Second, the world shows forth its brokenness in nature itself as well as through societal ills and human evil at all levels. These can also be readily observed, for example, in the destruction of hurricanes and in genocides. But the fallen creation also includes a third component which does not have a natural correspondent, namely, the fallen angels. Because these entities are not readily observed or sensed, their existence and influence is not readily able to be apprehended. It is this *super*natural component about which the most confusion and debate occurs. The differences that cause this confusion are not restricted to the church. Western secular culture exhibits great interest in the topic of the supernatural in general and more specifically in concepts of spiritual warfare. The existence of unseen forces enlivens curiosity today just as it has through most of humanity's past.[1] But the contemporary situation has its roots in Enlightenment influences.

The Enlightenment and the Supernatural

The figures of the Enlightenment are many and wrote prodigiously and a close look at them is beyond this book. To better understand the current milieu, however, we can benefit from a brief look at the movement of Western philosophical thought in the area of the supernatural over the last few centuries. To even keep that brief, this is just an overview of English thought on the matter as representing what was typical of the times.[2] John Locke's *Essay Concerning Human Understanding* in 1670 is considered the beginning of formal deistic publications in England. The concept then rose in popularity and was the focus of other works such as Michael Tindal's *Christianity as Old as Creation* in 1730. Deistic principles which emerged maintained that God exists and created all things. God also gave men an innate sense of his nature and ethic through conscience and the observation of nature. Other than this, Deism argues, God largely left the nature of his creation to run on its own apart from his intervention. In this climate, organized religions based upon sacred writings which purported to be God's own message to mankind were suspect.[3]

David Hume's *The Natural History of Religion* and his later *Dialogues Concerning Natural Religion* rejected natural religion with its proposed God-given innate understandings of the world, and instead moved to an understanding of religious truth as limited to empirical and experiential

---

1. An intriguing (though occasionally thin) argument is made by J. H. Brennan concerning just how much of human history has been dictated by unseen beings. In the theological realm, the direction of Judaism, Christianity, Hinduism, and Islam all claim supernatural authority for their teachings. In the secular and political realm, there are records of influence of the spiritual on the political life of ancient times (e.g., Egypt, Assyria, Babylon) and of several more recent leaders, including the Romanovs (Rasputin) and some members of the Third Reich. Brennan argues that the majority of the large movements in Western history were influenced by curiosity about and perceived contact in some way with an unseen world of spirits. See Brennan, *Whisperers*.

2. I have restricted this history to a focus on a few main English works. For example, Montaigne, Voltaire, Rousseau, and Nietzsche are important to the development into and even the movement out of deism in France and other European lands. The goal of this portion of the work is not a close reading of the philosophical underpinnings of the rejection of the supernatural, but the flow from philosophical thought to popular discourse.

3. Orr, *English Deism*, 13.

findings. The philosophical tradition continued to move away from the supernatural to a purely empirical view of creation. By 1839, Sir Walter Scott, speaking of the supernatural in general and devils in particular, could confidently open his writing to J. G. Lockhart saying, "You have asked me, my dear friend, that I should assist . . . with the history of a dark chapter in human nature, which the increasing civilisation of all well-instructed countries has now almost blotted out."[4]

Despite Scott's assuredness and that of academics who continued in the same vein,[5] there were others who took the notion of learning by experience not as a dismissal of the supernatural but as a framework for what they considered methodical inquiry into the subject. Allen Kardec's *The Spirits Book* (1857) reached the masses in France and England with its call for an organized exploration of the beyond. Such groups as the London Theosophical Society[6] and the Society for Psychical Research[7] were formed toward the end of the nineteenth century to systematically investigate the paranormal and the supernatural. In the early twentieth century, formidable names, including Sir Oliver J. Lodge, physicist and pioneer of electromagnetism and the radio, and *Sherlock Holmes* author Sir Arthur Conan Doyle were strongly convinced of the existence of a world unseen where spirits yet dwelled and could contact the living.[8] Such explorative groups never went away despite the rise of modernism, though they were usually relegated to the fringes of society.

Over the last half century, as the culture has moved away from modernism to post-modern subjectivity, the debate on the supernatural has continued amid groups with interest in the subject. Laser pioneer Russell Targ writes of his quest for evidence of the existence of paranormal powers and believes that he has proven their existence.[9] Mathematician and professor James D. Stein writes of the mathematical possibility for the

---

4. Scott, *Demonology and Witchcraft*, 2.

5. For example, British anthropologist Conway, *Demonology and Devil-Lore*, and Graf, *Story of the Devil*.

6. Founded in 1875 by self-proclaimed medium Helena Petrovna Blavatsky.

7. Founded in 1882, spearheaded by journalist Edmund Rodgers and physicist William F. Barrett.

8. Lodge mourned the loss of his son Raymond during World War I and sought solace by trying to contact his spirit. He details this exploration in Lodge, *Raymond, or Life and Death*. Doyle's books include *New Revelation* and *Vital Message*.

9. Targ, *Reality of ESP*.

The Spiritual Salad Bar and the Excluded Middle

paranormal (abilities and beings) to exist.[10] Against such existence, Brian Clegg recounts the history of those once thought to exhibit supernatural powers or able to contact the dead and shows how they were constantly exposed as frauds.[11]

The Supernatural in Western Thought and Media Today

Popular interest in the subject has now moved mainstream. Although polls show participation in mainline Christian denominations are on the wane in the West,[12] simultaneous to this decline, three out of four teens and adults today claim to have had a paranormal experience,[13] and at least half of all Americans believe in the existence of some type of devil.[14]

The belief in the existence of the supernatural but suspicion of established religion points us to the concern of C. S. Lewis for what he called the Materialist Magician, "the man, not using, but veritably worshipping, what he vaguely calls 'Forces' while denying the existence of 'spirits.'"[15] Here, by "spirits" Lewis is referring to angels and demons in contrast to a vague, supernatural accommodation for an otherwise materialistic viewpoint (the "Forces"). Belief in God, with formal doctrines, is rejected but belief in supernatural mystery remains. Each person is left to their own spiritual devices, experiences, and expressions.

Secular Western thought concerning the supernatural has led in many different directions over the last fifty years. There are those who dismiss personal supernatural beings other than a god of some type. This view is seen in the works of such best-selling authors as Rhonda Byrne and Eckhart Tolle. Byrne's books extol the power of positive thinking to claim the benefits of a benevolent universe.[16] Tolle is more nuanced but

---

10. Stein, *Paranormal Equation*.

11. For example, Clegg, *Extra Sensory*. A more direct route is taken by paranormal evidence skeptics who put up money for real proof. The most prominent is James Randi, who put up an increasing amount of money for anyone who professed paranormal or supernatural affiliation to prove their ability in a controlled setting. By the time he ended his offer in 2015, the amount had become one million dollars. It was never claimed.

12. Jenkins, *New Faces of Christianity*, 8–9.

13. Moore, "Three in Four Americans."

14. Robinson, "Devil and the Demographic Details."

15. Lewis, *Screwtape Letters*, 33.

16. Byrne, *Secret*; Byrne, *Power*; Byrne, *Magic*; and Byrne, *Hero*.

posits a view of true enlightenment as being fully present in the now (as opposed to past and future).[17] He says God has created all things but has stepped back to allow humans to search for their true potential, which is oneness with the Being in our being.[18] Tolle pulls selectively from the Bible, the Tao Te Ching, the Upanishads, and other religious writings to support his conclusions.[19]

A more direct acknowledgment of the supernatural is found in the reemergence of ancient pagan worship and witchcraft. A few of the more influential voices have been Margot Adler,[20] Starhawk,[21] Juliet Diaz,[22] and Scott Cunningham.[23] Starhawk (Miriam Simos) teaches that the goddess Earth is the world and in everything that is of the world so "Witchcraft can be seen as a religion of ecology."[24] She argues that while contemporary, her tradition of witchcraft is still tied to its ancient roots. "My own covens are based on the Faery tradition, which goes back to the Little People of Stone Age Britain, but we believe in creating our own rituals, which reflect our needs and insights of today."[25]

Witchcraft moves further into the exploration of the supernatural with trances. Starhawk speaks of astral entities which one encounters in

---

17. He defines the power of Now as "none other than the power of your presence, your consciousness liberated from thought forms." Tolle, *Power of Now*, 75.

18. Tolle, *Power of Now*, 96–97. See also Tolle, *New Earth*.

19. For example, he uses Jesus' observance that "before Abraham was, I am" to demonstrate that Jesus was not deity, but that he was fully enlightened. Because Jesus used the phrase "I am" in this way, "He had gone beyond the consciousness dimension governed by time, into the realm of the timeless. The dimension of eternity had come to this world . . . Thus, the man Jesus became Christ, a vehicle for pure consciousness" Tolle, *Power of Now*, 86.

20. Adler, *Drawing Down the Moon*. This book is a chronicle of witchcraft and paganism in the 1970s and an invitation to join Wiccan culture.

21. Starhawk, *Spiral Dance*. In addition to recounting the rise of the feminine in witchcraft, this book is also a resource for group (coven) exercises in magic, with invocations, chants, blessings, spells, and herbal charms.

22. Diaz, *Witchery*. Diaz provides a guide to the inner self's connection to magic and the use of a book of shadows for pagan observances as well as to communicate with one's ancestors.

23. Cunningham, *Wicca*. The distinction of Cunningham's work is his emphasis on Wiccan work which can be done individually rather than in a coven. He even provides a copy of his own Book of Shadows, the Wiccan's personal book of rituals, spells, and magical lore, which was uncommon at the time of his publication.

24. Starhawk, *Spiral Dance*, 35.

25. Starhawk, *Spiral Dance*, 35.

a trance as a combination of internal energies and external entities.[26] She speaks to the benefits of trances with words similar to those of Byrne and Tolle. As she puts it, "finally, in trance we find revelation. We invoke and become Goddess and God, linked to all that is. We experience union, ecstasy, openness.... We not only hear the music, but we dance the whirling, exhilarating, spiral dance of existence."[27] And yet in the midst of the trance discussion, the author cautions about those entities met and who may help grant transcendence, arguing that "no entity can possess a soul that denies it entrance."[28]

The Wiccan movement continues to gain popularity today.[29] The main thrust of the Wiccan movement is in harmony with a polytheistic worldview, and only touches on direct contact with unseen entities in such ways as Starhawk discusses above with trances. A much more direct route to contact the unseen today is attempted in mediumship, ghost hunting, and by some psychics. The difference between the earlier generations' fascination with the supernatural and today's milieu is how openly mainstream and accepted these explorations have become,[30] especially when seen as reality entertainment.[31]

Ghost hunting involves going to locations which are purportedly haunted to try to generate evidence for the reality of supernatural entities by seeking to contact the dead through a variety of pseudo-scientific means. Popular shows just over the past dozen years have included *Ghost*

---

26. "Whether those entities are internal forces or external beings depends on how one defines the self. It is more romantic and exciting (and probably truer) to see them as at least partially external; it is psychologically healthier and probably wiser to see them as internal" Starhawk, *Spiral Dance*, 169.

27. Starhawk, *Spiral Dance*, 171.

28. Starhawk, *Spiral Dance*, 169.

29. For example, the news station 12 in Westchester, New York, broadcast a story on local witchcraft, which they claim is one of the fastest growing religions in the region. See "Speak No Evil." They are not alone. See also Bosker, "Why Is Witchcraft On the Rise?"; Fearnow, "Number of Witches Rise Dramatically"; and Yellin, "'We're in the Middle of a Witch Moment.'"

30. One good example is the placement of the spirit board, *Ouija*, trademarked by Parker Brothers, in the board game section of department and toy stores.

31. This section explores the media of film and television, excluding written media. Exploring secular books which depict the supernatural and spiritual warfare within fiction would be a project of its own. The perennial popularity of Stephen King's works such as *IT* and *The Stand*, and J. K. Rowling's *Harry Potter* series, are examples of the diversity of audience and exploration of the general topic of the supernatural in popular fiction.

Hunters, *Destination Truth*, and *Ghost Adventures*. There are shows which recount and reenact paranormal encounters of persons, such as *Paranormal Witness*. One show, *The Haunted Collector*, has followed the cases of objects which are purported to be haunted.

These shows are slightly different than those which are explicitly mediumistic, where the host supposedly contacts the dead for others. Recent successful fictional dramas with a medium as the main protagonist include *Ghost Whisperer* and *Medium*. Nonfictional shows have also been successful, including *John Edward Cross Country* and *Long Island Medium*.

A great media example of Western secular confusion about the supernatural in general is found in the television show *The Dead Files*, where one can find an amalgamation of traditions used. The show depicts a medium who goes to the houses of families experiencing hauntings and encounters the entities there. Her partner, a former police officer, looks into the history of the place and conducts interviews. At the end of the program, the two come together to discuss the case with their clients. The medium, Amy Allen, fully explains to the family what is going on supernaturally and how to get rid of or appease the problematic entities. Her solutions often contain a mishmash of religious strains. For example, in the episode "The Beast," to keep an evil entity away from the home she recommends that the family use a protective powder made by a Wiccan around their property. Then, they are to apply black salt, a practice from hoodoo, to seal "every conceivable entrance" to the house. Finally, they are to burn frankincense each night, which "they use in churches to dispel any negativity and to cleanse the area."[32]

Within the broad cultural spread on the supernatural, spiritual warfare has its own wide and varied niche. The depictions in the media over the last half-century regarding the relationship between angels, devils, the world, and the church can give secular consumers, and nominal Christians, widely disparate (and inaccurate) accounts of the unseen realities even before entering the maze of available literature. Shows depict angels in various states of need to gain their wings or a place in heaven[33]

---

32. Traegler, *Dead Files*, "The Beast."

33. Not in the last fifty years, but the most famous of these is *It's a Wonderful Life*, directed by Frank Capra, in which an angel, in order to earn his wings, helps the protagonist fix his life. See also Wenders, *Wings of Desire*; Silberling, *City of Angels*; successful television series *Highway to Heaven* and *Touched by an Angel*.

The Spiritual Salad Bar and the Excluded Middle

or persons moving from human to angel.[34] Movies, television, and comic books portray all sorts of visions concerning Satan and what powers and plans he has including temptation schemes for various souls,[35] and his opportunity to produce his own son, the Antichrist, to doom the world rather than save it.[36] The church (usually Roman Catholic) or various independent Christians are in the business of vampire hunting,[37] witch hunting,[38] and battling demons of amazing power through exorcism and self-sacrifice.[39] Television heroes of the past few decades such as Buffy,[40] John Constantine,[41] or Sam and Dean Winchester[42] tend to portray an amalgamation of magical symbology and traditional Western superstition with various Christian symbols and rites.

As Christians are exposed to the secular Western accounts of the supernatural and spiritual warfare, they are faced with a portrayal in which

---

34. For example, Cornell, *Almost an Angel*.

35. Movie examples include: Heston, *Needful Things*; and Hackford, *Devil's Advocate*.

36. Such as Lawrence, *Constantine*; Hyams, *End of Days*; and Miner, *Warlock*.

37. One might argue that this tradition on film begins with the "magical" use of holy water and a crucifix in 1931 with Browning, *Dracula*. See also Carpenter, *Vampires*, where the hunter works directly for the Vatican.

38. Eisner, *Last Witch Hunter*, in which the immortal hunter also works for the Roman Catholic Church.

39. Well-known examples include Friedkin, *Exorcist*; Blatty, *Exorcist III*; Derrickson, *Exorcism of Emily Rose*; Stamm, *Last Exorcism*; and Häfstrom, *Rite*. Also, recently James Wan's 2013 film, *The Conjuring*, led to several tie-in movies, including Leonetti, *Annabelle*; Wan, *Conjuring 2*; Sandberg, *Annabelle: Creation*; and Hardy, *Nun*, with more in development. All of these movies depict demonic hauntings of places or objects.

40. As well as its spin-off series *Angel*.

41. Mainstream comic book characters have many encounters with the demonic (some being demonic themselves) including such characters as Image Comics' *Spawn*, Marvel Comics' *Mephisto* and *Doctor Strange*, and DC's collection of characters including *Jason Blood/Etrigan the Demon*, *Hades*, *Deadman*, *Dr. Fate*, *Spectre*, and *Sandman*. DC also has the character *John Constantine*, which is the same character as the eponymous movie and television show noted above. With his own comic book (*Hellblazer*), live-action movie, and live-action television series (with crossover appearances in other DC shows such as *Arrow* and *Legends of Tomorrow*), Constantine's media spread, among DC characters, is only rivaled by Superman, Wonder Woman, and Batman, the latter with whom he shares main billing in the animated film *Justice League Dark*, directed by James Oliva. And none of this considers the influence on Western secular views of spiritual warfare by Japanese manga like *Blue Exorcist* and *Death Note* or the myriad of video games with similar plots.

42. From *Supernatural*, which ran for fifteen seasons.

Jesus has little part. In that view, there are many intermediary beings, including human souls, roaming the unseen world. Crucifixes are reduced to holy talismans rather than symbols of salvation and baptismal waters are really for defense against monsters. What is portrayed is a universe in which God is indifferent or even antagonistic toward humanity, the Bible is only one version among equal ancient holy books and stories used for protection from unseen forces, the demons are (usually) set on taking over earth, and humans must depend on themselves to find a way to safety or victory against monsters, Satan,[43] and vast demonic hordes. Any persons, including Christians, encountering the media of Western culture on spiritual warfare can find a plethora of sources on the topic, and within them will only find amalgamation and confusion. It is the Western version of what the character Egg Shen, of another popular supernatural movie entitled *Big Trouble in Little China*, describes regarding Eastern mysticism: "There's Buddhism, Confucianism, and Taoist alchemy and sorcery: *we take what we want and leave the rest, just like your salad bar.*"[44]

Ecclesiastical Diversion and the Excluded Middle

The popular secular account of the supernatural and spiritual warfare is full of confusion. But the Western church has found itself in a similar situation. Despite how much has been written on the matter, large sectors of the Western church have ignored or dismissed the issue of spiritual warfare. For many Western denominations, the subject has received scant attention in the face of other concerns brought on by modern academic treatment of the Bible, leaving those seeking for direction in spiritual warfare to sift through the disparity available and come to their own conclusions.

Such a loss of spiritual warfare as a topic of consideration and concern is problematic, yet it is an unsurprising outcome of Enlightenment-influenced theology. For many in theological academia, the Enlightenment brought, over time, a denial of the existence of any created supernatural order.[45] The whole idea of the supernatural, and spiritual

---

43. Including a somewhat sympathetic Satan in *Lucifer*; and the series *Evil*.

44. Carpenter, *Big Trouble in Little China*.

45. I use the word "created" here because many believed in the existence of God, who is himself supernatural, but rejected all other forms of the unempirical unseen.

warfare in particular, was quaint and not worth contemplation. This is the foundation of the dismissive approach to spiritual warfare.

Albert Schweitzer traces the thought of the biblical critical school into the early twentieth century in his classic *The Quest of the Historical Jesus*. Incidental to the discussion of the authentic historical Jesus, he explores rationalistic thinking against miracles and the supernatural. D. F. Strauss is held up by Schweitzer as the first to thoroughly question the life of Jesus as presented by the church.[46] Christian Herman Weisse and Christian Gottlob Wilke introduced the Marcan Hypothesis and Bruno Bauer offered an early skeptical inquiry into the life of Jesus and the early church. By the time that Schweitzer reaches his own day in the first decade of the twentieth century, he concludes that the Marcan narrative has imposed a Messianic narrative onto the life of Jesus,[47] and concludes that the "Jesus of Nazareth who came forward publicly as the Messiah, who preached the ethic of the Kingdom of Heaven upon earth, and died to give His work its final consecration, never had any existence."[48] In his view, Jesus had to be removed of any strange trappings, including miracles and the supernatural.

Moving away from a focus on the eschatological messianic concerns, a few decades later Bultmann eschews a straight dismissal of all of the supernatural narratives of the Gospels and instead attempts to find the "real" meaning behind the narratives as they are given. The supernatural in Scripture, the angels and demons, miracles, and preaching on the parousia were just metaphors and symbols for other aspects of faith which could be mined to bring lasting truths out of their mythological trappings. To take these texts literally though, for Bultmann, was still absurd, as he notes in one of his famous quotes:

> Now that the forces and laws of nature have been discovered, we can no longer believe in *spirits, whether good or evil*. . . . It is impossible to use the electric light and the wireless and to avail ourselves of modern medical and surgical discoveries, and at the

---

46. "Strauss's 'Life of Jesus' has a different significance for modern theology from that which it had for his contemporaries. For them it was the work which made an end of miracle as a matter of historical belief, and gave the mythological explanation its due. We, however, find in it also an historical aspect of a positive character, inasmuch as the historic Personality which emerges from the mist of myth is a Jewish claimant of the Messiahship, whose world of thought is purely eschatological." Schweitzer, *Historical Jesus*, 95.

47. Schweitzer, *Historical Jesus*, 339–40.

48. Schweitzer, *Historical Jesus*, 398.

same time to believe in the New Testament world of spirits and miracles.[49]

By the middle of the twentieth century, proponents of the biblical critical method used their hermeneutical approach to not only question the notion of spirits, but also core Christian beliefs such as the veracity and historicity of the Bible as well as most of Jesus' life, ministry, passion, resurrection, and ascension. Questioning had moved to dismissal, and the scriptural accounts of the life of Jesus and of the supernatural were relegated to myth.

Yet in the midst of the assuredness of the biblical critical scholars, a new movement was burgeoning in the West. The Azusa Street revival of 1906 in Los Angeles, California is generally regarded as the beginning of the Pentecostal movement. According to Harvey Cox, the movement is harder to pin down than other movements because it lacks a consistent, definitive dogma.[50] But regardless of the lack of formal doctrine, the movement spread across the country and across the world over the twentieth century. Cox offers three features through which Pentecostalism tapped into the spiritual hunger of the masses over the last century: (1) primal speech, or praying in the Spirit with ecstatic utterance; (2) primal piety, which "touches on the resurgence in Pentecostalism of trance, vision, healing, dreams, dance, and other archetypal religious expressions";[51] and (3) primal hope, the "insistence that a radically new world age is about to dawn."[52]

The theological import of these points varies among stripes of Pentecostalism. But for those outside of Pentecostalism, the outward manifestations of these points, with glossolalia, dance, the uncontrollable laughing and falling of the "holy rollers," were disconcerting. The charismatic movement spread to other denominations during the 1960s. The signs and wonders emphasis began to emerge, particularly healing and deliverance ministries, with the rise in popularity of Pentecostal teachings.

The dearth we find in mainline denominations on spiritual warfare often comes from two simple, related sources. First, as influenced by the Enlightenment, discussion of the supernatural was stymied by a

---

49. Bultmann, "New Testament and Mythology," 4–5 (emphasis original).
50. Cox, *Fire from Heaven*, 71.
51. Cox, *Fire from Heaven*, 82.
52. Cox, *Fire from Heaven*, 82.

rationalistic view and so it was moved away from central theological concepts. Second, the issue of the supernatural was then of low priority compared to more immediate concerns. The Lutheran Church—Missouri Synod (LCMS), a confessional Lutheran church body, is no exception to this. One can look at the discussions and reports which came out from 1966 to 1975 and see that the integrity of Scripture and ecstatic experience were being dealt with nearly simultaneously. On one side, there were fundamental issues at stake regarding biblical inerrancy and the content of the gospel.[53] On the other side, there was a need to respond to groups claiming to speak in tongues and perform other works that exhibit the validity of the Spirit's work in their lives. One such work often claimed was deliverance ministry.[54] As a result, the LCMS and other traditional Western denominations turned the focus of their apologetics onto biblical critical issues (for better or worse) and tried to avoid (with varying degrees of success) associating with subjects affiliated with Charismatic assertions.

The path of modern biblical critical scholarship denied that the realm of the supernatural, apart from God, existed. The Charismatics asserted that the Holy Spirit, but also the angels and demons, were all around us all of the time. Both groups, unknowingly, were trying to address what Paul Hiebert calls *the excluded middle*. Hiebert summarizes

---

53. In the LCMS, for example, one can trace the concern in the documents produced by its Committee on Theological and Church Relations. Within the span of nine years, 1966–75, seven documents were published by them regarding issues of the authority and interpretation of Scripture: Committee on Theological and Church Relations, *Lutheran Stance Toward Biblical Studies*; Committee on Theological and Church Relations, *Seven Theses on Reformation Hermeneutics*; Committee on Theological and Church Relations, *Gospel and Scripture*; Committee on Theological and Church Relations, *Comparative Study of Varying Contemporary Approaches*; Committee on Theological and Church Relations, *Guiding Principles*; Committee on Theological and Church Relations, *Report on Dissent*; and Committee on Theological and Church Relations, *Inspiration of Scripture*.

For the LCMS, the inerrancy of Scripture was one of the main factors in the split of the faculty of Concordia Seminary, St. Louis, in 1974. For more on this event, see Zimmerman, *Seminary in Crisis*; and Marquardt, *Anatomy of an Explosion*.

54. "When a conference of Lutheran pastors in the charismatic movement was held at Concordia Seminary, St. Louis, in May 1971, it was estimated that there were over 200 pastors in the Synod claiming to have received the baptism of the Holy Spirit." Committee on Theology and Church Relations, *Charismatic Movement and Lutheran Theology*, 5. See also: Committee on Theology and Church Relations, *Lutheran Church and the Charismatic Movement*; and Committee on Theology and Church Relations, *Spiritual Gifts*.

how the modern Western church had dealt with the supernatural in terms of planes of existence. First, he says there is a materialistic view in which people do not believe the existence of spiritual warfare because they deny a celestial plane of angels and demons. But there is an acknowledgement of injustice and suffering in the world, and the Christian who comes from this materialist view demythologizes the text (like Bultmann) in light of this commitment: "The battle, they claim, is between good and evil in human social systems. The church is called to fight against poverty, injustice, oppression, and other evils which are due to oppressive, exploitative human systems of government, business and religion."[55]

Similar to this material view, Hiebert argues, is what he terms "Cartesian dualism" in which there is a realm of God and angelic beings, but they have nothing to do with daily life, which is about rationalism and science. "People pray to God for their salvation, but turn to modern medicine for healing and psychology for deliverance from so-called demon possession, because demons exist in the heavens, not on earth."[56] The lack of an intersection of these two planes, the celestial and the terrestrial, whether in the first pattern by denying the celestial, or in the second pattern by the bifurcation of the planes, is what he calls the excluded middle.

Hiebert then looks to the tribal and Indo-European views of non-Western, non-enlightened cultures, and sees in them an understanding that unseen beings interact with the concrete world.[57] These cultures have the right idea about the reality of this interaction, but do not properly understand what is going on. Hiebert wants the church to recognize that it is in error to separate the seen and the unseen. Pentecostalism has tried to bring back the concept of this intersection into Western theology. Most of what is written on spiritual warfare comes from a Pentecostal background that, Hiebert contends, works from the same motifs as the Indo-European view,[58] and little of it seems to be systematic and thoroughgoing in its academic rigor, operating largely on an experiential basis.

Thus, the Western church has found itself in a state similar to Western popular secularism. There are different attempts to account for Scripture's depictions of a spiritual realm. The dismissive and social approaches try to cast it out with an "angelology of the weary shrug of the

---

55. Hiebert, "Spiritual Warfare and Worldviews," 1.
56. Hiebert, "Spiritual Warfare and Worldviews," 1.
57. Hiebert, "Spiritual Warfare and Worldviews," 2–3.
58. Hiebert, "Spiritual Warfare and Worldviews," 3.

shoulders,"[59] as if a theology concerning the supernatural is an unimportant curiosity of little interest, or by a demythologization of the supernatural texts. The bifurcated approach, unsure of what to do with the supernatural, tends toward Hiebert's Cartesian dualism. The Pentecostals try to bridge the gap but overemphasize the status of the fallen angels in contrast to divine sovereignty. With a particular focus on the bifurcated approach, the average churchgoer who might have questions about these issues is left to find answers for themselves, and will cast about for books or media, finding a flurry of contrasting views. The result of such a search is an amalgamation of ideas which Christians attempt, consciously or not, to reconcile with the theology they learn in the worship setting, from the theological voices with whom they resonate, and the cultural influences with which they interact.

Our project takes a different approach than Hiebert. The main problem is not the issue of the excluded middle; that is a symptom. The underlying problem is a misunderstanding of how Jesus reigns in these days of the church, and how that dynamic plays out for God's people on earth in relation to the fallen powers. If one tries to fit angels and demons into what is an otherwise "complete" theology, then that theology is really deficient on the meaning of Christ's atonement, his sovereign authority, and the place of vocation in God's creation.

Perhaps the most quoted text outside the Bible related to spiritual warfare is from C. S. Lewis in his preface to *The Screwtape Letters*:

> There are two equal and opposite errors into which our race can fall about the devils. One is to disbelieve in their existence. The other is to believe, and to feel an excessive and unhealthy interest in them. They themselves are equally pleased by both errors, and hail a materialist or a magician with the same delight.[60]

Most works use this quote to express their desire to strike a proper balance between the two extremes of disbelief or fascination.[61] What is usually missed in the attention to the first two sentences of this quote

---

59. Barth, *Church Dogmatics*, 3:369. Barth argues that fallen angels are simply a negation of creation, not personal entities but also not just symbolism related to social justice.

60. Lewis, *Screwtape*, 3.

61. "That 'balance' is important in this area is a widely shared conviction among evangelicals. However, this unity quickly gives way to diversity when it comes to the questions of just *how* this balance should be achieved." Beilby and Eddy, *Understanding Spiritual Warfare*, 22 (emphasis original).

is the point of the third, namely, that there is a more fundamental issue than the amount of attention paid to the devils, which is right understanding of the subject. The right amount (and right kind) of attention to the unseen will be paid when spiritual warfare is rightly understood; the latter will sort out the former. The next chapter begins this process with a constructive and critical examination of the dismissive approach and the social approach as put exemplified by Walter Wink.

3

The Social Approach to Spiritual Warfare and Walter Wink

Wink's Influence

The previous chapter showed an urgent need for clarity on the topic of spiritual warfare within the Western church. The church, unsurprisingly, finds no help from the secular culture for a proper orientation toward the unseen.

In this uncertainty, the church should turn to the Bible to find its basis for an account of the supernatural. As noted in the previous chapter, however, the approach to the text will greatly affect what is drawn from Scripture. One of the more influential approaches toward the spiritual warfare texts in Scripture is that of Walter Wink.

One approach to biblical texts on spiritual warfare is to focus upon New Testament texts which discuss concepts and entities of power, particularly in the letters of Paul. Wink's study of these texts about power is laid out in his three-volume work often called *The Powers Trilogy*,[1] "which has profoundly shaped the conversation on spiritual warfare over the last few decades."[2] Before the third volume was finished, his views were of such impact that he was called on to write about a spiritually healing path forward from apartheid in South Africa[3] and produced the

---

1. In addition to *Naming the Powers*, the other two books are: Wink, *Unmasking the Powers*; and Wink, *Engaging the Powers*.
2. Beilby and Eddy, *Understanding Spiritual Warfare*, 27.
3. Wink, *Violence and Nonviolence in South Africa*.

first in a series of volumes about paths to world peace for the Life and Peace Institute of Sweden.[4]

Walter Wink comes out of the biblical critical school and its dismissive view of the supernatural, but he comes to different conclusions than are typical of other authors from that school of thought. Before he wrote his influential works on the Powers[5] and spiritual warfare, Wink wrote a book about his hermeneutical method. There, he lays out why and how he diverges from the normal biblical critical school methodology. An examination of his revised biblical critical approach to Scripture will aid in examining his subsequent work on the Powers.

Wink's Hermeneutical Method

In his first book, *The Bible in Human Transformation*, Wink critiques the dismissive view's approach to Scripture in its classic biblical critical formats. This is not a wholesale, fundamental breakdown of the critical method; Wink uses the tools of source, form, and historical criticism in his own thinking.[6] However, he examines, and ultimately questions, the stated objectivity of the overall biblical critical method.

The historical critical method of biblical exegesis, he says, merely applies modernism to Scripture and lacks the claimed neutrality or detachment.[7] For Wink, the various biblical critical methods had been on the right trail but had gone astray into attempts at pure objectivism, noting, "For since truth is not absolute, but only approximate and relational, its relevance can only emerge in the particularity of a given community's struggles for integrity and freedom."[8]

Moreover, he contends, the biblical critical method undercut its own intended purpose. He says the original purpose of the method was to "undermine Protestant dependency on the Bible as the sole source of authority." It was then used by Reimarus to assault Christianity's roots

---

4. Wink, *When the Powers Fall*.

5. The common parlance in discussion of the biblical powers is to capitalize when discussing the powers themselves, distinguishing from their abilities and effects.

6. Wink, *Bible in Human Transformation*, 24.

7. Wink, *Bible in Human Transformation*, 3–4. Again, Wink is not rejecting higher criticism, only pointing out the perceived flaws in its purported objectivity.

8. Wink, *Bible in Human Transformation*, 11.

in history.⁹ This was followed by the Graf-Wellhausen hypothesis "destroying the conservative view of biblical origins and inspiration, thereby destroying its entire ideology."¹⁰ He approves of these efforts because he believes they were freeing biblical consideration and interpretation from the chains of orthodoxy and theological tyranny. "As long as this ideological onslaught was made for the sake of desirable fundamental change, i.e., as long as it was seeking breathing room for the spirit and the right of the intellect to free inquiry its thrust was utopian in the best sense of the term: it sought to destroy an existent state of reality for the sake of one which it conceived to be better."¹¹

However, once the biblical critical school of thought became the *status quo*, it also became entrenched and restraining, no longer seeking truth but maintaining the preeminence of its methodology and ideology.¹² In light of this, Wink joins Paul Ricoeur in looking for a "second naiveté" to again bring faith to perform "an iconoclastic function in respect to criticism."¹³

He admits he is not the first to see the problem and search for the way forward. He cites Schlatter, Barth, and Bultmann as examples of those who have made attempts to find a way forward through the "general malaise and a crisis of morale in the field,"¹⁴ but believes he has found a yet better way forward into the post-critical era.

He brings a three-step diacritical approach to the biblical text: fusion, distance, and communion. The first stage, *fusion*, recognizes that a person comes into contact with the biblical material as part of a heritage and culture. One cannot come to the Bible without these entailments, consciously or unconsciously, including provision of the "available believable" for the boundaries of what can be believed and the orientation for the reasoning process.¹⁵ Wink contends that the biblical critical process is an aid at this point in recognizing the inherited intellectual residue of culture and orthodoxy so we can question the tradition and distance ourselves from our heritage by means of objectification of the text apart

---

9. Wink, *Bible in Human Transformation*, 11.
10. Wink, *Bible in Human Transformation*, 12.
11. Wink, *Bible in Human Transformation*, 12.
12. Wink, *Bible in Human Transformation*, 29.
13. Wink, *Bible in Human Transformation*, 13.
14. Wink, *Bible in Human Transformation*, 18.
15. Wink, *Bible in Human Transformation*, 21.

from its cultural baggage.[16] The Bible, thus understood, is then open to critical scholarship since it is merely written by persons and no longer simply treated "as an immediate Thou" from God.[17]

Wink is trying to make the distinction between *objectivism*, the false assumption that one can truly analyze the Bible from a perfectly neutral position, and *objectivity*, which he says should be sought as one seeks to extricate analysis from inherent biases. For Wink, "the 'criticisms' serve the function then of decomposing the 'picture' of Jesus and the early church delivered by Christendom. It is only after the negation of the ecclesiastical and intrapsychic images of Jesus and primitive Christianity that we ourselves are thrown into the open space where genuine questioning, and hence freedom and truth, becomes possible."[18]

Thus far, Wink's approach is in step with the tradition of standard biblical criticism and the mythical view of spiritual warfare. In this first step of fusion he has proposed the self-awareness which must reject tradition and culture to approach the text "as it really is" instead of how it has been interpreted and reinterpreted over the past two millennia. In the second step, *distance*, Wink's critique of the critical method surfaces.

For that second step, he argues that the *method* of objectivity, to be freed from the baggage of the past and culture, became the goal of interpretation and so the whole process became objectivism. At that point, the meaning and purpose of objective distance was lost. Wink then uses Satan as a paradigm for the perceived problem with classic biblical criticism. Just as Satan has to repress all knowledge of the Father to claim mastery of the world, so the critical methodology had come to repress all self-knowledge and faith to claim mastery of the Scripture. "Objectification can thus be seen as a special form of the problem of 'fallen consciousness,' of which Satan is the archetypal representation. Objectification is the consequence of an independence which is out of communion with its own ground: an alienated consciousness."[19]

Wink is not arguing that biblical criticism does not work. He is arguing that it "'got stuck' in the second moment of the dialectic of

---

16. "Negation here is an essential objectification and hence distancing of oneself from prevailing cultural and intrapsychic images and preunderstandings, and consequently a dialectical moment of necessary alienation on the way to freedom and truth." Wink, *Bible in Human Transformation*, 22.

17. Wink, *Bible in Human Transformation*, 23.

18. Wink, *Bible in Human Transformation*, 24–25.

19. Wink, *Bible in Human Transformation*, 27.

understanding."[20] He contends that a person cannot remain at a distance from the Scripture if one intends to gain real meaning and insight from the text. The method is not the goal. The text must return upon the examiner. The one who is doing the objectifying also needs to be addressed critically by the text. An examination of the critical biblical scholar, Wink says, finds secularist tendencies ingrained into his perspective.[21] This, he says, leads to the heart of the issue for the scholar:

> On the one hand, he studies the Bible because it witnesses the reality of God, and because he wants to let that reality be effective in his personal and corporate life. On the other hand, he must study as a functional atheist. The method itself alienates him from his very objective. It establishes a gulf which can never be bridged as long as he is frozen in distance.[22]

In response to this dilemma, Wink provides his direction for getting unstuck and making use of the distance he claims biblical criticism provides. He turns to Freud for his way forward through the distance to relevance. He sees Freud's self-criticism in the face of his own responses to others' dreams as a type of public psychoanalysis of self.[23] This allows for the subject to be vulnerable to the object. In the biblical critical case, such self-criticism frees the critic to again be opened to the influence of the biblical text.[24]

The quest for the subject to again be affected by the text is, Wink argues, one of overcoming the repressions we place in the way of the text acting upon the subject. This is more than demythologizing the text. Like the initial work of struggle against the ecclesial baggage of the text, the subject now has to be open to the text's impact on his life. The reader must regain the ability "wherein the primal question can once again address us as the question of our own being."[25] This is the second naiveté of Riceour which allows for a return to the "powerful immediacy of

---

20. Wink, *Bible in Human Transformation*, 31.
21. Wink, *Bible in Human Transformation*, 38–39.
22. Wink, *Bible in Human Transformation*, 39.
23. Wink, *Bible in Human Transformation*, 33.
24. "Interpretation must now pass through a second negativity: the loss of our own emotional predisposition not to be unsettled, our easy acquiescence to contemporary questions, languages, and perspectives. We must pass through a fiery river of social and self-analysis in order to make possible what Ricoeur calls 'an archaeology of the subject.'" Wink, *Bible in Human Transformation*, 34.
25. Wink, *Bible in Human Transformation*, 48.

symbols," but only after the needed distance of criticism and demythologization. In other words, once the critical methods have been applied, the reader needs to take the time for psychoanalytical examination of how that interpretation of the text is to actually impact his own life, rather than consider the critical interpretation as an end in itself.

Practically speaking, this impact of the text on the subject is depicted by Wink as a type of reader-response theory applied to the critical interpretation of the biblical passage.[26] Technique becomes subordinate to the "overarching purpose of enabling transformation." Wink argues that this move gives a deeper meaning to the text than the critical school was capable of on its own.[27]

This leads us to the third aspect of Wink's proposed dialectic, *communion*. What he means by communion is that the text is no longer merely an object to be studied, nor is the subject only the objective observer of the text, standing apart from it. Rather, the text, properly interpreted, should inform the life of its reader, and that insight should then construct deeper and further conclusions about the text. "If the subject-object *relationship* dialectically supplants the subject-object *dichotomy*, and in doing so establishes a communion of horizons, then there is worked a transformation of our life-relation to the text."[28]

In summary, Wink considers the various biblical critical approaches to Scripture as essential; the demythologization of Bultmann's school of thought and the symbolism of Ricoeur are vital. However, he argues the purported objectivity of the critic is a flawed assumption and leads to an anemic impact of the text upon the reader. Instead, the reader should critically interpret the text but then use that text to question his own assumptions about life, looking at how the themes found apply to his life and, in such examination, shed new light on the given text.

---

26. "For, even if, unlike a dream, I did not produce the story of the text, its capacity for evocation depends on its resonance with psychic and sociological realities within or impinging upon me. It is therefore legitimate to introject the characters in the Gospel story as probes into one's own self-understanding." Wink, *Bible in Human Transformation*, 55.

27. "Such exploratory analysis is not subjectivism or intrapsychic reductionism, for the understanding of ourselves which the text evokes makes possible a far more profound understanding *of what the text itself actually says*." Wink, *Bible in Human Transformation*, 62 (emphasis original).

28. Wink, *Bible in Human Transformation*, 68 (emphasis original).

Wink and the Powers as Social Ethic

Wink's primary test case for applying his hermeneutical method is in the study of the biblical Powers. As noted earlier, the Powers are terms for concepts and entities of power at work in the world as used in the New Testament, particularly by Paul. Wink links these Powers to concepts of liberation theology. Liberation theology largely arose from the need for the church to seriously address social justice issues, particularly in the Global South. It was brought to Western attention through the translation of books like Boff and Boff's *Introducing Liberation Theology* and Gustavo Gutiérrez's *The Theology of Liberation*. These and other theologians made a case for God's special concern for the plight of the poor and the need for the church to practice a "preferential option for the poor" or a priority of love towards the neediest neighbor.[29]

Walter Wink came into contact with the issue of institutionally inflicted suffering in a concrete manner. He had become interested in the concept of the Powers after reading and being inspired by William Stringfellow's *Free in Obedience*.[30] As part of his study, he traveled to several South American countries that lived under military dictatorships to speak with the priests and nuns and others who struggled against oppression. By the end of those four months, he was emotionally and spiritually overwhelmed by his exposure to the struggles against evil in those places.[31] His experience in the South had a profound effect on his view of the size, scope, and depth of evil in the world.[32] Wink focused his study of the concept of social action related to the Powers, particularly upon the New Testament, and produced his study in his *The Powers Trilogy*.

---

29. Boff and Boff, *Introducing Liberation Theology*; and Gutiérrez, *Theology of Liberation*.

30. Wink, *Naming the Powers*, xi. Stringfellow's book offers a challenge to the church to follow Jesus' call to obedience. Pertaining to our issue, part two of the book criticizes the church for trying to use the "principalities and powers," the institutions and ideologies of the world, to further the church's purposes. He argues that the church is trying to use tools not given to it to gain its ends in a manner which is improper to its calling. Yet, we are to be fully engaged with the world. Christ, freeing us from the bondage of death, ultimately also frees us from the bondage to the preservation of worldly institutions. So, we can bring truth to bear on the world by proper social action without need to identify with prevailing socio-cultural paradigms.

31. Wink, *Naming the Powers*, ix.

32. Wink, *Naming the Powers*, ix.

In the first volume, *Naming the Powers*, Wink presents an exegetical examination of terms for power in the New Testament and traditional Jewish literature of the intertestamental period. He separates the documents in a biblical-critical manner, looking at the undisputed passages of the New Testament in light of the Jewish writings and follows that discussion with the critically disputed passages of Paul.[33]

At the outset, Wink is consistent with the same assertions made in his hermeneutical work. He dismisses outright the belief in personal supernatural beings, but is also critical of the dismissive view's overt rejection of all supernatural accounts in Scripture.[34]

To analyze terms of Power in the New Testament, he outlines his analytic approach based on his preliminary observations. He notes that the language of Power pervades the whole of the New Testament.[35] The wording is "imprecise, liquid, interchangeable, and unsystematic"[36] yet clear patterns of usage will emerge.[37] Wink contends that different lists of Powers are really all shorthand for the same overall concept[38] which encompasses "heavenly and earthly, divine and human, spiritual and political, invisible and structural" aspects[39] that can be both good and evil.[40] He later adds one more observation, namely, that the terms for Power should be understood in their most comprehensive sense unless context further specifies.[41]

He brings up each term of Power he sees mentioned in the New Testament and makes some assertions on how each is used. These terms are *arche* (ruler) and *archai* (usually translated as "principalities"), *exousia* (authority or power), *dynamis* (power), *thronos* (throne), *kyriotes*

---

33. Wink, *Naming the Powers*, 39. By the term "disputed," Wink means those passages that are more controversial in provenance for the biblical critical tradition. But he also claims they are disputed in that they are ambiguous in their usage of the terms of power when compared with the passages he first examines. So, in one sense, he is trying to use an aspect of proper hermeneutic here, to use those passages deemed clearer "to specify who or what the Powers are in these more clouded texts," but it is on the basis of the biblical critical viewpoint.

34. Wink, *Naming the Powers*, 4–5.

35. Wink, *Naming the Powers*, 7.

36. Wink, *Naming the Powers*, 9.

37. Wink, *Naming the Powers*, 10.

38. Wink, *Naming the Powers*, 10–11.

39. Wink, *Naming the Powers*, 11.

40. Wink, *Naming the Powers*, 12.

41. Wink, *Naming the Powers*, 39.

(ruling power), and *onoma* (name).[42] He asserts that the terms of angels, fallen angels, evil spirits, demons, and angels of the nations are equivalent terms of power to those earlier mentioned.[43] He argues that each of the terms has both a political and spiritual reference, and that the language of Power in the New Testament is "far too rich and complex to reduce either to the human structures and institutions of the liberation theologians or the spiritual beings of traditional theology."[44] He then applies these findings to what the biblical critical school considers the disputed passages of the Pauline corpus. As he looks at the passages, he attempts to apply the general meanings he found in his word study to their Pauline instances.

For example, in regarding the familiar spiritual warfare text in Eph 6:10–20, Wink posits that the list of Powers in Eph 6:12 has to be demonic in interpretation, but also must adhere to his rules. Thus, he speaks of this list of enemies as "not only divine but human, not only personified but structural, not only demons and kings but the world atmosphere and power invested in institutions, laws, traditions, and rituals as well," including also the rich and powerful who seem to be of a higher order than the masses, the spirit of empire among nations, and institutional idolatry. Understood from a biblical critical viewpoint, he rephrases what he assumes Paul is saying: "we contend not against human beings as such ('blood and flesh') but against the legitimations, seats of authority, hierarchical systems, ideological justifications, and punitive sanctions which their human incumbents exercise and which transcend these incumbents in both time and power."[45]

In response, the Christian is to put on the whole armor of God, which Wink says are both defensive and offensive items.[46] He focuses primarily on the nature of the sword in the Vulgate being translated as *gladius*, the legionnaire's sword which could have been used offensively.[47] Likewise, he says of the repeated use of "stand" in verses 11, 13, and 14 that it highlights how persons are either drawing up for military formation in combat or taking the stance of a victor. He concludes about

42. Wink, *Naming the Powers*, 13–22.
43. Wink, *Naming the Powers*, 22–35.
44. Wink, *Naming the Powers*, 15.
45. Wink, *Naming the Powers*, 85.
46. "It is humorous to watch the statement bob from scholar to scholar that the weapons listed here are all 'defensive.' The Pentagon says the same about nuclear missiles." Wink, *Naming the Powers*, 86.
47. Wink, *Naming the Powers*, 86n101.

the armor and stance, "The writer has no notion here of Christian life as a last-ditch, rear-guard, defensive operation; this is war with the powers of evil. He depicts the church taking the fight to the enemy, and *he expects the church to win.*"[48] He then ties this observation with Eph 3:10 to conclude that all of the descriptions of fighting are a form of making known God's wisdom to these demonic Powers.[49]

This social understanding of the Pauline terminology of the Powers leads Wink to conclude that, "Paul has already taken key steps toward 'demythologizing' or at least depersonalizing it [i.e. the anthropomorphic character of the text] by means of the categories of sin, law, the flesh, and death. I suggest we follow Paul's lead in this, and attempt to reinterpret the mythic language of the Powers."[50]

By the end of his textual analysis, Wink concludes that the Powers of the New Testament are not personified, supernatural realities, nor abstractions of such realities that are only myths, nor just vessels of a primitive view to be summarily dismissed. Rather, the Powers are "the inner aspect of material or tangible manifestations of power."[51] The Powers are a part of the material world, the innermost essence of that reality.[52] The demons of the New Testament, then, are not an independent reality but "the name given that real but invisible spirit of destructiveness and fragmentation that rends persons, communities, and nations."[53] This inner aspect is always linked to an outer aspect, which is its natural manifestation within human systems. The "spiritual" inner aspect and the "material" outer manifestation are not two separate powers or entities, but *"simultaneously the outer and inner aspects of one and the same indivisible concretion of power."*[54]

These aspects, if negative, take on demonic nature. But when good is done and lived the aspects take on a heavenly disposition. "If heaven is not some other reality but the inner essence of present reality in its fullest potentiality, then the mystical 'ascent' is not out of the body and into a

---

48. Wink, *Naming the Powers*, 88 (emphasis original).
49. Wink, *Naming the Powers*, 95–96.
50. Wink, *Naming the Powers*, 104.
51. Wink, *Naming the Powers*, 104.
52. Wink, *Naming the Powers*, 105.
53. Wink, *Naming the Powers*, 107.
54. Wink, *Naming the Powers*, 107 (emphasis original).

wholly incorporeal spiritual realm, *but into the body's very own essence as the temple of the Holy Spirit within us.*"[55]

Now that Wink has established that these powers are anchored in the material order, they can be confronted. He contends they are confronted with Jesus, who is the exemplar of confrontation with such powers. "For if the crucified Jesus is 'Lord'—if the marred and disfigured form of the one truly human being who ever lived has become the criterion and norm of ultimate truth, life, and reality—then we and every power in heaven and on earth and under the earth are forever after utterly without excuse."[56]

Having performed the fusion and distance portions of his hermeneutic, Wink then moves on to his conclusions for communion with the text. For the Christian, Wink says there are three parts to the confrontation with the Powers. The first is to provide the communion with the text and reader. Before the powers can be engaged, a rigorous self-examination must take place to recognize our own inner evil and also our participation in institutional and cultural evil, which is easy to merely project upon opponents. "We must ask how we are like the very Power we oppose, and attempt to open these parts of ourselves to divine transformation."[57] It is only when we recognize the same evil in ourselves that we will not replace the evil we confront with our own version of the same thing. Having completed personal communion with the text, the second and third parts of the confrontation involve action dealing with the inner and outer aspects of the problematic, oppressive, power.

The church is to confront earthly powers and their outer aspects by pointing out repeatedly to whom they belong.[58] "Evangelism is *always* a form of social action. It is an indispensable component of any new 'world.' Unfortunately, Christian evangelism has all too often been wedded to a politics of the status quo and merely serves to relieve stress by displacing hope to an afterlife and ignoring the causes of oppression . . . all liberation involves conversion."[59] Conversely, Wink also asserts that social action is always evangelism, "if carried out in full awareness of Christ's sovereignty over the Powers."[60]

---

55. Wink, *Naming the Powers*, 122 (emphasis original).
56. Wink, *Naming the Powers*, 115.
57. Wink, *Naming the Powers*, 130.
58. Wink, *Naming the Powers*, 116.
59. Wink, *Naming the Powers*, 117 (emphasis original).
60. Wink, *Naming the Powers*, 117.

But faith and prayer also have a job, which is to intercede before God to deal with the inner aspects of evil. So Wink argues Christians should call on God to act on the inner aspects while we attend to the outer aspects of the broken institutions that assail the world.[61] Thus, the job of the Christian is "to work with determined persistence at the outer [aspect], and trust God to change the inner [aspect]."[62] Christians are called upon to be socially active against the outward actions and policies of oppressive systems at all intrapersonal and personal levels, but also are to pray for God to change the heart of such systems from demonic to heavenly so that they may, in turn, achieve their true, God-given potentials in society and world.

Wink expands on the inner aspect of his theory in *Unmasking the Powers*, looking more closely at the use of angelic and demonic terms in the biblical and extra-biblical literature.[63] For Wink, "Satan" is merely a term used for the dark side of our human natures, which we try to unconsciously repress. Ultimately, though, we must work to redeem as much of our lives as we can as Christians, and only then recognize and consciously repress what cannot be redeemed of our natures.[64]

For Wink, the demonic is the dark inner aspect of corrupted collective entities of Power.[65] Wink uses the event of the Gerasene demoniac as an example of a meta-narrative depicting such corrupted entities. By Wink's account, the episode is not about Jesus and personal exorcism, but a narrative about the Decapolis region stifled and struggling under oppressive foreign rule, most recently of Rome. The people of the region had focused their angst upon the man who became a "demoniac," really being used as a scapegoat for their frustrations and stress while under Roman subjugation. The demonic scapegoat was a personified story of their plight. The move of the demonic to the herd of pigs by Jesus represented the removal of the scapegoat motif, where Jesus freed the demoniac from

---

61. Wink, *Naming the Powers*, 126–27.

62. Wink, *Naming the Powers*, 127.

63. His approach is to treat all period literature equally. On the one hand, this is good because he is adamant that all biblical literature is equal so that he will not "elevate any part of it . . . to implicit supremacy." But on the other hand he also says, in an attempt to recover the New Testament worldview, "virtually any scrap of papyrus, however dubious its literary or religious value, can help us recover the basic cosmology of the epoch." Wink, *Unmasking the Powers*, 7–8.

64. Wink, *Unmasking the Powers*, 40. He again invokes Freud for this analysis.

65. Wink, *Unmasking the Powers*, 44.

the role forced upon him by the social structures. The people then begged Jesus to leave and, now without a scapegoat to vent upon, would become the rebels against Rome that Vespasian would come down upon in AD 68.[66] Consistent with his first volume, Wink continues in this manner of demythologization with examinations of angels,[67] gods,[68] and elements of the universe.[69]

The proper Christian response to the exterior aspect of these Powers is considered by Wink in the final volume, *Engaging the Powers*. Wink says that the Powers of the world can be good, and some are, but many are fallen. When fallen, they need to be redeemed from being a Domination System.[70] "The gospel is a context-specific remedy for the evils of the Domination System."[71]

Jesus was executed, Wink says, because he had set out to expose the domination systems of his day, and those in power killed him to maintain concealment of their system from the masses.[72] Jesus' ministry was one which preached, taught, and exemplified a domination-free order.[73] Such is the substance of Jesus' gospel message. "If Jesus had never lived, we would not have been able to invent him. There is, in the integrity of his teaching and living, an exposé and repudiation of the Domination System that no one trapped within that system could possibly have achieved. No wonder he was regarded as God's Son, descended from heaven."[74]

---

66. Wink, *Unmasking the Powers*, 43–48. This view has emerged elsewhere, including in a guest lecture by theologian Richard Horsley, who used this exact example when making his case for demythologization of the exorcistic events in Jesus' ministry. Horsley, "Jesus as Exorcist and Healer."

67. Angels of the churches are the spiritual health of congregations, angels of the nations are the stability of the spirituality of a nation, and angels of nature are "the code name for the numinous interiority of created things." Wink, *Unmasking the Powers*, 78, 93, 169.

68. Wink, *Unmasking the Powers*, 117. Gods are just the repressed powers of Jungian archetypes that occur to different degrees in every nation and every generation.

69. Wink, *Unmasking the Powers*, 145. The "elements of the universe" is the idolization of matter.

70. "The Domination System is what obtains when an entire network of Powers becomes hell-bent on control. The Domination System is, so to speak, the system of Powers, in a satanic parody of God, who might be called the System of the systems." Wink, *Engaging the Powers*, 49.

71. Wink, *Engaging the Powers*, 48.

72. Wink, *Engaging the Powers*, 110.

73. Wink, *Engaging the Powers*, 112.

74. Wink, *Engaging the Powers*, 136.

Wink concludes that Jesus' embodied gospel offers a third way of action against domination. Christians are called not to fight or flight, but to nonviolent direct action.[75] Such is not merely pacifism, which might be construed with submission and passivity, but includes measures of civil disobedience, such as seizing the moral initiative, refusing the humiliation inherent to victimization by a Domination System, exposing the injustice of the system, and shaming the oppressor into repentance, while seeking the oppressor's transformation.[76]

After the *Powers Trilogy*, Wink went on to further explore the ramifications of his approach. He examines just war theory and "the myth of redemptive violence" as he calls it, in comparison to his developed method of non-violence.[77] Violence, he says, is contrary to the gospel, but acknowledges humanity cannot always live up to the gospel. Instead of accepting terms like "just war" or "pure pacifism", he contends for terms of violence-reduction.[78] The enemy is not an enemy in traditional terms, but one who also needs redemption by God, so solutions minimizing violence toward the enemy, seeking redemption of the other, should be sought.[79]

He also applies his inner and outer aspects of social structures of Powers to Hiebert's issue of the excluded middle. Wink contends that his view is complementary to the ancient view of everything natural having a corresponding supernatural component. Where the primitive view saw personal supernatural, divine beings tied to each object, Wink has merely removed the personal supernatural and divine elements, substituting the inner aspect as the actual force such primal views were striving to ascertain.[80] Thus, he says, the excluded middle problem is solved by his approach.

When Wink applies his view to the crucified Jesus, he sees Jesus' life, ministry, suffering, and death as his commitment to nonviolence. Jesus' life and mission is then exemplary for his people, enabling all who are oppressed to identify with him and find comfort in him. Imitating Jesus'

---

75. Wink, *Engaging the Powers*, 175.

76. Wink, *Engaging the Powers*, 186–87. These are part of an 18-quality list for direct nonviolent action.

77. Wink, *Powers That Be*, 132–41.

78. Wink, *Powers That Be*, 140. This does not mean that violence is acceptable, just minimized when it does happen, a "restrained bellicosity."

79. Wink, *Powers That Be*, 176.

80. Wink, "Biblical Theology," 264.

nonviolent life also exposes the Powers in their rebellious state against God's intention for them so they may have opportunity for repentance and transformation.[81]

Finally, Wink applies these principles to the notion of the Cosmic Christ, noting that Christians contending with fallen Powers "do not have to 'make' the Cosmic Christ their Lord. We do not have to install Christ as the System of the systems. That is what the Cosmic Christ already *is*."[82] But that Cosmic Christ is himself cosmic because he is the apex of human potential. He argues that Jesus' work fulfilled Jewish Law and also every pagan myth to show us who we ought to be, and in doing so, Jesus' "own history became mythic, universal. By historicizing the myths he mythicized his history. Jesus' death on the cross was like a black hole in space that sucked into its collapsing vortex all the meanings of the universe, until in the intensity of its compaction there was an explosive reversal. . . . So Jesus as the Cosmic Christ became the universal human, and as such, the bearer of our own utmost possibilities for living."[83]

An Analysis of the Social Approach

Wink's formulation of the Powers and the Domination System has received positive reception, consideration, and attention by authors over the recent decades, both in terms of pneumatic demythologization[84] and social justice issues.[85] There are several aspects of his observations and calls to social action that ought to be considered by God's people. He raises the needed issue of the Christian life in society, culture, and politics, seeking to ingrain faith into life rather than compartmentalizing the sacred from the secular in daily living.

His way of getting to his destination, and the conclusions he has to make as a result of his path, are problematic. Some of his methodology is questionable within his own context. The suppositions from which he constructs his approach have some built-in contradictions. When he sets out his approach to explore the biblical terms of Power, for instance, he

---

81. Wink, "Biblical Theology," 270–71.
82. Wink, "Biblical Theology," 271 (emphasis original).
83. Wink, "Biblical Theology," 271.
84. For example, see Lane, *Unseen World*, in which nine of eleven theological essays on various aspects of the supernatural address Wink's teachings.
85. See, for example, Yong, *In the Days of Caesar*, 139–51.

notes their fluidity and interchangeability but then goes on to carefully delineate what many of the terms specifically mean. Moreover, a close reading of the biblical texts depicts, even within his standards, the angels and fallen angels as specifically supernatural beings without reference to a concrete social reality.[86]

Having rightly criticized the higher-critical method for the feigned objectivity of its day, Wink has embraced the idea of communion between life and the biblical text. However, he has succumbed to the philosophy of his time, post-modern subjectivity. His approach is painted with his Latin American experience and urgent need to legitimize social justice and civil disobedience. He uses a Jungian archetypal process of symbolic demythologization, similar to Paul Riceour, to create distance between himself and the text. In doing so, however, he also pursues his agenda of creating general concepts from the Powers so that he can apply them to the social constructs which concern him. Because he has presupposed the legitimacy of applying the Powers texts to social justice issues, he is unable to properly apply his Freudian self-examination to extricate his own initial motives from his hermeneutical conclusions.

In addition, by equally relying on Jewish intertestamental literature as on Scripture, his analysis implies that Jesus and his apostles are just as culturally conditioned and limited in understanding the meaning and direction of the Old Testament as all first-century Jews. As a result, the New Testament authors and those about whom they write (including Jesus), are assumed not to have a deeper, richer, and more accurate understanding of God's intentions and truth than any other first century Jew.

Also, the implications of his hermeneutic for interpretation beyond the Powers is left unexamined and unexplored. He contends that the angelic hosts (both holy and fallen), the principalities and powers, heaven and hell, are all merely symbolic of human systems. He is arguing that all unseen aspects of Scriptural reference are merely symbolic archetypes of sociocultural realities. However, he never gives a reason for stopping there in his dissection of the supernatural aspects of the scriptural account. By his criteria, he should also call into question the reality of prayer, of an

---

86. The terms of "angels" and "fallen angels" are not interchangeable biblically, which Wink distinguishes in practice but not in his guiding principles. Additionally, he is not consistent in his analysis of passages speaking of such beings. When it comes to explicit action by angels as proclaimers of Jesus' birth as the fulfillment of God's plan of salvation in the events of Luke, chapters 1–2, he dismisses them as a part of the mythic narrative which grew around Jesus' legacy; they do not fit into his Powers paradigm, so they are relegated to myth. Wink, *Engaging the Powers*, 113.

afterlife, and the existence of God.[87] For example, Wink commends the church to pray against the interiority of fallen systems,[88] but he leaves his skepticism and criticism he applied to the pneumatic passages out of his commendation for men to speak, even think, words upon which an unseen entity is supposed to hear, perceive, and act.

Wink's account of evil as the interior aspect of external social systems, while powerful, scales down the problem of evil merely to humanity and, more concerning, to human perception. Most of his examples of spiritual warfare involve political and climatological forms of justice as the highest good. Discerning what is institutionally good or evil, in the present, is only as powerful or validating as humanity's ability to discern the future consequences of present courses of action. Wink gives political examples of triumph in his approach, including such examples as Jesus' methods being parallel to Saul Alinsky's *Rules for Radicals*,[89] or assuming that Nicaragua's history would have been better if the United States had not backed the Contras.[90]

Other calls to action described by Wink such as nuclear disarmament, ecological justice in light of deforestation,[91] and the dismantling of oppressive regimes with nonviolent action might be positive, but are not the primary purpose of the church.[92] By placing social concerns at the fore of God's purpose for his people, the heavenly is replaced with the earthly, and the focus on death and rebirth, on the fulfillment of recreation, and the complete but future eradication of all sin and evil in Christ's action

---

87. Marva Dawn makes an accurate observation about Wink's theology when she says, "He reduces Jesus simply to a person with immense integrity and diminishes the atonement to an idea confused by Paul. Wink himself is not thoroughly Trinitarian and thereby elides an essential requirement for the atonement to be properly understood without ramifications of patriarchal oppression." in Dawn, *Powers*, 16.

88. Wink, *Engaging the Powers*, 297–317.

89. Wink, *Jesus and Nonviolence*, 39–50.

90. Wink, *Powers That Be*, 140–41. My critique is not a defense of the foreign military policy of the United States, but is to point out the presumption by Wink that he knows a brighter alternate future was in store for the Nicaraguans if the United States would have ignored the Nicaraguan situation. Even if Wink thinks it *likely*, he cannot *know*.

91. Wink, *Unmasking the Powers*, 163–65.

92. David Powlison insightfully notes, in response to Wink, that the list of social ills listed by Wink is decidedly politically liberal, ignoring other legitimate social concerns that are normally considered politically conservative. See Powlison, "Response to Walter Wink," 74n10.

for us is replaced with the concern for eradicating injustice today. Wink has reduced spiritual warfare, and the gospel, to social justice.

By the end of his trek down this theological road, Wink attempts to rewrite the "Jesus Myth" for the present Western culture in order for the culture to learn what it is to be human and for us to then transcend our perceived limitations. He sees this as the most important theological enterprise since the Reformation. This remythologization of Jesus goes far beyond scriptural boundaries, he notes, "In our Father/Mother's house, there are many mansions, with rooms for Moses, Elijah, Enoch, Metratron, Melchizedek, and—why not blurt it out—everyone who has served to reveal the Humanchild since history began. Any number of traditions can nurture the archetype of human transformation."[93]

Jack Miles, intending praise, describes Wink's observation above precisely when agreeing with Wink that the Reformation was really about reframing Jesus' story to become relevant for that day, Miles comments:

> What Wink understands to be the "most important theological enterprise since the Reformation" is, yes, on one level the old Reformational enterprise merely reprised. And yet, on another level, and why not blurt this out, it is not merely post-Reformational but post-Christian.[94]

Thus Wink, by the end of his theological journey, has made Jesus not King of kings and Lord of lords, but Myth of myths.

On the positive side, Wink has challenged the historical-critical tradition by taking the pneumatic texts more seriously. He has also challenged those in the West who hold to an inspired view of Scripture to find their own (heretofore missing or weak) solid account of how God and his people encounter evil in the world. He has responded to and incorporated concepts from other influential works beyond Ricoeur, including Berkhof's notion that these evil systems might be redeemed,[95] and Yoder's path of repudiating violence as an option for the church, both of which are worthy of closer consideration.[96] He exposes, to great depth, the durability and extensive nature of institutional evils. The call to the

---

93. Wink, *Human Being*, 229. Here, "Humanchild" is the term he coins for any contribution to the mythos of the ideal human person to which all persons should aspire.

94. Miles, "Myth of the Suppressing Church," 293.

95. Berkhof, *Christ and the Powers*, 42.

96. Wink, *Engaging the Powers*, 163–64.

people of God to be responsible voices and actors against evil in the world is needed and commendable, and many of his suggested practical actions may be viable. In the end, Wink's highlight of the social concern of spiritual warfare is commendable, but his imposed biblical critical limitations and, at best, anemic Christology (and Trinitarian theology) are unacceptable and unnecessary losses for what he is attempting to gain.

4

The Pneumatic Approach and C. Peter Wagner

C. Peter Wagner Becomes a Charismatic

Besides the social approach championed by Wink, another common Western account of spiritual warfare emphasizes its pneumatic dynamics. By "pneumatic" we mean a paradigm that accounts for a supernatural worldview in which the Christian fights against evil spirits with the help of the Holy Spirit. One of the best-known advocates for this approach is C. Peter Wagner. He was an evangelical missionary in Bolivia and later the director of the Andes Evangelical Mission. Wagner, like Wink, repudiated the notion of Christian violence as a legitimate reaction to oppressive regimes.[1] In his book on Latin American theology, he helpfully notes that conservative Evangelicals were right to be criticized for a lack of social vision for cultures under oppression.[2] He goes on to argue that the Bible speaks of two kingdoms, a kingdom of God and a kingdom of the devil, between which a temporal dualism is being waged.[3] The job of the church is to preach the kerygma in order fulfill the Great Commission and expand God's kingdom.[4] Social service is not the primary work of the church, but is the *diakonia* of the Christian, done out of love for others and because of the compulsion that faith without works is dead.[5]

---

1. Wagner, *Latin American Theology*, 86.
2. Wagner, *Latin American Theology*, 100.
3. Wagner, *Latin American Theology*, 104.
4. Wagner, *Latin American Theology*, 105.
5. Wagner, *Latin American Theology*, 106–8.

The Pneumatic Approach

When Wagner and other Evangelical missionaries were returning from their southern mission fields, where the Christian numbers were growing, they faced declining or plateauing numbers in their own denominations in the West and particularly in the United States. It caused Wagner to look to his mission experience for answers. Wagner combined what he had learned from Donald McGavran[6] about church membership strategies with his own Latin American mission experience. Wagner's work in and witness to the growth of Christianity in South America and his analysis of mission techniques made him a leading voice of the Church Growth Movement.[7]

His work in the area of spiritual warfare came in fits and starts. First, he wrote observations on the exploding Pentecostal movement, particularly in Chile, and noted the healing aspects of the ministry there.[8] Later, as a professor at Fuller Theological Seminary, he became friends with Pentecostal pastor John Wimber,[9] and teamed up with him to offer a course at Fuller entitled "Signs, Wonders, and Church Growth."[10] An aspect of the class was prayer for immediate healing for members of the class itself, in which "night after night I saw words of knowledge verified on the spot, sick people instantly healed, evil spirits cast out, and many other manifestations of supernatural ministry."[11] These experiences altered his views on the Christian life and ministry, which he discusses in his book *The Third Wave of the Holy Spirit*. The term "Third Wave" was subsequently taken up as the name for the signs and wonders movement.[12]

Wagner contends that a Western worldview has barred Christians in the West from recognizing the excluded middle. With Hiebert, he asserts that the Western worldview has two tiers, a cosmic religion of a supernatural reality which is aloof and detached from physical creation,

---

6. McGavran, *Understanding Church Growth*.

7. Wagner, *Frontiers in Mission Strategy*. Others influential works on the subject include: Wagner, *Your Spiritual Gifts*; Wagner, *Leading Your Church to Growth*; and Wagner, *Strategies for Church Growth*.

8. Wagner, *Third Wave of the Holy Spirit*, 23. Wagner writes about his observations from Chile in Wagner, *Spiritual Power and Church Growth*.

9. Wagner, *Third Wave of the Holy Spirit*, 23.

10. Wagner, *Third Wave of the Holy Spirit*, 24.

11. Wagner, *Third Wave of the Holy Spirit*, 24.

12. "The label 'Third Wave' surfaced while I was being interviewed on this subject by *Pastoral Renewal* magazine. . . . It is simply a term which I found convenient at the moment, and which some others have picked up, to describe this new activity of the Holy Spirit." Wagner, *Third Wave of the Holy Spirit*, 15.

and the physical realm of daily life governed by science.[13] But most of the non-Western world has a third, middle, tier in which "everyday phenomena are influenced by superhuman and supernatural forces."[14] For Wagner, the lack of this middle, of an integrative pneumatic approach, is a key reason for the difficulty of the Western churches to flourish and for their lack of the Spirit's dynamic presence.[15]

Ignoring this middle tier has also caused Westerners to miss some critical facets of faith, Wagner contends, citing four types of faith for Christians: saving faith,[16] sanctifying faith,[17] possibility-thinking faith,[18] and fourth-dimension faith.[19] Westerners, he says, normally have the first two facets, but rarely the third and not at all the fourth.[20] But it is the fourth dimension, Wagner argues, in which spiritual warfare occurs.

Based on Dan 10:10–21, Wagner argues that demons rule over portions of the earth not yet reclaimed by the church. In these places, Christian activity in the area of fourth-dimension faith can unbind the geographic area, as well as its people, from demonic rule, and open it to the gospel.[21]

These discoveries propelled Wagner from considering the possibility of signs and wonders to becoming a leading voice on spiritual warfare, including his four-volume Prayer Warrior series,[22] especially his work on Strategic-Level Spiritual Warfare (SLSW). This is a method of spiritual warfare dependent upon fourth-dimension faith and the diligence of the Christian to seek out and, in authoritative prayer, engage in the removal of oppressive territorial spirits.

---

13. Wagner, *Third Wave of the Holy Spirit*, 32.
14. Wagner, *Third Wave of the Holy Spirit*, 31.
15. Wagner, *Third Wave of the Holy Spirit*, 45.
16. Wagner, *Third Wave of the Holy Spirit*, 37.
17. Wagner, *Third Wave of the Holy Spirit*, 38.
18. Wagner, *Third Wave of the Holy Spirit*, 38–39. This third dimension is faith for setting goals toward possibility and growth. His inspiration for this facet is Robert Schuller. This facet is a central tenet of Wagner's popular approach to church growth.
19. Wagner, *Third Wave of the Holy Spirit*, 40–41. This fourth dimension is the expectation of God's supernatural action in Christian ministry today.
20. Wagner, *Third Wave of the Holy Spirit*, 41.
21. Wagner, *Third Wave of the Holy Spirit*, 58–60.
22. This series includes: Wagner, *Warfare Prayer*; Wagner, *Prayer Shield*; Wagner, *Confronting the Powers*; and Wagner, *Praying with Power*.

Wagner's Hermeneutical Approach

Scripture and Experience

Like with Wink, we can better follow how Wagner comes to these conclusions by first understanding how he approaches the Bible. Wagner lays out his hermeneutical approach to spiritual warfare in the third book of his Prayer Warrior series, *Confronting the Powers*. Unlike Wink, Wagner holds a high view of Scripture, referring to himself as a "biblical inerrantist."[23] But he also notes the centrality of experience for his view: "Though good theological understanding informs good ministry, I believe that ministry ordinarily comes first and then theology follows."[24] He argues that Paul ministered this way: "Paul's theology was much more rooted in what he *experienced* and what he *did* than in his rabbinical training."[25]

Wagner believes that the fourth (pneumatic) dimension is encountered primarily through observational and experiential knowledge of events rather than intellectual knowledge.[26] To validate these experiences, Wagner creates a set of seven criteria to discern proper methodology and verify warfare events while still adhering to Scripture. The method or event can be considered valid if, first, it does not contradict the clear teaching of Scripture or biblical principles; second, it brings glory to the Triune God; third, the results conform to God's will; fourth, it blessed those involved; fifth, it advances God's kingdom on earth; sixth, it is affirmed by at least two witnesses; and lastly, its conclusion "merits agreement by responsible and like-minded colleagues."[27]

He goes on to make an important, further distinction in his first criterion between biblical proof and biblical concepts. He states that if the Bible does not prohibit a concept or method, and if a collation of biblical data allows for a concept, and the other criteria still hold, then that concept or method is still biblical, "but in a somewhat broader sense of the term."[28]

---

23. Wagner, *Confronting the Powers*, 51.
24. Wagner, *Confronting the Powers*, 44.
25. Wagner, *Confronting the Powers*, 44 (emphasis original).
26. Wagner, *Confronting the Powers*, 50–51.
27. Wagner, *Confronting the Powers*, 63.
28. Wagner, *Confronting the Powers*, 86–87.

To support SLSW, Wagner pursues this broader method of hermeneutic collation. He begins by arguing for general exorcistic practice. He highlights the parts of Jesus' ministry of healing which had demons as a cause for ailments and other issues.[29] He "counts 150 references to conflict in the spirit world of the Gospels."[30] Based on Jesus' interaction with the demonic, for example, Wagner notes, "it is not far-fetched to understand Jesus' coming to earth as analogous to a military invasion."[31] This leads to Jesus' later commission to the disciples in Matthew to baptize and teach which, Wagner contends, would have included confronting pneumatic issues along the way.[32] In particular, he argues that Acts records the apostles continuing in the confrontation of the demonic, and adds that John, Peter, and Paul all speak to this conflict in their epistles.[33]

In the first few centuries of the church, Wagner notes that we also find anecdotes about the early Christians exorcising demons, including references by Justin, Irenaeus, Tertullian, and Cyprian.[34] In addition, Wagner places great significance on historian and Yale professor Ramsay MacMullen's conclusion to his exploration of the rapid rise of Christianity in the Roman Empire, arguing that the extraordinary faith change in the empire resulted from an "emphasis on miraculous demonstration, head-on challenge of non-Christians to a test of power, head-on confrontation with supernatural beings inferior to God, and contemptuous dismissal of merely rational . . . paths toward true knowledge of the divine."[35]

Wagner affirms that the source of the power to confront the demonic is the Holy Spirit. He notes that Jesus relied on the Holy Spirit's action throughout his life and ministry in these demonic encounters, and that the apostles, the early church, and Christians today do the same: "Everything Jesus did by way of power ministries He did by the Holy Spirit. Furthermore, He let the disciples know in very clear terms that they would only be successful in ministry if they did the same. Good

---

29. Wagner, *Confronting the Powers*, 122.

30. Wagner, *Confronting the Powers*, 124. Figure cited from Murphy, *Handbook of Spiritual Warfare*, 290.

31. Wagner, *Confronting the Powers*, 124.

32. Wagner, *Confronting the Powers*, 126–28.

33. Wagner, *Confronting the Powers*, 128–29.

34. Wagner, *Confronting the Powers*, 101–16.

35. Wagner, *Confronting the Powers*, 101. Cited from MacMullen, *Christianizing the Roman Empire*, 112.

Christology leads to good pneumatology, and vice versa."[36] Further, he says that for the Holy Spirit to empower a person to perform spiritual warfare one must "be holy before the Lord, have no unconfessed sin and be free of carnal motives."[37]

At this point Wagner concludes, "The kingdom of God [Jesus] brought was resisted at every turn by Satan and his forces of darkness. When Jesus left the earth, He left His disciples with the same power source He used . . . Jesus left His disciples to carry on the war."[38] By extention, then, if the disciples were to carry on the war, then so are all of God's people even today.[39]

In this war, different levels of spiritual warfare can take place, often simultaneously: ground-level, occult-level, and strategic-level.[40] The ground-level takes place by breaking demonic influence on individuals.[41] The occult-level "involves resistance to a more ordered level of demonic authority" as found in pagan and eastern religions.[42] But the highest level of action is found in strategic level warfare, which "requires confrontations with high-ranking principalities and powers as described by Paul in Ephesians 6:12."[43]

Having established his different levels of spiritual warfare, Wagner then addresses SLSW in particular. The demonic entities at the strategic-level, Wagner asserts, are powerful territorial spirits that oppress whole geographical regions, constantly pushing the masses toward sin and chaos and against God's will and good order.[44] He derives this idea from Dan 10:10–20, in which the Prince of Persia delays the angel Michael from assisting Daniel.[45] He then links this to Deut 32:8 and its mention of the boundaries of peoples corresponding to the number of God's angels,

---

36. Wagner, *Confronting the Powers*, 133.

37. Wagner, *Confronting the Powers*, 156.

38. Wagner, *Confronting the Powers*, 141.

39. Wagner, *Confronting the Powers*, 143.

40. Wagner and Greenwood, "Strategic-Level Deliverance Model," 178; also Wagner, *Confronting the Powers*, 20–22.

41. Wagner, *Confronting the Powers*, 213–15.

42. Wagner and Greenwood, "Strategic-Level Deliverance Model," 179; Wagner, *Confronting the Powers*, 215–16.

43. Wagner and Greenwood, "Strategic-Level Deliverance Model," 179; Wagner, *Confronting the Powers*, 22.

44. Wagner and Greenwood, "Strategic-Level Deliverance Model," 179–80.

45. Wagner, *Confronting the Powers*, 172–73.

agreeing with F. F. Bruce who asserts on this passage, "in a number of places some at least of these angelic governors are portrayed as hostile principalities and powers."[46]

Other Authorities than the Bible

Wagner then points to Jesus' depiction of the strong man as "a key text for understanding the concept that Jesus commissions us to do strategic-level spiritual warfare."[47] Wagner examines the confrontation of Jesus and the Pharisees in Luke 11:14–26. There, Jesus casts out a demon that is causing a man to be mute. The Pharisees see this and conclude that Jesus has received this power from Beelzebub, the prince of demons (Luke 11:15). Wagner argues that when the Pharisees move from talking about the demon Jesus removed to discussing Beelzebub, they have turned the conversation from ground-level to strategic-level spiritual warfare.[48] Wagner goes on to assert that Beelzebub is a general under Satan, and that other names, which he says are also demonic entities, such as Wormwood and Apollyon, are also principality demons separate from Satan.[49]

On this point, he says, "the Bible does not provide us with sufficiently clear evidence to prove either the point that Beelzebub *is* the same person as Satan or that he is *not*. Our conclusions either way are most likely based much more on certain assumptions we bring to the text rather than an exegesis of the text itself."[50] Since he cannot argue for his demonic hierarchy by way of clear biblical teaching, he asserts "it may be possible to receive selected, but valid, information from the world of darkness itself."[51]

Regarding this concept of gleaning information from the demonic realm, on the one hand, Wagner recommends caution since demons are known deceivers. On the other hand, he also asserts that "certain people such as shamans, witch doctors, practitioners of Eastern religions, New Age gurus or professors of the occult on university faculties" as well as

---

46. Wagner, *Confronting the Powers*, 173. Cited from Bruce, *Epistle to the Hebrews*, 33.
47. Wagner, *Confronting the Powers*, 145.
48. Wagner, *Confronting the Powers*, 147.
49. Wagner, *Confronting the Powers*, 147.
50. Wagner, *Confronting the Powers*, 147.
51. Wagner, *Confronting the Powers*, 148.

former occultists who are now Christians, may have knowledge which might be considered accurate.[52] From this basis, he asserts, "The reason I have concluded [Beelzebub] is a principality under the command of Satan is that the consensus of written materials I have examined and of the personal interviews I have conducted with experts about the occult lead me to that judgment. I have seen those who know this smile somewhat patronizingly when I suggest that Beelzebub may be Satan. They generally know very well who the notorious Beelzebub is, and to ask whether he is Satan seems absurd to many who operate professionally in the spirit world."[53]

Having argued for his derivation of the demonic hierarchy, Wagner then makes further assertions about the events in Luke 11. He notes that Jesus' use of the term "finger of God" in the text is talking about the Holy Spirit, derived from the parallel account in Matt 12:28. This is important to the construction of the SLSW argument because it reiterates that all Christians have the same source of power for deliverance that Jesus used.[54]

In Luke 11:21, Jesus notes the strong man is armed, guards his place, and his goods are at peace. Wagner interprets the strong man being Beelzebub, the goods as unbelievers, and notes that, if nothing happens to prevent it, Beelzebub is armed and able to keep people in his territory from believing with his protective power over that territory.[55] He then concludes that territorial spirits have kept whole parts of the world away from the gospel because their armament has been allowed to stay intact.[56]

The next verse, Luke 11:22, points to the remedy for this when it says that one stronger than the strong man can go and bind him and plunder his goods. Wagner argues that the stronger one is not Jesus, but the Holy Spirit.[57] This, again, is crucial to Wagner's argument because the Holy Spirit resides with God's people today. So if Jesus was able, by the Holy Spirit, to overcome all demons, then we share that same source

---

52. Wagner, *Confronting the Powers*, 148.
53. Wagner, *Confronting the Powers*, 148.
54. Wagner, *Confronting the Powers*, 149.
55. Wagner, *Confronting the Powers*, 149–50.
56. Wagner, *Confronting the Powers*, 150.
57. Wagner, *Confronting the Powers*, 151.

of power and authority to likewise overcome them, including all of the territorial strong men.[58] This is Wagner's central point:

> One high-priority use of this Holy Spirit power by those who wish to serve Jesus in evangelism is to overcome whatever strongman may be holding a particular neighborhood or city or people group in spiritual captivity. Nothing I know of could be more important for winning the lost. If we are not satisfied with the fruit of our current evangelistic activities, whatever they may be, strategic-level spiritual warfare might at least be worthy of some experimentation. Possibly a strongman needs to be bound by the power of the Holy Spirit given to us.[59]

Wagner then jumps from Luke 11 to Matt 16:13–19 to discuss Jesus' commissioning of the church. There, Wagner says, Jesus announces that the church will prevail against the devil's forces when he declares that the gates of hell will not overcome the church. The way in which the church overcomes Satan and the demons and their work is by the power given to her to bind and loose in Matt 16:19. Wagner concludes that the actions of binding and loosing are actually about binding and loosing the territorial spirits.[60] This is where discernment is needed, he says. One must be able to gain a *rhema* (word of insight) from God as to the name of a spirit to bind it, and for direction for when to mount an attack.[61]

SLSW is, Wagner concludes, a valuable way of removing powerful demonic barriers to evangelism in that territory.[62] Once the spirit is removed, it must also be kept from returning. Often, Wagner says, the church has not sufficiently removed all of the legal claims that the demonic powers have over a territory and so they have a right to return.[63]

To supplement his hermeneutical analysis, Wagner asserts that there are biblical accounts of SLSW where the apostles take on such

---

58. Wagner, *Confronting the Powers*, 152.

59. Wagner, *Confronting the Powers*, 152.

60. Wagner, *Confronting the Powers*, 154–56.

61. "It is foolish, as well as dangerous, to confront the enemy by binding and loosing outside the will of God or outside His timing." Wagner, *Confronting the Powers*, 155.

62. Wagner, *Confronting the Powers*, 156.

63. Wagner uses Western Europe's post-Christian attitude as an example, saying that not all of Satan's legal claims on Europe were removed, indicating this as the source of the continent's growing Christian apathy. He makes no thorough argument for this idea of legal rights except in a footnote claiming one might make the case from Satan's assertions to God in the book of Job. Wagner, *Confronting the Powers*, 158–59n2.

entities. He claims that such examples include: Peter's encounters with Simon Magus[64] and King Herod,[65] and Paul's encounters with Bar-Jesus,[66] the Python spirit,[67] and Diana of Ephesus.[68]

Wagner's Implementation of Strategic-Level Spiritual Warfare

Having made his argument for the reality of SLSW, Wagner then speaks to the different aspects of actually carrying it out. To engage in this level of warfare, Wagner cites four components for the warrior's strategy: spiritual mapping, divine insight (*rhema*), identificational repentance, and prayer walking.

Wagner says that warfare at this level requires preparation in the form of spiritual mapping. This involves gathering spiritual information about the community, city or nation, such as the history of the land and the peoples, locations of destruction and evil in its history, broken covenants among the peoples, and other egregious sins perpetuated by the people, as well as their general faith history.[69] The concept of spiritual mapping comes from Charismatic leader George Otis Jr.[70] Wagner explores this concept even further in his book *Breaking Strongholds in Your City*, where he calls on Otis and other Charismatic leaders who participate in SLSW to confirm the system by their own use of it.[71]

Wagner asserts biblical support for this concept in 2 Cor 4:18, where Paul says that we look at the things unseen rather than those which are

---

64. Wagner, *Confronting the Powers*, 174–77.

65. Wagner, *Confronting the Powers*, 177–80. This is an important assumption by Wagner. Jesus cannot actually get at the world because the devil gained possession of it in the fall. So, saved humans must be God's instruments to take back parts for God through careful, rigorous prayer.

66. Wagner, *Confronting the Powers*, 190–95.

67. Wagner, *Confronting the Powers*, 195–97.

68. Wagner, *Confronting the Powers*, 203–17.

69. Wagner, *Confronting the Powers*, 236–37.

70. Otis, *Last of the Giants*, 85.

71. *Breaking Strongholds in Your City* is primarily a book of anecdotes and testimonials of how mission work struggled until the unseen demonic powers and unrepented regional sins were exposed. Once these were addressed, the mission efforts were more fruitful. In particular, the work of Victor Lorenzo in La Plata, Argentina, is noted in the epilogue. Wagner, *Breaking Spiritual Strongholds*.

seen, and in Ezek 4:3, where God charges Ezekiel to make a map of the city to lay siege to it.[72] Wagner says that spiritual mapping is an essential tool for spiritual warfare in addressing the unseen needs of a community.[73] This is combined with the Christian's impressions, dreams, and visions from God to create a complete understanding of what is broken and what entity or entities are behind the issues.[74] Such spiritual mapping lays open the historic and present sins of the peoples in that place.

The second step of SLSW is called identificational repentance,[75] in which intercessory prayers of repentance are said on behalf of the sins of a people group in that place.[76] "Those of us who contend with territorial spirits on a professional level believe that no expression of spiritual warfare prayer is more significant than identificational repentance."[77] These prayers may include past cultural sins, such as racism, slavery, and related land issues,[78] bloodshed in a place,[79] the idolatry of false religions such as freemasonry or more explicit forms of occultic activity,[80] or broken cultural or governmental covenants.[81]

Wagner concedes that there is nothing in the New Testament about this type of repentance, but points to Old Testament evidence, such as Exod 20:5 concerning the sins of the fathers visited upon the children,

---

72. "Obviously, this refers to spiritual, not conventional, warfare." Wagner, *Breaking Spiritual Strongholds*, Preface.

73. "I understand Paul's message to mean we must recognize that the essential battle for world evangelization is a spiritual battle and that the weapons of this warfare are not carnal but spiritual. We must also recognize that God has given us a mandate for intelligent, aggressive spiritual warfare. If we understand this, the more the process of world evangelization will be accelerated. Understanding the differences between the visible and the invisible is one important component of the overall battle plan to break the hold the enemy has on lost and perishing souls." Wagner, *Breaking Spiritual Strongholds*, chapter 2.

74. In addition to the anecdotes in *Breaking Spiritual Strongholds*, see also: Wagner and Greenwood, "Strategic-Level Deliverance Model," 181–87.

75. The pioneer of this proposed mechanism is John Dawson in Dawson, *Healing America's Wounds*.

76. Identificational repentance is discussed by other authors besides Wagner and Dawson, including Jacobs, *Possessing the Gates of the Enemy*.

77. Wagner and Greenwood, "Strategic-Level Deliverance Model," 187; Wagner, *Confronting the Powers*, 239.

78. Wagner and Greenwood, "Strategic-Level Deliverance Model," 183–84.

79. Wagner and Greenwood, "Strategic-Level Deliverance Model," 185.

80. Wagner and Greenwood, "Strategic-Level Deliverance Model," 185–86.

81. Wagner and Greenwood, "Strategic-Level Deliverance Model," 186–87.

Nehemiah confessing the sins of his fathers (Neh 1:6), and David remitting Saul's sins against the Gibeonites in 2 Sam 21:1–14.[82] Collating these passages into a biblical justification, he confirms his assumptions through his and others' experiences. He sees this step not only as crucial for opening a place for evangelism, but also for keeping the evil spirits from returning:

> We know a great deal more about [blocking evil spirits from returning] than we did previously, largely through our understanding that a crucial part of much strategic-level spiritual warfare should be identificational repentance. Through accurate and sensitive spiritual mapping we can identify strongholds rooted in unremitted sins of past generations and we now understand the ways and means of dealing with those sins of the past in our own generation.[83]

Third, yet intertwined with the other components, God gives special messages and instructions to the Christian which involve prophetic decrees or actions. This is referred to as *rhema*. These can be divine insights giving information such as the names of demonic entities, or God's directives of command to use against these principalities. With God's directives, he argues, the Christian announces those directives against the demonic forces, expressing the prophetic actions that God urges.[84]

Lastly, one practices prayerwalking. This component involves wandering the area and praying about the spiritual bondage and oppression of the place. This includes praying for what one encounters in the journey, praying for the items uncovered by the spiritual mapping, professing repentance for those things if required, and any other revelations God gives as one walks and prays.[85] Through these steps, the spiritual bondage of a place is broken and the gospel can then be shared without obstruction.

Though deliverance ministry had been a part of the Charismatic movement for decades, it was Frank E. Peretti's fictional book *This Present Darkness* which brought notions of SLSW into the mainstream Christian consciousness. Wagner's efforts at some systemization of SLSW theology and his already-recognized name from his work on church growth brought him sizable influence in the evangelical world and led to his

---

82. Wagner, *Confronting the Powers*, 79.
83. Wagner, *Confronting the Powers*, 159.
84. Wagner and Greenwood, "Strategic-Level Deliverance Model," 188.
85. Wagner and Greenwood, "Strategic-Level Deliverance Model," 190–91.

leadership in proposing SLSW at Lausanne II.[86] From there, his influence in this area continued to grow to make him the most prominent representative of SLSW.[87] His leadership in the New Apostolic Reformation also increased the influence of SLSW as a predominant model for Western Charismatic leaders in removing demonic obstacles from a place in the greater advancement of God's Kingdom.[88]

An Analysis of the Pneumatic Approach

Through a Lutheran lens, there are some fundamental issues to address in Wagner's pneumatic paradigm. First, his hermeneutic is inconsistent and problematic. Wagner begins with personal experience and observation in ministry. After this, he says, one turns to Scripture to find a basis or validation for an event. If one does not find the Bible explicitly contradicting one's assertion, then one can move on to collect biblical data which supports the assertion. Wagner's approach falters at this point. For Wagner, the biblical data does not have to be contextual; the context of a sentence or thought in Scripture is immaterial if the words, in isolation, can be made to fit the topic. Like Wink, Wagner approaches Scripture from a personally subjective stance, albeit one that claims Scripture as holy. Yet, that holiness does not include Scripture as a primary means by which the Holy Spirit acts upon humans. Rather, the Bible is a sourcebook from God for guidance, confirming the immediate action of the Spirit in one's life. The result is a hermeneutical system where it is easy to back up one's subjective, experiential viewpoint with Scripture, disregarding the context of the text.

---

86. By the Lausanne II conference in 1989, his views were influential enough to warrant special consideration by the international assembly; the official Lausanne statement expresses some reservations about an overemphasis on SLSW. But it has been very influential nonetheless. The general statement can be found here: Lausanne Movement, "Statement on Spiritual Warfare (1993)." For further development and discourse building off of the Lausanne statement, see: Moreau et al., *Deliver Us From Evil*.

87. "The remarkable interest in workshops on the Holy Spirit, spiritual warfare, and prayer offered at Lausanne II eventually led to the birth of the AD 2000 Movement and its United Prayer Track, as well as the Spiritual Warfare Network. At the intersection of these groups was a man who has become the most widely recognized advocate for strategic-level spiritual warfare today, C. Peter Wagner." Beilby and Eddy, *Understanding Spiritual Warfare*, 40.

88. For a thorough examination and critique of the New Apostolic Reformation and its relation to SLSW, see Geivett and Pivec, *New Apostolic Reformation?*, 150–65.

This approach leads Wagner, as noted earlier, to the assertion that we can build our knowledge of the devil and the fallen angels on the words and revelations of the demons themselves and from occult practitioners. In this way, he maintains, one can discern such information as names of the demons, their motives, their organization structure, and more.[89] Wagner asserts that the demons always spoke the truth in the New Testament.[90] Yet this romantic epistemology ignores the deceptive character of the words of the serpent in Genesis,[91] that Jesus called the devil "the father of lies,"[92] the twisting of Scripture into lies by the devil in the temptation narratives,[93] and Revelation depicting the devil as the ultimate deceiver.[94] Wagner merely culls the data which supports his experiential inferences.[95] Further, his dependence upon, on the one hand, the information from demons and occultic practitioners and, on the other hand, the reliance on the various *rhema* of visions and dreams and other signs for dealing with demonic powers sounds very much like the discernment of the Wiccan practitioners discussed in chapter 2. Such similarities are not condemning of his method, but they are disturbing.

Second, though Wagner went through a paradigm shift in working with John Wimber, a consistent thread in his teaching from his mission days to the present day is that the world is ruled by the devil and the fallen angels, and the inauguration of the kingdom of God is an invasion by God into enemy territory.[96] This position unveils a temporal dualism to which he admits.[97] God's sovereignty is misplaced in this paradigm.

Third, from his hermeneutical foundation, Wagner argues that the experience of signs and wonders can be linked to the Holy Spirit's desire to work powerfully through humans against the devil. He uses sensory

---

89. Wagner, *Confronting the Powers*, 64–70.

90. Wagner, *Confronting the Powers*, 69–70.

91. Gen 3:1–5.

92. John 8:44.

93. Matt 4:1–11; Mark 1:12–13; Luke 4:1–13.

94. Rev 13:14; 20:10.

95. Moreover, even when the demons spoke the truth in the New Testament, it was to thwart the will of God. For example, during his ministry, Jesus did not want his identity known, so the demons pronounced it openly. For example, see Mark 1:21–28, 34.

96. Wagner, *Latin American Theology*, 104.

97. "I have no problem in affirming a *limited* dualism, because Satan and his forces of evil are not yet all under Jesus' feet as they will be sometime in the future." Wagner, *Confronting the Powers*, 64.

experience and anecdotal evidence as a fundamental part of his argument for describing the pneumatic dimensions of the Christian battle. He uses these as confirmation of all he is saying rather than, at best, a possible correlation between individual experience and biblical narrative. As he reads his experiences back into the texts, his method does not really affirm his approach, but instead displays his epistemological priorities in his readings of Scripture and the writings of the early church. By placing the believer's experiences at the center of his evidence for warfare, Wagner creates an anthropological maximalism in which God's ability to act is contingent on the believer. The human is, like with Wink, placed at the center of successful spiritual warfare. Through the prayer of a believer, for example, the Spirit acts out miracles and also gives the person the insights and powers needed to wage war against the fallen angels to take back the world for God. This makes God's purposes in history "contingent, by His own design, on the effectiveness of believing prayer."[98] Such assertions threaten to put the human person as central to God successfully enacting his will in the world.

Compounding this anthropological maximalism, Wagner comments that the Spirit will work power only through persons leading pure lives so that the channel of the Spirit is clean and clear.[99] While morality is important for the Christian life, this view asserts the Christian must reach a certain level of sanctification for the Holy Spirit to make use of him/her. Such a stance denies the power of original sin and implies that the Spirit's ability to act is limited by the level of our active sanctification.[100]

Fourth, Wagner's pneumatic approach is confined to the spiritual realm. It addresses direct confrontation with evil spiritual forces but does little to address the daily needs of the neighbor, particularly those who are poor, oppressed, or face other social concerns. This pneumatic approach has effectively suppressed the social concerns.

However, there are gains from Wagner. First, he takes the Scriptural accounts of demonic activity seriously, treating them as personal entities who harass and attack persons, including Christians. This forces the

---

98. Wagner, *Confronting the Powers*, 253.

99. Wagner, *Confronting the Powers*, 156.

100. This stance puts all of the onus for a proper relationship with God upon the Christian, which also has implications for justification and his view of the Trinitarian economy of salvation. How Wagner delineates the line between the Son's work for salvation, God the Father's approval, and one's usefulness to the Holy Spirit is unclear, but appears all to be related to one's piety.

Christian to take the experiences of others into account when they speak of supernatural experiences or occult involvement rather than simply dismissing them as mere psychological expressions. His regard for the Scriptural accounts also causes Wagner to take the world's idols seriously. They are not seen as innocuous concepts of primitive cultures but as real enemies of the gospel proclamation; they are not competing narratives born of equal cultural validity to the Western Christian narrative (as biblical critical authors and secular voices claim),[101] but active demonic entities seeking to subvert the work of the church.

Second, he significantly emphasizes the prayer life of the Christian. While Wink also gives a place to prayer in his paradigm, Wagner makes it an integral aspect of spiritual warfare. Prayer is used in every level of spiritual warfare including SLSW. He puts emphasis on the use of prayer to call upon the Holy Spirit to give information and for the strength to act against the demonic.

Related to this, Wagner acknowledges that the Holy Spirit's action is essential for spiritual warfare to succeed. In his approach, the Christian must be empowered by the Holy Spirit to make any advance against the powers of darkness in a place. God's help is essential for success.

Both Wink and Wagner have tried to fill in a theological gap they perceived after encountering the theology and mindset of cultures less affected than the West by the Enlightenment. Wink's focus on the social concerns of the oppressed removed all pneumatic concerns expressed in the Scriptures, despite the fact that strong belief in the supernatural is a part of the very culture which inspired him. Wagner has created a paradigm for his pneumatic approach in which humans fight against the unseen cosmic powers of evil spirits with the power of the Holy Spirit. However, this approach has lost almost all talk about his main evangelistic concern as a missionary in his earlier works, or about addressing the social concerns of oppressed peoples so that the gospel might have freer course among them.

Both Wagner and Wink began with a hermeneutic based on subjective experience and observation, and subsequently looked to the Bible to support their views, rather than grounding experience in a comprehensive biblical account of spiritual warfare. Missing from these approaches is a creedal hermeneutic, one which begins and ends not with self, or the world, or the neighbor, but with a narrative of spiritual

---

101. See chapter 2.

warfare grounded in the work of the Triune God, the salvation given in Christ Jesus, and his inaugural reign. Such a different foundation will enable not only a more biblically faithful and consistent approach to spiritual warfare, but also robustly address both the pneumatic and social concerns of these theologians.

5

The Bifurcated Approach and Lutheran Voices

The Common Critique Re-examined

Paul Hiebert's assessment of the Western church and its division of the natural and supernatural realms has been visited already in chapters 2 and 4. There, we noted Hiebert's criticism of mainline denominations was centered on how they functionally and theologically consider the spiritual or supernatural realm to have little to do with the natural realm in any meaningful way, saying:

> God, angels and demons are involved in a cosmic battle in the heavens, but the everyday events on earth are best explained and controlled by science and technology. People pray to God for their salvation, but turn to modern medicine for healing and psychology for deliverance from so called demon possession, because demons exist in the heavens, not on earth. Western missionaries influenced by this dualism affirm the cosmic battle between good and evil, but deny the realities of witchcraft, spirit possession, evil eye and magic in the cultures where they serve. Consequently, they fail to provide biblical answers to the people's fears of earthly spirits and powers, and to deal with the reality of Satan's work on earth.[1]

Hiebert's time in mission work, like that of Wagner, led him to believe that this separation was in error. Instead, he proposed an overlap of

---

1. Hiebert, "Spiritual Warfare and Worldviews," 1–2.

the supernatural and the natural realms. He is correct that ignorance of the supernatural realm's interaction with the natural is a deficiency.

However, Hiebert's assessment is not an entirely accurate representation of the doctrinal work of Western mainline denominations over the last two centuries. The churches of the bifurcated approach do not hold the two realms as *completely* separate in daily life as Hiebert assumes, but they do hold the connections between them to very specific, limited roles. The first is temptation, in which the fallen angels work to entice the Christian into sinful thoughts and actions. Second is possession, in which a demonic entity can, on some level, enter into and control a person. Third is the connection of the fallen angels to occultic activity.

Temptation and the Fallen Angels

Unlike the dismissive or social accounts of spiritual warfare, those who hold to the bifurcated view acknowledge that the supernatural realm, beyond the existence of God, is a created reality. A. M. Ramsey, the former Archbishop of Canterbury, said regarding the supernatural related to miracles,

> What do we understand by the supernatural? "Well," said Humpty Dumpty, "when I use a word it means just what I choose it to mean." Anyhow some word is required to express the phenomena inherent in the divine activity in the world, if there is a living God who has a dynamic relation to the world and to human beings, and if providence, grace and revelation have any place at all . . . if divine grace can create saintly lives . . . then the word supernatural serves to express this.[2]

If God works in a hidden manner, then that manner must be through supernatural means.

The *Catechism of the Catholic Church* points to the reality of the supernatural realm,[3] and so do the Lutheran Confessions.[4] Within this belief, those who take the bifurcated approach also acknowledge the existence of angels and fallen angels.[5]

---

2. Ramsey, *Christianity and the Supernatural*, 4.
3. *Catechism of the Catholic Church*, 326.
4. CA XVII, 1–3 in Kolb and Wengert, *Book of Concord*, 50–51.
5. See *Catechism of the Catholic Church*, 328; also John Paul II, *Catechesis on the Angels*, secs. 1–9; and Hermann, "What You Don't Know." For a brief Lutheran

The Bifurcated Approach

In the discussion which emerges in the bifurcated approach concerning Satan and the fallen angels, as well as spiritual warfare, the demonic enticement of men to sin—that is, temptation—is a common topic. The *Catechism of the Catholic Church* states, "The whole of man's history has been the story of dour combat with the powers of evil, stretching, so our Lord tells us, from the very dawn of history until the last day. Finding himself in the midst of the battlefield man has to struggle to do what is right, and it is at great cost to himself, and aided by God's grace, that he succeeds in achieving his own inner integrity."[6]

A typical Protestant example is David Powlison's *Power Encounters*, where he attempts to diminish the perceived role of demons from the pneumatic approach by instead emphasizing human depravity as the source of sin and suffering.[7] He works to disabuse his reader of notions of demons *causing* sin and thus the need for the sinner to be exorcised. Moral sin, he contends, has its source in the depravity of sinful man which collectively creates situational evils. "Moral evil causes situational evil; sin is the sting that causes death. Suffering is the consequence of sin in two ways: first, sin causes others to suffer; second, sin will be paid back justly with harm sooner or later. Satan, of course, exploits both moral and situational evil for his evil purposes."[8] So, Satan can exploit our penchant to sin but is not the cause of it; in other words, he simply tempts persons to sin.

Similarly, Joel Beeke, president of the Puritan Reformed Theological Seminary, categorizes the devil's works as enticing to sin by temptation, hindering spiritual discipline, twisting God's truth, and opposing sanctification.[9] Dennis MacCallum limits the work of the demonic to keeping people from the gospel by distraction and deceit and tempting Christians to lives of sin and thus rendering our work and message ineffective.[10] The Byzantine Orthodox classic *Unseen Warfare* by Scupoli focuses exclusively on the devil as the one who tempts Christians away from the

---

introduction, see Pieper, *Christian Dogmatics*, 1:498–99.

6. *Catechism of the Catholic Church*, 408.
7. Powlison, *Power Encounters*, 52.
8. Powlison, *Power Encounters*, 65.
9. Beeke, *Striving Against Satan*, 73–86.
10. McCallum, *Satan and His Kingdom*, 51–56.

pursuit of Christian perfection and union with God.[11] Satan as a source of temptation is also noted by Lutherans.[12]

Possession and the Fallen Angels

Of those in the bifurcated approach, not all voices are willing to admit possession as a relevant aspect of theology today, or some try to relegate it simply to another category. Using Powlison as an example again, the one way in which the demonic stands out for him is in the instances of possession mentioned in the New Testament. He acknowledges them, but he then puts them into the same category as illnesses. He does so not because he ignores the reality of the evil spirits, but because he does not see Jesus or the apostles treating the situation of a possessed person any differently from those who are ill. He notes that the "confrontations between Jesus and the spirits do not have the feel of titanic combat between forces of moral good and immoral evil. Instead, they have the feel of a compassionate alleviation of human misery."[13] His focus here is not on the one doing the possessing but the one who is possessed.[14] However, he omits that Jesus' method of exorcism is set apart by the texts as different from physical healing.

Other than this observation, Powlison has very little to say regarding the phenomenon of possession or about the activity of the fallen angels. He justifies this by saying that among the world, flesh, and the devil, Scripture focuses less on the third than the first two.[15] He concludes that more overt cases of demonic affliction should be met just like sickness, with "fervent, believing prayer with the sufferer for God's healing mercy; second, an exploration of possible medical causes and treatments, applied as appropriate in the Lord's name; and third, probing pastoral care to turn these adverse circumstances into an opportunity for ongoing repentance and growth in grace."[16] He later says spiritual warfare "is less about casting out supposed demons than it is about assisting those, who through enthrallment to sacred violence, justify their exclusionary

---

11. Scupoli, *Unseen Warfare*.
12. For example, Pieper, *Christian Dogmatics*, 1:533.
13. Powlison, *Power Encounters*, 71.
14. This concept is revisited in the epilogue.
15. Powlison, *Power Encounters*, 110.
16. Powlison, *Power Encounters*, 120.

The Bifurcated Approach

and violent tactics to see that overcoming the principalities and powers is already accomplished in the cross of Christ."[17]

Powlison rejects the social approach which denies the reality of angels and demons and rejects the centralizing of the demonic so often found in the pneumatic approach. But, as Gregory Boyd notes, Powlison's rejection of the need for exorcism treatment distinct from illness is less biblically accurate than it is a moderate westernization of the biblical account.[18] In reaction to the excesses of some pneumatic deliverance ministries, Powlison has confined the demonic to temptation and a form of illness. This is a very limited view, yet it is broader than Beeke, McCallum, or Scupoli, who don't mention possession at all.

In contrast to the minimization of possession, the Roman Catholic Church has been particularly noted for its acknowledgement of it. In the West, their voice has particular strength due, in part, to the cultural impact of *The Exorcist* and other similar movies which consistently portray Catholic priests as the ones on the front lines of such tales of demonic wrestling. Thus, this connection of the Roman Catholic Church to demonic possession continues to surface in the consciousness of the culture.[19] In recent decades though, the denomination itself has been more forthcoming on its own about the concept of possession and its treatment. Their Catechism speaks of it briefly, saying:

> In a simple form, exorcism is performed at the celebration of Baptism. The solemn exorcism, called "a major exorcism," can be performed only by a priest and with the permission of the bishop. The priest must proceed with prudence, strictly observing the rules established by the Church. Exorcism is directed at the expulsion of demons or to the liberation from demonic possession through the spiritual authority which Jesus entrusted to his Church. Illness, especially psychological illness, is a very different matter; treating this is the concern of medical science. Therefore, before an exorcism is performed, it is important to ascertain that one is dealing with the presence of the Evil One, and not an illness.[20]

---

17. Beilby and Eddy, *Understanding Spiritual Warfare*, 116.
18. Boyd, "Response to David Powlison," 121.
19. This is discussed in more detail in chapter 2.
20. *Catechism of the Catholic Church*, 1673.

More extensively, Fr. Gabriele Amorth,[21] the late head exorcist in Rome, published two books discussing his work.[22] They contain some of the cases of possession he has encountered, and detail both how he discerns possession[23] and how he handles the issue.[24] Joan Cruz's book about angels devotes twenty-two pages to the subject of possession, though large portions of it concern brief historic anecdotes and the role of Mary in exorcism.[25] A more recent account of the training of an American Roman Catholic priest as exorcist is given in *The Rite*.[26] Peter Kreeft also writes briefly about possession.[27]

The Lutheran church has, comparatively, had little focus on the subject of possession, but it has been in the periphery of its doctrine since the time the first generation of Missouri Lutherans landed in Perry County, Missouri. The first president of what would later become The Lutheran Church—Missouri Synod (LCMS), C. F. W. Walther, in his 1872 work *Pastoral Theology*, regarded pastoral visits to the possessed as part of the legitimate work of the office.[28] He reflects on dealing with possession in an anecdote from his 1884–85 doctrinal lectures *Law & Gospel*, where, in talking about blaspheming the Holy Spirit, he relates, "I once had to counsel a girl who even *spoke* thoughts of this kind, but at the same time fell on the ground, weeping and moaning to be delivered by God from her affliction. She did not find peace until she realized that it was not she who was speaking these thoughts. Satan had taken possession of her lips."[29]

Francis Pieper, a former president of Concordia Seminary in St. Louis, an LCMS institution, writes of possession briefly in his *Christian Dogmatics*, saying that Christians can be possessed, but mainly defers

---

21. Amorth was publicly vocal about the issue of the reality of Satan and the fallen angels. For example, he pointed to the sexual abuse cases within the Roman Catholic Church as proof of the devil's reality. See Owen, "Chief Exorcist Father Gabriele Amorth Says Devil is in the Vatican." He also comments on the rise in demand for exorcists in the Western world, in Squires, "Surge in Satanism Sparks Rise in Demand for Exorcists"

22. Amorth, *Exorcist Tells His Story*; and Amorth, *Exorcist: More Stories*.

23. Amorth, *Exorcist Tells His Story*, 67–89.

24. Amorth, *Exorcist Tells His Story*, 117–21, 153–63.

25. Cruz, *Angels and Devils*, 238–60.

26. Baglio, *Rite*.

27. Kreeft, *Angels (and Demons)*, 114–15, 122–27.

28. Walther, *Pastoral Theology*, 343–47.

29. Walther, *Law & Gospel*, 445.

back to Walther's pastoral work.[30] John Fritz, in his 1945 *Pastoral Theology*, merely summarizes Walther's earlier discussion. More recently, Kenneth Klaus pointed out that exorcistic practice is in line with the historic church and should not be ignored in today's church.[31] Darrell McCulley pulls from some popular works and offers his thoughts on diagnosing possession and exorcism in his work *The House Swept Clean*.[32] Harold Ristau, a pastor of the Lutheran Church of Canada, recently published a memoir recalling his encounters with possessed persons and what he learned from those events.[33]

There are also anecdotes of more local provenance, like the recollection of a possession encounter recorded in a history of St. John's Lutheran Church, New Minden, Illinois,[34] or the pieces of information concerning a case of believed possession in 1949, which is the Lutheran part of the events that inspired *The Exorcist*.[35]

All of these, to some degree, discuss exorcism in terms of its reality, whether a Christian can be possessed, briefs on how to determine if a person is truly possessed, and occasional suggestions on what to do should such a possession occur. But none of them speak of possession in the broader context of the scope or aims of the fallen angels to do such a thing, nor how it fits into the larger context of the devil's schemes. Possession and temptation are not linked by any larger conception—much like the third area of discussion, the occult.

The Occult and the Fallen Angels

Some perspective from the occult point of view was touched upon in chapter 2. But from the Christian side, occultic activity is the third common point at which the fallen angels are brought into the conversation. The Catholic catechism alludes to demons connected to the occult.[36] Merrill Unger wrote about demons in his landmark book *Biblical Demonology*, using a full quarter of the book to describe the demonic connection

---

30. Pieper, *Christian Dogmatics*, 1:509–10.
31. Klaus, *Exorcism*.
32. McCulley, *House Swept Clean*.
33. Ristau, *My First Exorcism*.
34. Mueller, *Our God, Our Help*, 44–45.
35. The Lutheran elements of this event are, as of yet, unpublished.
36. *Catechism of the Catholic Church*, 2117.

to magic, divination, and necromancy.[37] Speaking from experience on both sides, Sharon Beekmann describes her time as a psychic medium and the revelation that her familiars (the supposed friendly spirits who revealed information to her) were really demonic, and how she found Christ despite their terrors.[38]

Among Lutherans, we find mainly brief mentions regarding the occult. Luther refers to magicians and sorcerers as making pact with the devil.[39] Pieper asserts that all pagan sacrifices are sacrifices to demons[40] and spiritism is devil worship.[41] Theodore Graebner addressed spiritism in his 1919 book, *Spiritism: A Study of Its Phenomena and Religious Teachings*, and summarizes his assessment by saying, "We have seen enough of the doctrines and morals of Spiritism to convince any honest searcher after truth that it is born in the abyss; that its chief head and leader is the devil, and that it is not only a wretched counterfeit, but one of the worst enemies of Christianity."[42] John Warwick Montgomery wrote at length about different aspects of the occult, loosely tying demons to the issue.[43] More recently, Robert Bennett wrote his second book to raise awareness of how occultic ritual and tradition is not only tied to the demonic, but how much of the spirituality of the pagan religions has been incorporated into the worldview of American culture, and also that of Christians.[44]

The accounts above show that Hiebert's accusation of an excluded middle in the Western church is somewhat exaggerated, though not entirely without merit. These three points of contact with the supernatural realm in relation to discussion of fallen angels and spiritual warfare are narrow in scope. However, unlike the solutions of the social and pneumatic approaches to this perceived deficit, I submit that what is offered by the bifurcated approach in terms of a biblical account of temptation,

---

37. Unger, *Biblical Demonology*, 107–64.

38. Beekmann, *Enticed by the Light*.

39. On idolators, Luther says, "In this category also belong those who go so far as to make a pact with the devil so that he may give them plenty of money, help them in love affairs, protect their cattle, recover lost property, etc., as magicians and sorcerers do," LC I, 12 in Kolb and Wengert, *Book of Concord*, 387.

40. Pieper, *Christian Dogmatics*, 1:11, 3:44.

41. Pieper, *Christian Dogmatics*, 3:515.

42. Graebner, *Spiritism*, 128.

43. Montgomery, *Principalities and Powers*. This book is unfortunately named, as the author never ties the work into Ephesians and barely into spiritual warfare at all.

44. Bennett, *Afraid*, 10–12.

possession, and the occult is closer to the truth than the other views and their proposed attempts at a spiritual warfare theology.

Where the social approach only sees the evil of people and the pneumatic approach often categorizes sin in terms of demonic influence or subjugation in need of deliverance ministry, the bifurcated approach recognizes that while it is the human person who sins, the fallen angels are eager to tempt man into sin. Where the social approach denies possession and the pneumatic approach sees the demonic in control of everything that is not overtly Christian, the bifurcated approach acknowledges the reality of demonic possession, but does not allow for a theology of demonic domination. Where the social approach denies any supernatural power to the occult and the pneumatic approach gives it great power to curse across generations, the bifurcated approach recognizes the connections of the occult to the fallen angels but not at the expense of God's supremacy.

Yet, while the bifurcated approach, when the concepts are combined, is more comprehensive and accurate than the other solutions, these points of insight do not encompass all that may be said, or needs to be said, concerning spiritual warfare. In pursuit of a more complete and robust theology of spiritual warfare, there are three particular contemporary Lutheran voices who have broadened these links between the natural and supernatural realms, or even forged new ones, bringing some additional insights to enhance the bifurcated tradition and a move toward an antifragile approach.

Extended Contributions by Contemporary Lutheran Theologians

The academic discussion of biblical supernatural themes among Lutherans in the West has largely been ignored since the Enlightenment.[45] However, aspects of the topic have been explored explicitly and implicitly in the past century by theologians with roots outside North America. Three Lutheran voices which have spoken at some length on issues related to spiritual warfare include Gustav Wingren (Sweden), John W. Kleinig (Australia), and Leopoldo Sánchez M. (Chile, Panama). Each voice speaks on topics related to a proper Lutheran account of spiritual warfare, addressing either aspects of the pneumatic or social concerns

---

45. See chapter 2.

and laying out proper hermeneutical approaches to the Scriptures that bear upon the topic.[46] An assessment of their potential contributions, including strengths and weaknesses, is critical for constructing a fuller account of spiritual warfare.

Gustav Wingren

Vocation as a Battle between Two Governments

As a youth, Swedish Lutheran theologian Gustav Wingren began to see the connections between faith and life.[47] When he matriculated at university, he approached theology as it met with practical living, commenting, "I have always sought to choose topics that throw light on the integrating function of the Christian faith in human life as a whole."[48] One of the great theological tragedies, he contends, is when the church is cut off from ordinary human life.[49]

For Wingren, the description of the interaction of theology and Christian daily life is found most poignantly in Martin Luther's work on vocation.[50] Wingren's first book, in 1942, was *Luthers Lehre vom Beruf* or *Luther on Vocation*. In this work, Wingren discusses Luther's understanding of the relationship between our daily works and God's work in the world.[51]

One's vocation (*beruf*), says Wingren, is every office a Christian occupies at a given time, including both occupational and biological orders.[52] Each legitimate office a person has in life is given by God

---

46. Two other Lutheran voices on the subject include Aulén, *Christus Victor*; and more recently Bennett, *I Am Not Afraid*. Aulén's work is primarily historical, speaking of the nature of Christ's triumph over the devil as a part of his examination of atonement narratives. Bennet's *I Am Not Afraid* is a sociological survey regarding possession, demon veneration disguised as ancestor worship, and the impact of Christ regarding a portion of the Lutheran Church in Madagascar.

47. Wingren, *Flight from Creation*, 13–15.

48. Wingren, *Flight from Creation*, 15.

49. Wingren, *Flight from Creation*, 15.

50. Wingren, *Flight from Creation*, 17.

51. "Here we are inquiring only into Luther's conception of earthly work, not vocation in any other sense." Wingren, *Luther on Vocation*, 2.

52. Wingren, *Luther on Vocation*, 4–5. "Every attempt to differentiate between the sphere of the home, where personal Christian love rules, and the sphere of office, where the more important rules of vocation hold sway, immediately runs afoul of

The Bifurcated Approach

as he orders and sustains his creation.[53] These vocations are not about salvation, but about the welfare of our neighbor, as Wingren notes, "so vocation belongs to this world, not to heaven; it is directed toward one's neighbor, not toward God."[54] But this does not mean that God stands aloof from the works of men. Rather, God acts underneath the work of man for his neighbor:

> The good that man does on earth is God's creation, and it is to be directed toward his neighbor. Before God the good is not man's but God's. Only before one's neighbor does the good done appear as coming from him who does it. Through this we can understand the concept of man as "mask" of God.[55]

In this earthly life with the neighbor, contends Wingren, man's action is not limited to a prescribed list of good works but acts in the freedom of love for the neighbor in need. "Love's action may proceed in keeping with usual practice or against it. It acts according to a principle which cannot be construed in advance, but which makes its decision afresh in the light of the need of the neighbor, who steadily changes, bearing now one burden and then another."[56]

Wingren then sets a larger framework for this action of love for the neighbor in terms of kingdoms and governments. There are two kingdoms, Wingren observes, the *earthly kingdom* and the *heavenly kingdom*. The earthly kingdom is the realm of daily life ruled by God through the law and the two governments. It is also where God works through his people in love toward their neighbor. The heavenly kingdom is also ruled by God and membership is solely based on faith in Christ and the forgiveness of sins, not on works.[57]

Wingren looks more closely at those two earthly governments. First, God has established the *worldly government* to curb evil (and so in this sense "to thwart the devil").[58] Second, he has created the *spiritual government* of the church, through which he maintains and gives access to

---

Luther's terminology."
- 53. Wingren, *Luther on Vocation*, 9.
- 54. Wingren, *Luther on Vocation*, 10.
- 55. Wingren, *Luther on Vocation*, 18–19.
- 56. Wingren, *Luther on Vocation*, 49–50.
- 57. Wingren, *Luther on Vocation*, 10.
- 58. Wingren, *Luther on Vocation*, 79.

heaven.[59] However, these governmental orders, along with all of the vocations of each person, become the devil's tools when abused. "As soon as vocation is abandoned, God loses hold of man, both faith and love cease, and, since there is no free will before God, the devil, that objective power that opposes God, has gained control of man. This view of vocation, cannot be emphasized enough."[60]

Wingren uses these governments as a lens by which he examines Martin Luther's work *De servo arbitrio* (*The Bondage of the Will*). Wingren notes that God's acts of love upon humanity (and through each person as his masks in creation) are in the earthly kingdom. In the earthly kingdom, each person seems free but is not in reality. Every person is either subject to God or, in rejecting God and his will, subject to the devil.[61] Since the governments are comprised of a collective of persons, the whole of each government, worldly and spiritual, is only as faithful as the degree to which each person in that government faithfully carries out his or her work.[62]

For Wingren, the implication of these governments as God's mechanism against worldly evil is that there is a devil working against God.[63] The struggle between God and the devil is for the sake of humans. "God wishes man to be saved from the power of sin, and the devil wants man kept in it. Out of that invisible combat, which goes on even when man does not think on it, come all the agony and anxiety that enter into human life."[64]

Wingren focuses on a further aspect of the abuse of given offices in God's two governments. Not only are offices abused by humans, but the devil's work against God is fought across the spectrum of God's two earthly governments.[65] So the offices in either of these governments are

---

59. Wingren, *Luther on Vocation*, 23–24.
60. Wingren, *Luther on Vocation*, 33.
61. Wingren, *Luther on Vocation*, 78.
62. Wingren, *Luther on Vocation*, 79.
63. Wingren, *Luther on Vocation*, 79. Wingren's line of reasoning is that man's active hostility toward God implies an instigator of that hostility. If the issue was merely ignorance, God would use intellectual enlightenment rather than the law. This is not a convincing argument for the existence of the devil, unless Wingren equates the devil with sin rather than as a personified entity. But it might be used to discuss sin in society and the need for God's two governments in this age.
64. Wingren, Luther on Vocation, 80.
65. Wingren, Luther on Vocation, 85.

good, but can be misused. "Abuse involves an action directly opposed to the work of God . . . the devil's onslaughts consist of temptations to misuse a good and divine office, to mismanage one's vocation."[66] In either the worldly or the spiritual government, deviation from the path of the office stems from the devil as an impelling force.[67]

Moreover, within the offices of both governments, Wingren notes that only a Christian can have a vocation in an office.[68] As the Christian attempts to be faithful to God in his office, vocation "is a focal point of decision in the combat between God and the devil. In this combat the word of God is God's weapon. The spiritual government modifies the shape of vocation under the worldly government."[69] There is an interaction between the two governments, such that faithfulness to God in one's earthly vocations modifies the worldly government toward faithfulness itself, the part affecting the whole.

The Christian in an office, says Wingren, has freedom to enact his faith as love for the neighbor in any way that is required at that time, by action or inaction, whichever love requires. Wingren posits this was Luther's understanding of Christian liberty. Wingren describes these opportunities as "doors through which God creatively enters into the orders of creation."[70]

The devil can also turn this use into abuse. "That God is a hidden God means, among other things, that man can oppose God, that he can set himself up against God, or, in other words, that the devil can exist."[71] The devil corrupts the proper use of office and corrupts the message of the Gospel into one of salvation by works. Such corruption confuses humans, turning freedom and bondage upside down so that the gospel appears to be bondage and the law freedom.[72]

---

66. Wingren, *Luther on Vocation*, 87.

67. Wingren, *Luther on Vocation*, 89.

68. "Man's office gives tangible direction about works, but 'faith and love' modify the work done in the office. Apart from relation with God, man has an office, established by God, but not a vocation." Wingren, *Luther on Vocation*, 91.

69. Wingren, *Luther on Vocation*, 92.

70. Wingren, *Luther on Vocation*, 96.

71. Wingren, *Luther on Vocation*, 100. This is an interesting turn of phrase, sounding as if the sinful rebellion of the "old man" is equal to the devil's actions.

72. Wingren, *Luther on Vocation*, 100.

This happens because a person's will is always bound either to God or to the devil.[73] Wingren considers these two forces on even footing when it comes to a person's will, though captivity to God is really freedom while captivity to the devil is thralldom.[74] The confusion of the kingdoms and perversions of the governments occurs when the devil works through the evil in human hearts.[75] The two problems are connected. When one perverts the governments in the earthly kingdom, one will misunderstand the nature of the heavenly kingdom. So vocation and faith are linked. "In general, the devil mixes the two kingdoms through a person's deviation from vocation and violation of vocation, i.e. through misuse of one's proper offices. Satan tempts humans to do this."[76] This distortion of kingdoms and offices causes them to work contrary to God's intention and will.

Therefore, Wingren argues, understanding the spiritual dynamics at work in the confusion of the exercise of vocation in the two governments is important because such dynamics and confusion show how vocation is precisely the context where God and the devil do battle: "The strife between God and the devil surges back and forth through the whole world and through every heart. . . . Both God and the devil transform all things, each make use of everything in the struggle against the other."[77] To find our way in this struggle with discernment, Wingren argues that it is God's word and vocation together which ground the human person in God the Creator and against the devil as usurper.[78]

On the Law and Spontaneous Love

Generalizing this connection between word and vocation to daily life, Wingren argues that we then cooperate with God in our earthly works.[79] Works are directed toward our neighbor in vocation, but we are also co-workers with God against the devil by resisting temptation, living humbly, reaching down to the neighbor in need, and relying on God to sustain

---

73. Wingren, *Luther on Vocation*, 105.
74. Wingren, *Luther on Vocation*, 106.
75. Wingren, *Luther on Vocation*, 113.
76. Wingren, *Luther on Vocation*, 115.
77. Wingren, *Luther on Vocation*, 121.
78. Wingren, *Luther on Vocation*, 122–23.
79. Wingren, *Luther on Vocation*, 124.

us against evil.[80] Wingren reminds us that Luther sees the human person in vocation as God's mask, through which God acts to bring good and help to our neighbor. "In co-operation in vocation, man becomes God's mask on earth wherever man acts. A mask of God is therefore found only in the earthly realms where man labors and does his work for others. In his toil he is a tool in God's hand."[81] The devil seeks to confuse Christians and pull them from their vocations.[82]

Wingren notes that vocation is further complicated when Christians try to discern God's will in a given situation. "To Luther, the law is not a fixed magnitude that is codified, either in the Bible or in any other book. . . . Each of God's masks is just such an embodied law: parents, neighbors, etc. The law is a sum of living points."[83] But man, in his limitation, "cannot tell if something new is of God or the devil in the moment, and we must risk a position."[84]

Wingren argues that Luther's position on good works was relative situational ethics and rejected the concept of a third use of the law.[85] Rather, the neighbor mandates action by the need of the moment.[86] The laws of God still have their place in curbing evil when Christians and non-Christians look to abuse their office,[87] but God acts by spontaneous love through the Christian and by law through the non-Christian, using both for his recreative work. Therefore, "on earth there is no decisive difference between Christians and non-Christians. . . . Where works and external behavior are concerned it is not merely difficult to make a sharp demarcation between Christians and non-Christians, it is erroneous."[88]

---

80. Wingren, *Luther on Vocation*, 128.

81. Wingren, *Luther on Vocation*, 137. Of note here is Wingren's own loose use of his terms. He uses "realms" here to speak of the two governments in the earthly kingdom, though "realm" is synonymous with "kingdom" rather than with "governments." He also uses the term "earthly" for both the earthly kingdom and the worldly government. He additionally makes occasional references to those under the devil as being in the "kingdom of the devil" instead of the "kingdom of God," and will refer to this contrast as two kingdoms, adding further ambiguity to his discussion.

82. Wingren, *Luther on Vocation*, 143.

83. Wingren, *Luther on Vocation*, 143.

84. Wingren, *Luther on Vocation*, 145.

85. Wingren, *Luther on Vocation*, 146–47.

86. Wingren, *Luther on Vocation*, 148.

87. Wingren, *Luther on Vocation*, 149–50.

88. Wingren, *Luther on Vocation*, 151.

In the freedom of the Christian, Wingren argues, God acts creatively when the devil tries to calcify works. God would permit the world to be steady and unchanging if the devil was not always acting.[89] To this end, the combat against the devil is seen by Wingren as Luther's foundation for God's creative action: "Fresh creation takes place all the time *contra diabolum*, against the devil. God's new measures in the external world are combative actions."[90] In such combat, no rule of law is set up as a norm because God's freedom is not constrained.[91] Because God acts this creative, combative work through humans for the neighbor, a person discerns the will of God not by any codified guide, but by a willingness to be used by God and in prayer.[92]

In the final part of the book, Wingren more closely examines what his model means for the Christian in daily life. For the life of a Christian, he says, the human person in vocation not only is a mask by which God helps the neighbor, but God also brings the gospel to the self as we work by encouraging us to look for a greater meaning than the daily work; if vocation points to the cross, then it also points to resurrection and renewal.[93]

Prayer and Discernment of Vocational Action

Yet, this cross is the lonely burden of our unique vocations where we have no guidance but God's command to do and pray.[94] Not only is the law not a guide but, Wingren contends, there is no imitating others who have gone before us. There is no imitation of conduct because "no particular form of conduct is fixed in advance as holy,"[95] and because each situation

---

89. Wingren, *Luther on Vocation*, 160.
90. Wingren, *Luther on Vocation*, 160.
91. Wingren, *Luther on Vocation*, 160–61.
92. Wingren, *Luther on Vocation*, 161 says, "[God] gives access to himself to all who come in faith, which does not see or scrutinize God, but which suffers him and prays. By willingness to receive God, whatever he may do, this open faith . . . accepts it as true that God is love. God enters in with a person with an open faith like this."
93. Wingren, *Luther on Vocation*, 166.
94. Wingren, *Luther on Vocation*, 171.
95. Wingren, *Luther on Vocation*, 178.

is unique in life and the world without repetition.[96] Guidance, Wingren concludes, can only come through prayer.[97]

Wingren reveals the complexity of this prayer discernment by observing that prayer must be accompanied by full effort on the part of Christians to do the work given or else the prayers will not be as well heard by God.[98] Prayer comes into the picture from desperation, when one has done all that can be done but cannot succeed. Only then in prayer will God act to finish the work.[99] One's vocation, he concludes, can only be properly fulfilled by constantly renewed prayer,[100] and so in prayer and action a person in his vocation becomes the mask of God.[101] Prayer opens the Christian's mind to God's creative action,[102] which has no formula but ventures into new expressions of love for the neighbor.[103]

This freedom to act in prayer for the neighbor is of the Spirit and also entails being "free from the law even in external matters."[104] Wingren argues that if his framework of Luther's view is correct, then the third use of the law, as a guide for Christian living, is rejected as being a teaching of Luther.[105] Understanding God's command for action in a given situation does not arise from any written law or standard, but is brought about by the Spirit in guiding the spontaneity of love and faith in action.[106] The devil tries to distort and trouble this communication,[107] but "a sound reason carefully judges the outward situation, and prayer seeks guidance from God. In this double receptivity, toward God and vocation, one becomes certain that a particular thing ought to be done."[108]

This insight should give us comfort, Wingren says, because God is in charge of all of the movements and happenings in creation.[109] One

---

96. Wingren, *Luther on Vocation*, 182.
97. Wingren, *Luther on Vocation*, 184.
98. Wingren, *Luther on Vocation*, 185.
99. Wingren, *Luther on Vocation*, 186.
100. Wingren, *Luther on Vocation*, 192.
101. Wingren, *Luther on Vocation*, 195.
102. Wingren, *Luther on Vocation*, 196–97.
103. Wingren, *Luther on Vocation*, 198.
104. Wingren, *Luther on Vocation*, 202.
105. Wingren, *Luther on Vocation*, 202n72.
106. Wingren, *Luther on Vocation*, 205.
107. Wingren, *Luther on Vocation*, 204–5.
108. Wingren, *Luther on Vocation*, 207.
109. Wingren speaks this way to the point of a fatalism that sounds like double

indicator Wingren notes for knowing what is the will of God is that a God-pleasing task, when done properly and at the right time, will go smoothly and with ease.[110] Doing the right thing at the right time is crucial for Wingren's understanding of vocation. "Both prayer and God's commandment are more clearly understandable in the light of the concept of 'the time.' These three concepts can be said to clarify each other. In prayer man commits all to God, lets God direct all events; man himself heeds God's command, the command which in that hour gives him the form of God's direction. God's work with the factors of man's environment and God's work through man, by way of commandment and the Spirit, coincide, so to speak, in 'the time.'"[111]

Trying to get away from God's command in the moment is to leave the freedom of God for the bondage of the devil.[112] The battle between God and the devil plays out in humanity and in the life of each person. The Christian struggle with this, says Wingren, is that the "devil, sin, evil is actively present in the form of the old man,"[113] whereas God acts by law and gospel in such a way that "the gospel acts in man's conscience, and extinguishes sin; wherefore the new man has no sin. The law acts in the body, and there it does not at once efface sin, but drives out sin slowly."[114]

The law without the gospel, though, will only condemn and is the tool of the devil[115] where unbelief reigns. Wingren argues that every human must struggle to persevere in a positive relationship with God, lest

---

predestination, though he never explicitly goes that far: "Therefore all anticipatory anxieties and all precise planning for the future are fruitless and meaningless. Man cannot escape that which is to be." Wingren, *Luther on Vocation*, 213.

110. Wingren, *Luther on Vocation*, 215.

111. Wingren, *Luther on Vocation*, 220.

112. Wingren, *Luther on Vocation*, 234.

113. Wingren, *Luther on Vocation*, 239. I am not sure if this is a mistake in the translation or Wingren is here saying the devil, sin, and evil are synonymous terms.

114. Wingren, *Luther on Vocation*, 239. Wingren elaborates on his idea of the slow sanctification of man in this life in his later book, *The Living Word*, where he states, "Man is destined to grow, to develop, by receiving without intermission from the hands of God. Adam, had he not fallen, would have developed more and more and at last would have received the heavenly life in the Spirit. But now, in addition, there is the fact that Adam was overthrown by Satan and that Christ's conquest, which casts down the corrupting power, only little by little and in stages gains control in man. So then conflict and the growth that belonged even to creation in its purity are intertwined." Wingren, *Living Word*, 171.

115. Wingren, *Luther on Vocation*, 240.

the devil may seduce one into his power, but even this is the will of God.[116] This threat of condemnation leads to the desperation of faith which will accept hardship and all things as faith turns to Christ, who endured in the face of condemnation.[117] Faith changes desperate moments in life from despair unto condemnation into good and the path to resurrection.[118]

Wingren concludes from this that all life is a struggle to maintain faith, and salvation is always uncertain since we depend on faith alone.[119] But when the last day comes, the burden of labor in vocation shall cease just as uncertainty will cease, the devil will be vanquished, and the law will no longer rule.[120]

An Analysis of Wingren's Views

Wingren's arguments have several facets to contribute toward a Lutheran understanding of spiritual warfare. Wingren echoes Luther's *De servo arbitrio* to emphasize rightly that there is no neutrality any person may take as an independent, observing entity between God and the demonic. Unlike Wink's approach, in which a person is a neutral party capable of good, for Luther one is either a child of God by faith in Jesus or a child of wrath, under the devil, in unbelief.[121] This cosmic truth helps to create part of the foundation for a narrative of the Lutheran account of spiritual warfare as an existential reality of daily life. The spiritual reality, contra Wink, is a constant part of our lives since we, ourselves, are spiritual and never neutral.

Wingren also helpfully highlights the usefulness of Luther's teaching on vocation. Though Wingren never gives a full definition of the term,[122] he lays out vocation as the will of God[123] acted through the Christian in

---

116. Wingren, *Luther on Vocation*, 243, notes, "It is incomprehensible how God can will that that should happen; but since Scripture says that that will happen for some, God must will it. Otherwise it would not happen."

117. Wingren, *Luther on Vocation*, 245.

118. Wingren, *Luther on Vocation*, 246.

119. Wingren, *Luther on Vocation*, 246.

120. Wingren, *Luther on Vocation*, 248.

121. Wingren, *Luther on Vocation*, 105.

122. Wingren, *Luther on Vocation*, 1. Wingren narrows the general use of the term "vocation" to "the work which each one does" but does not further elaborate. Subsequently, he will speak of facets of vocation but never give a full definition.

123. Wingren, *Luther on Vocation*, 10.

love[124] for the benefit of the neighbor.[125] While these actions do not affect the status of salvation, which Christ alone has fully accomplished,[126] God yet wills that his children by faith act in love for those around them as the "masks" through which he enacts that will.[127] Because the devil tries to remove faith from the Christian, a part of his work toward that end is to attempt to confuse vocation with devotion to other pursuits or actions without regard for faith.[128] This concept of a person's conscience toward neighbor as a battleground of faith[129] adds depth to the social aspect of a coherent account of spiritual warfare. The temptation of the devil to cause us to sin must be related to a confusion concerning the nature and use of vocation. Confusion of vocation causes a person to wrongly view the neighbor.

In this battle, Wingren highlights the centrality of prayer in our moments of desperation. The scope of the proper use of prayer for Wingren is much smaller than that of Luther,[130] but is important. Wingren focuses on desperate prayer, namely, that when we have done all yet our work remains insufficient, the moment of stringent and fervent appeal to God arrives.[131] This insight recognizes the power of prayer to bring real change in our lives as God's hand fulfills that prayer for us. Desperate prayer acknowledges our dependence upon God and stands in contrast to Wagner's charismatic and anthropocentric view of faith-powered prayer.

Finally, Wingren's treatment of governments reflected the idea that the collective of persons had the same issues as the individual person regarding proper use of office and vocations. The governments, he contends, are corporate battlegrounds for the wills of God and the demonic, of the proper use of vocation and confusion of vocation.[132] This parallel between individual and collective is an intriguing counternarrative to

---

124. Wingren, *Luther on Vocation*, 9.
125. Wingren, *Luther on Vocation*, 4.
126. Wingren, *Luther on Vocation*, 13.
127. Wingren, *Luther on Vocation*, 137–40.
128. Wingren, *Luther on Vocation*, 115.
129. Wingren, *Luther on Vocation*, 121.
130. Luther writes, for example, "We are to fear and love God so that we do not curse, swear, practice magic, lie, or deceive using God's name, but instead use that very name in every time of need to call on, pray to, praise, and give thanks to God." SC, The Ten Commandments, 4 in Kolb and Wengert, *Book of Concord*, 352.
131. Wingren, *Luther on Vocation*, 189.
132. Wingren, *Luther on Vocation*, 121.

Wink's account of inner and outer aspects of domination systems. Rather than the inner and outer aspects of the ideology and culture of entities of power, it is the collective confusion of or adherence to the offices God gives (and the Christian vocations in them) which constitutes the faithfulness or depravity of such powers. Yet there is also an echo of Wink's concerns for dealing with oppressive structures in Wingren's work. Wingren says that rulers in the worldly government are held in check by still higher rulers, but if the highest earthly ruler is tyrannical, then under him "a Christian can only suffer; revolt is sin. Within God's order there is no power which may legitimately punish a tyrannical sovereign ruler."[133] However, God himself may use a revolt or a foreign power to remove the ruler, but in that case he is using what is clearly sin by humans to do his sovereign work. Like Wink, Wingren opposes the use of force to tear down oppressive systems.

While Wingren offers important insights into the general concept of vocation which add to a Lutheran understanding of the pneumatic and social aspects of spiritual warfare, there are several deficiencies with his treatment of the subject and his portrayal of Luther's thought.[134] The most egregious issue with Wingren's account of Luther is in regard to the proper use of the law. Wingren rightly finds support from Luther that the law, in its first and second uses, applies to the non-Christian as well as to Christians when they stray from their vocations.[135] But then Wingren moves to an antinomianism position regarding the Christian's vocational ethic. He claims Luther denies the third use of the law, that is, the law as a guide for the Christian.[136] Wingren favors spontaneous acts of love brought on through faith by the Spirit in accordance with the *mandatum Dei*.[137] The support he finds in Luther, however, is deficient.[138] Instead,

133. Wingren, *Luther on Vocation*, 92.

134. A general issue which makes Wingren difficult to use is his own inconsistency. For example, one of his presuppositions he lays out is that Luther's teaching on vocation is only consistent after his work *De votis monasticis* of 1521 (Wingren, Luther on Vocation, xvii). Yet he cites with regularity earlier works of Luther's, such as Commentary on Romans (1515–1516), Treatise on the Sacrament of Baptism (1519), On the Papacy of Rome (1520), Treatise on the Sacrament of Penance (1519) and several other sermons and works of that early period.

135. Wingren, *Luther on Vocation*, 56.

136. Wingren, *Luther on Vocation*, 202, n72.

137. Wingren, *Luther on Vocation*, 199.

138. Wingren, *Luther on Vocation*, 202–04. For example, Wingren quotes Luther contrasting the faithfulness of vocation to the self-chosen works of meritorious

Luther argues clearly for the need of the Ten Commandments to be the guide for the Christian's life with the neighbor. For example, in the *Large Catechism* he notes that the Decalogue is critical for the Christian to act rightly: "Here, then, we have the Ten Commandments, a summary of divine teaching on what we are to do to make our whole life pleasing to God. They are the true fountain from which all good works must spring, the true channel from which all good works must flow."[139] We find support as well in the Augsburg Confession, which Luther did not write, but endorsed.[140] How one understands the role of the law affects one's understanding of social justice and shapes concern for the neighbor.

This leads us to the second issue with Wingren, which is a lack of the use of God's word in the Christian life and vocation. Jesus and Paul certainly spoke in positive terms of godly conduct in various roles in daily life. God's word is a cornerstone of the Reformation and the foundational work that Luther used to support his theology. Luther directly connects our daily work to God's word.[141] The Confessions make direct connection between a discussion of God's *mandatum* and the word, but this is not found at all in Wingren.[142]

There are notable aspects to take from Wingren's observation of how the two governments of the earthly kingdom are the stage for vocation and the enactment of faith. His effort to highlight the concept of vocation as central for understanding Luther's perspective on the Christian life is valuable, providing a pneumatic aspect and a social aspect that relate to a Lutheran account of spiritual warfare. But Wingren's arguments, in important respects, are lacking in substantial fundamentals and do not accurately represent the broader view of Luther or the Lutheran Confessions. A different, more nuanced narrative will be needed as a basis for a confessional Lutheran account of spiritual warfare.

---

pilgrimages promoted by the Roman Catholic Church. But this does not provide support for a rejection of the third use of the law.

139. LC I, 311 in Kolb and Wengert, *Book of Concord*, 428.

140. For example, CA VI, 1–2; and CA XX, 27 in Kolb and Wengert, *Book of Concord*, 40–41, 56.

141. LC I, 91–93 in Kolb and Wengert, *Book of Concord*, 399.

142. This is one of the critiques of Wingren's conclusions also given by Fagerberg, *New Look at the Lutheran Confessions*, 287–88.

John Kleinig on the Intercessory Character of Spiritual Struggle

Another Lutheran author who has tackled the subject of spiritual warfare in a substantive way is John W. Kleinig. He is professor emeritus at Australian Lutheran College in Adelaide. Kleinig's approach to the topic of the Christian life and spiritual warfare varies greatly from that of Wingren and is most fully laid out in his book *Grace Upon Grace: Spirituality for Today*.[143]

Receptivity is at the heart of Kleinig's view of the Christian life.[144] He applies the doctrine of original sin to the life of the Christian, using Luther's *simul justus et peccator* (the Christian is simultaneously righteous and a sinner) as his driving motif, of which he says: "so we have a dual status, spiritually. As the fallen children of Adam and Eve, we are beggars before God. Yet in Christ we are holy beggars with angelic status."[145]

Kleinig's receptivity is not vacuous. He highlights the importance of living within God's calling, that proper piety "has to do with participation in the life of the triune God through knowing Jesus and trusting in His promises."[146] Such piety involves interaction with God's word and a life of prayer.[147]

In contrast to Wingren, Kleinig is emphatic about the need for God's word in the daily life of the Christian, "Our conscience functions properly only when it is governed by faith in God's Word and when it attends both to the voice of the Law and the voice of the Gospel."[148]

God's word, Kleinig contends, brings the reality of Jesus to bear upon the Christian life. "We interact with Christ, who is actually present with us invisibly."[149] The word of God is the means by which one also receives the Holy Spirit and, by the faith given in Christ by that word, one is justified by the Father and before him.[150] This presence of God by the word is crucial for Kleinig, who argues "we can achieve nothing spiritually by ourselves. Only as long as we are attached to Christ and receive

---

143. Kleinig wrote an earlier paper on this topic: Kleinig, "Oratio, Meditatio, Tentatio," 255–67.
144. Kleinig, *Grace Upon Grace*, 28.
145. Kleinig, *Grace Upon Grace*, 30.
146. Kleinig, *Grace Upon Grace*, 41.
147. Kleinig, *Grace Upon Grace*, 45.
148. Kleinig, *Grace Upon Grace*, 53.
149. Kleinig, *Grace Upon Grace*, 96.
150. Kleinig, *Grace Upon Grace*, 97.

the Spirit from Him can we live the life of Christ and do the work of God the Father. Our spiritual life depends entirely on our ongoing reception of the Holy Spirit."[151]

Such reception of the Spirit has fourfold benefits. First, as one meditates upon God's word, one receives strength from the Lord as one focuses physically and mentally on his word in intentional meditation.[152] Second, one receives guidance from his word and picks up something relevant to one's current situation.[153] Third, one receives help from the Lord as one has his word memorized, which the Holy Spirit then uses to provide protection for the Christian even when one is unaware.[154] Fourth, one is also given vision and insight by "contemplating His hidden presence with us," which reassures a Christian of God's abiding presence and brings to mind his perspective on the situation.[155]

In addition to the word of God, Kleinig highlights the importance of prayer. The ability to pray is a gift, in which the Holy Spirit prompts and encourages the Christian to pray to the Father, who desires to hear his children.[156] In contrast to Wagner, Kleinig argues that in prayer, Christians do not have their own latent power, or even some special independent power bestowed at Baptism. Rather, "we borrow prayer from the risen Lord Jesus. . . . Thus, while we do receive His power by faith in prayer, we can never take hold of it and possess it for ourselves."[157]

It is in prayer that Kleinig sees Christian vocation. "Our vocation is to work with Him here on earth as we daily go about our earthly business. We have been chosen to work with Him in administering God's grace by praying for His help in our work and for the needs of our co-workers."[158] Intercessory prayer, for Kleinig, is the central instrument of Christian activity in the world and the primary fulfillment of the "Golden Rule,"[159] as well as the method by which "the Church is created and sustained."[160]

---

151. Kleinig, *Grace Upon Grace*, 107.
152. Kleinig, *Grace Upon Grace*, 147–48.
153. Kleinig, *Grace Upon Grace*, 148.
154. Kleinig, *Grace Upon Grace*, 149.
155. Kleinig, *Grace Upon Grace*, 150.
156. Kleinig, *Grace Upon Grace*, 166.
157. Kleinig, *Grace Upon Grace*, 193–94.
158. Kleinig, *Grace Upon Grace*, 199.
159. Kleinig, *Grace Upon Grace*, 201.
160. Kleinig, *Grace Upon Grace*, 202.

Satan, therefore, will do all he can to stifle our life of prayer for one another.[161]

Contrary to Wink, Kleinig argues that intercessory prayer is not only powerful for the church but also for the direction of the world. "We can do more for international justice and world peace by our individual and corporate prayers than by anything else we ever do. Our prayers are our greatest contribution to the welfare of the world and the salvation of its people."[162]

Using receptive meditation on God's word and intercessory prayer as the foundations for Christian spirituality, Kleinig then addresses his final aspect of daily Christian life, which is spiritual warfare. He is rightly critical of many of the current trends around this topic[163] and offers two foci as correctives. First, we cannot rely on ourselves to understand the nature of spiritual warfare since it is beyond our sensory experience.[164] Second, Satan is an expert at deception, and so sober vigilance with God's word and prayer is essential.[165]

Kleinig notes that in the war between Satan and Christ, Christians find themselves torn. Because each Christian still has original sin, the old nature is hostile to God despite the new nature given in Jesus. Because of this dual nature, the individual conscience "becomes the main battleground."[166] Baptism, therefore, thrusts one into the battle, where the Christian becomes a soldier of the cross.[167]

Satan attacks the Christian, Kleinig says, by trying to "undermine our faith in Christ and its foundation, the forgiveness of sins and our acceptance by God the Father."[168] Therefore the main battle is not out in the world at all, but in each person's soul. Each fight is not a crusade, but a struggle to retain the reception of God's gifts, namely, forgiveness and a good conscience which comes through faith in Jesus.[169]

---

161. Kleinig, *Grace Upon Grace*, 202.
162. Kleinig, *Grace Upon Grace*, 212.
163. Kleinig, *Grace Upon Grace*, 219.
164. Kleinig, *Grace Upon Grace*, 219.
165. Kleinig, *Grace Upon Grace*, 219–20.
166. Kleinig, *Grace Upon Grace*, 223.
167. Kleinig, *Grace Upon Grace*, 225.
168. Kleinig, *Grace Upon Grace*, 225.
169. Kleinig, *Grace Upon Grace*, 226.

Kleinig then tries to provide a closer examination of the facets of this warfare. Since Jesus ascended into heaven and is mediator, Satan rebelled and was thrown from heaven and is now upon the earth. The two strongholds that Satan attacks now are the individual Christian conscience and the church,[170] which might be considered the collective Christian conscience.

Kleinig notes, "the vision from John shows that we have two main weapons to combat this attack (Rev 12:11). With these seemingly insignificant weapons we use the authority and power of Christ Himself to overcome Satan; with them in our hands we win the victory on our personal front in the cosmic battle."[171] The first of those weapons is the blood of Jesus given for a good conscience,[172] and the second is the word of testimony, the witness to Jesus in the confession of faith.[173] This includes both the law and the gospel.[174]

The word of God and intercessory prayer will also bring others into the faith. Therefore, conversion is also an aspect of Kleinig's view of spiritual warfare, saying "all people remain in darkness until Christ comes and teaches them the Father's Word with authority. . . . With that Word He sends Satan and his spirits packing. . . . All that remains to be done now in this period of history is to mop up the remaining outposts of darkness here on planet earth."[175]

Kleinig examines Eph 6:10–20 in order to further assess the weapons given to the Christian for spiritual warfare. The first of the weapons is Jesus' name used in prayer and confession of the faith.[176] Second, is God's word, which is "our main offensive weapon in spiritual combat" by which demons are banished.[177] The third weapon is the confession of faith, which includes creedal statements.[178] Last is the appeal in prayer to Jesus for help, since we receive all things from him.[179]

---

170. Kleinig, *Grace Upon Grace*, 230.
171. Kleinig, *Grace Upon Grace*, 231.
172. Kleinig, *Grace Upon Grace*, 231.
173. Kleinig, *Grace Upon Grace*, 232.
174. Kleinig, *Grace Upon Grace*, 246–47.
175. Kleinig, *Grace Upon Grace*, 239.
176. Kleinig, *Grace Upon Grace*, 251.
177. Kleinig, *Grace Upon Grace*, 251.
178. Kleinig, *Grace Upon Grace*, 252.
179. Kleinig, *Grace Upon Grace*, 253.

Kleinig particularly latches onto this last point, noting, "When we come under attack, we do not need to defend ourselves, let alone launch a counterattack. We need to do nothing except pray. . . . By praying, we stand firm in faith and rout our enemy. Christ engages and defeats the enemy for us in a most unexpected way. He joins us in the battle and prays for us. . . . The climax of Christ's battle against the powers of darkness came with His agony in the Garden of Gethsemane."[180] Prayer is so essential and decisive that Kleinig asserts the lack of it is the reason that the occult is now on the rise.[181]

For Kleinig, the saints are involved "with God the Father in battle for the liberation and restoration of the cosmos; God's plan is to reunite the citizens of earth with the citizens of heaven under the headship of Christ."[182] The role that each Christian plays as a soldier is like that of guards in the Roman legion of Paul's day. Kleinig argues that such a soldier "stood guard at his post and watched for his enemy. If he saw the enemy approaching . . . he was not allowed to leave his post. . . . He had to sound the alarm," and could only fight if his particular post was under attack. He was not allowed to give that ground once the fight was engaged.[183]

We are appointed such guard duty, asserts Kleinig, and are not responsible for any part of the battle but the part at our post.[184] To fight at our post, we are required to fight the right enemy,[185] Satan, in the right place (our daily life),[186] using the right armor of Christ,[187] with the right weapons, particularly prayer.[188] We must also use that weapon at the right time, by which Kleinig means as often as possible,[189] and for the right people, particularly our fellow saints and the ministers of the gospel.[190]

In practical terms, Kleinig concludes, we resist the devil by faithful attendance to the divine service, in our daily devotions, by trusting in the

---

180. Kleinig, *Grace Upon Grace*, 254.
181. Kleinig, *Grace Upon Grace*, 255.
182. Kleinig, *Grace Upon Grace*, 256.
183. Kleinig, *Grace Upon Grace*, 258–59.
184. Kleinig, *Grace Upon Grace*, 259.
185. Kleinig, *Grace Upon Grace*, 259.
186. Kleinig, *Grace Upon Grace*, 260.
187. Kleinig, *Grace Upon Grace*, 261.
188. Kleinig, *Grace Upon Grace*, 262.
189. Kleinig, *Grace Upon Grace*, 263.
190. Kleinig, *Grace Upon Grace*, 263.

grace of God, staying under Christ and his word, by praying the Lord's Prayer and using it as a pattern for our personal prayers, and by the use of intercessory prayer.[191]

An Analysis of Kleinig's Views

Kleinig offers much to the pneumatic aspect of a Lutheran understanding of spiritual warfare. His emphasis on receptivity, that we as Christians cannot grasp or attain anything spiritually for ourselves is framed in an anthropological minimalism strikingly divergent from both Wagner and Wink. While they pursue arguments for independent Christian activity based on faith, Kleinig argues that such independence is an illusion. We are only beggars before a giving God.[192] The pneumatic aspect which Kleinig exposes is one in which the Holy Spirit, in bringing Christ's gifts to us, plays the central role in our spirituality and life of faith. Wagner holds the Spirit's presence as important, but Kleinig makes him central.

In contrast to Wingren, Kleinig offers up a portrayal of Scripture as essential in Christian spiritual life. It is through the word of God that the Holy Spirit comes to man and brings God to bear on human life. Thus for man to have any faith, much less a faith challenged by Satan, the word by which God brings such faith about has to be on hand. Kleinig's perspective also diverges from Wingren in understanding the nature of the battlefield. Wingren argues that the confusion of vocation in the civil and spiritual offices is the battlefield, whereas Kleinig sees the place of battle in the individual conscience.[193]

In addition, the emphasis on prayer, particularly on intercessory prayer, is a useful insight from Kleinig. He has constructed a faithful and profound portrait of the gift that is prayer and how Christians are to use this mighty tool as the people of God to appeal to the Father for aid. Kleinig sees the pneumatic life as one in which the Spirit prompts us to pray to God amidst spiritual attacks and encourages us to continue such practice in daily life. This view is more expansive than Wingren's view of desperate prayer.

---

191. Kleinig, *Grace Upon Grace*, 266–70.

192. Kleinig, *Grace Upon Grace*, 16.

193. Both of these are actually aspects of the same problem and will be addressed in the construction of the antifragile approach.

However, though the above points are powerful, Kleinig's weak area is his work on spiritual warfare. Here, his language of receptivity becomes much less pronounced. He does make reference to all victory being that of Jesus and not our own, but his wording vacillates between the active soldiering of the Christian and the dependency we have on God, between having some offensive weapons and work, and everything being a matter of defense.

The situation he presents related to spiritual warfare also changes. He speaks at some points about an active battle for the cosmos between Christ and Satan in which we have a part, and then at other times about the victory already being won in Christ, and yet at other times about our age as a "mopping up mission." While some reconciliation of these views might be made, Kleinig himself does not fill in the gaps.

Finally, while Kleinig has had much to say that has been helpful regarding the personal pneumatic aspects of spiritual warfare, he says almost nothing about the social aspects of this battle. He does make reference to the importance of vocation in Luther's theology, but he only makes reference to it as a caution against making social concerns the final goal of our spiritual life, limiting useful vocation mainly to prayer. Also, he limits the scope of spiritual warfare to the local action of daily life and the individual conscience, leaving no room for a larger perspective like Wink's of social justice or a Wagner's broader pneumatic perspective.

Kleinig offers many productive insights from which a spiritual warfare theology may be constructed. His insight on the importance of God's word and a life of prayer as foundations on which we might construct portions of a Lutheran account of spiritual warfare is crucial. But more is needed to bring about the robust approach a Lutheran confessional account of spiritual warfare is capable of engendering.

Leopoldo Sánchez on Spirit Christology and Models of Sanctification

Another significant Lutheran voice addressing aspects of spiritual warfare as part of a broader investigation of life in the Spirit is Leopoldo A. Sánchez M., a naturalized US theologian born in Chile and raised in Panama. His dissertation work, entitled *Receiver, Bearer, and Giver of God's Spirit*, later published, explores the relationship between a classic Logos-oriented Christology and his proposed Spirit-oriented Christology, arguing that the latter aspect of the mystery of Christ complements and invigorates the former. He contends that this additional pneumatological framework can enrich how we speak of God in a Trinitarian way and how we speak of the relationship between the church's life and Christ's life in the Spirit.

Spirit-Christology and the Church

In his works on the Holy Spirit, Sánchez also writes about some of the tactics of the demonic and what God reveals to Christians regarding the Holy Spirit's reaction to, even control over, those efforts. Finally, Sánchez also writes about issues of the neighbor, with an emphasis on immigration and ethnic disparity. These topics: Spirit Christology, the relation between the demonic and the Spirit in the Christian's life, and considerations of the neighbor in the West, are all useful for composing an account of spiritual warfare.

In his published dissertation, Sánchez seeks to correct an overemphasis in contemporary theology on a Logos-oriented reading of Jesus' life and mission—the focus being so overwhelmingly on Jesus' identity as God Incarnate that his Spirit-endowed humanity is overshadowed. Sánchez works to portray Jesus' humanity within a broader understanding of the Trinitarian nature of the redemptive act of God for us through the God-Man Jesus (the incarnate Logos) in the Spirit. He does this by reflecting on how the Spirit is received, borne, and given by Jesus in his life and ministry. On the reception of the Spirit by Jesus, Sánchez states:

> A Spirit-oriented Christology reads events in Jesus' life and mission as special instances of the Father's sending of his Spirit upon his incarnate Son in the economy of salvation. A pneumatic reading of the story of Jesus highlights the dynamic presence of the Spirit as an agent in its own right in the humanity of the Son throughout his life and work as obedient Son, Suffering Servant, and risen Lord. Such a Spirit-oriented reading establishes an economic-Trinitarian ground for Christology and soteriology, as well as a Christological ground for the Christian's participation by grace in the Spirit, who is given to us by the Father through Christ.[194]

---

194. Sánchez, *Receiver, Bearer, and Giver*, xxii.

The Bifurcated Approach

Sánchez notes the affinity of this thesis with teachings posited in the early church by Irenaeus[195] and Basil of Caesarea.[196] He examines key moments in which the Spirit is a pivotal presence in the narrative of Jesus' life and redemptive work. In his incarnation,[197] his baptism in the Jordan,[198] and his resurrection, ascension, and establishment at the right hand of God,[199] the Spirit is received by Jesus for our sake. All of these events are consequential for Jesus and for us in God's redemption and sanctification of human persons. But the third event, his resurrection, will be most relevant for our purposes and requires closer examination. In a classic Logos-Christology, Sánchez asserts, an emphasis is placed on Jesus as already being God from eternity, and thus always having his exaltation and lordship. This emphasis partially eclipses the defining place of the Spirit in his bodily resurrection as a new moment in history. A Logos-Christology can posit that during his life and ministry the eternal Logos' exalted status is hidden away, yet extant in his humanity. At his incarnation, the humanity of Christ is already endued also with his divine majesty and lordship. This lordship was unveiled to the world, however, in his resurrection. As Sánchez puts it, for a Logos-oriented reading, "Thus the exaltation of Jesus as risen and ascended Lord and Messiah has an unveiling character *for others*, but not a constitutive one *for Jesus himself*."[200]

In a Spirit Christology, the resurrection does not merely unveil a prior reality but brings about a new one in the Logos' human history. Sánchez highlights Peter's words in Acts 2:33, where Peter notes that Jesus' exaltation to the Father's right hand is marked by the Son receiving from the Father the promised Holy Spirit, whom Jesus then sends upon the disciples and the crowd at Pentecost.[201] The emphasis Peter places on the Spirit's active involvement in Jesus' exaltation, argues Sánchez, does not detract from the eternal divinity or incarnation of the Logos, but rather marks a new turn in the work of God for humanity through the humanity of the Logos: "Following Congar, we may say that a Spirit

---

195. Sánchez, *Receiver, Bearer, and Giver*, 17–20.
196. Sánchez, *Receiver, Bearer, and Giver*, 31–33.
197. Sánchez, *Receiver, Bearer, and Giver*, 34–39.
198. Sánchez, *Receiver, Bearer, and Giver*, 39–46.
199. Sánchez, *Receiver, Bearer, and Giver*, 46–52.
200. Sánchez, *Receiver, Bearer, and Giver*, 48 (emphasis original).
201. Sánchez, *Receiver, Bearer, and Giver*, 46.

Christology invigorates Logos-oriented approaches to the exaltation of Jesus by seeing his resurrection as a new *kairos* in which God has actually made him (not simply proclaimed or declared him as) ascended Lord and Messiah."[202]

This view does not deny the Logos-oriented view, but instead brings a Trinitarian lens to bear on the events of the exaltation of the Christ. The Father's will to save humanity is accomplished through Jesus who has the fullness of the Spirit upon him. Jesus' redemptive life, atoning death, and victory over sin, death, and the devil is verified and fulfilled in his glorifying resurrection, ascension, and enthronement, all of which are accompanied by the presence and activity of the Spirit whom Christ receives, bears, and gives to us in accordance with the will of the Father. Christ, then, is glorified not merely to be vindicated, but as part of God's will in the ongoing work of the salvation of humanity. God's raising of Jesus from the dead according to the Spirit of holiness (Rom 1:4) is thus a new phase in the salvific work of the incarnate and risen Son of God. To put the matter in pneumatic terms, we may say that in the resurrection event the Spirit of God affects the Son in his humanity, so that through his Spirit-raised humanity we might be raised in the Son by the same Spirit, The one who receives the Spirit is thus also able to give the Spirit.

In addition to receiving the Spirit, Sánchez remarks on Jesus bearing the Spirit in his life and mission, particularly in the working of Jesus' teaching and miracles. He describes the dynamic at play in Jesus' life with the Spirit as "a *joint mission* to bring God's kingdom on earth . . . Nothing less than an eschatological inbreaking of God's kingdom among sinners takes place through the Son who acts in the power of the eschatological Spirit. Where God rules both through his Son and in his Spirit, the rule of sin, death, and the devil comes to an end."[203]

Finally, Sánchez offers a look at Jesus as giver of the Holy Spirit. The life of Jesus in his humiliation and exaltation are both lived in the Spirit so that, upon completion of his mission, Jesus might give the Spirit to others. For Sánchez, "the paschal mystery stands at the center in the transition from one state of existence to the next and, therefore, *from Jesus' receiving and bearing of the Spirit as suffering Servant from Jordan to Golgotha to his giving of the same as exalted Servant and Lord at the*

---

202. Sánchez, *Receiver, Bearer, and Giver*, 49.
203. Sánchez, *Receiver, Bearer, and Giver*, 53–54 (emphasis original).

time of his resurrection."[204] There is a cruciform trajectory to the mystery of Christ's life in the Spirit, which bring Christ into conflict with the powers of the anti-kingdom in his mission, but also inaugurates Christ's endowment of the church with the power of the Spirit for her mission in the world.

The Holy Spirit is thus given by the glorified, risen, and exalted Christ to the church as a gift. "Jesus pours out the 'gift' and promise of the Holy Spirit whom he first received from the Father for the forgiveness of all who call upon his name with a contrite and trusting heart (Acts 2:32–39; cf. 5:30–32). The Holy Spirit is given to the church as the power for missionary witness to Jesus (Acts 1:8), and for this reason it is called 'the Spirit of Jesus.'"[205]

The cruciform trajectory of Jesus' work as receiver, bearer, and giver of the Spirit becomes important in Sánchez's contemplation concerning the material difference a right confluence of Logos and Spirit-oriented Christologies can have on the church's witness through proclamation. He proposes "that reading the story of 'Jesus in the Spirit' facilitates 'preaching in the Spirit' that aims at our being crucified and raised with Christ"[206]

Sánchez notes the distinction between looking at the Bible as a collection of historical references and religious points about the past and as God speaking through authoritative words to us now. The written word is authoritative but also there to inform the spoken proclamation of God's yes and no to transform lives:

> For Luther, both the written and spoken forms of the word are ultimately authoritative because through them the Spirit points to Jesus Christ, the enfleshed Word; but the reformer also teaches that the written word exists for the sake of the spoken one. . . . Behind the turn to the narrative lies the assumption that the Spirit addresses human beings in every age through the biblical texts by appropriating what their authors said in the past with the goal of creating in the present a new community of people whose identity is shaped after Jesus' story.[207]

Though Sánchez does not express it in quite these terms, the Spirit, sent by the enthroned Christ in accordance with the will of the Father, is

---

204. Sánchez, *Receiver, Bearer, and Giver*, 70 (emphasis original).
205. Sánchez, *Receiver, Bearer, and Giver*, 70.
206. Sánchez, *Receiver, Bearer, and Giver*, 183.
207. Sánchez, *Receiver, Bearer, and Giver*, 184.

the agent who mediates an ongoing communication from God to us by means of the word of God which orients us toward Jesus and, in turn, points us back to God in thankfulness for the gift given us as the church.[208] This pneumatic dynamic is important for a proper understanding of spiritual warfare because it highlights the continuity of God's promises of salvation across the different turnings of his plan in history to the current situation. In other words, the Spirit's work through the word of God is important because it reveals the manner in which God chooses to reign in this age, and also that such a manner of reigning is consistent with and in continuity with his way of reigning over every age.[209]

Spirit-Christology, the Devil, and the Neighbor

The idea that God is sovereign now is also explored as a component of Sánchez's earlier book *Pneumatología* which, in its second chapter, deals with the Holy Spirit, angels, and evil. Sánchez observes that God is the Almighty Creator, and as such has control over all of his creation. This means control over the good angels as well as over the demonic.[210] Sánchez examines the case of kings Saul and David and how their respective sins are handled. In Saul's refusal of God's command, God removes his Spirit from Saul and sends, instead, an evil spirit.[211] In this account, Sánchez finds both something to be said about God's actions over the spirits of men as well as his actions over the angelic spirits:

> At the pneumatological level, the basic lesson of 1 Sam 16:14–15 is that God reserves for Himself the power and initiative of acting upon all spirits (in this case angelic). In the case of human creatures, just as God gives His Spirit, or breath of life, into a human being and only He can remove it, in the same way only God can give us His Spirit (or Holy Spirit) and only He may remove Him. . . . The same way the power of God applies upon every human spirit also applies, in 1 Sam 16:14–15, to His power over every evil spirit. . . . The faith of the church allows us to say that God is not responsible for evil nor the action of evil spirits in the

---

208. Sánchez, *Receiver, Bearer, and Giver*, 185–86.
209. This will be discussed more below in chapter 6.
210. Sánchez, *Pneumatología*, 55.
211. Sánchez, *Pneumatología*, 55.

world and at the same time say that He can use these realities for the good of His people.²¹²

At first, God's omnipotence seems a problem when faced with evil spirits. But from this, Sánchez contends, one actually finds a blessing since "it assures us that evil actions have to be, somehow, under the control of God. It would be worse if it were not so. God would not, then, be God Almighty. The devil and his evil would have the final word."²¹³

Because God is in control, Sánchez observes, he can use evil for his purposes without being complicit in it. "He has the power to assume these realities for the benefit of His sons and daughters. The power of God over evil spirits manifests when He uses them as instruments of His will in such a way that He draws us closer to His love."²¹⁴ The Christian's suffering, by God's hidden actions, actually helps one not only have a greater faith and repentant heart, but identify with the needs of the neighbor in his suffering, and so the work of the devil backfires.²¹⁵

Sánchez expands on this conclusion in his second book on sanctification, *Teología de la santificación*, where he explores the productivity of a Spirit Christology as a biblical narrative and theological framework for exploring models of sanctification in the Christian's life. The holiness given in the Spirit is one in which "every Christian receives, by pure grace, the gift of holiness, by which he also has been called, according to the vocations in the world which God has given to him, in order to serve his neighbor."²¹⁶ Thus, humans have a twofold purpose in life. First, like Kleinig strongly emphasized, one has a purpose in which God created humans to pray.²¹⁷ But, like Wingren, one is also created as a social being, for work in the world with and for the neighbor.²¹⁸ Sánchez speaks in similar lines to Wingren's understanding of the devil bringing confusion into vocation to act against God, but notes that the source of the confusion is our human sinful nature, which the devil goads onward.²¹⁹ Work,

---

212. Sánchez, *Pneumatología*, 56–57. All translations are by me unless otherwise specified.

213. Sánchez, *Pneumatología*, 57. This conclusion is missed by Boyd, who moves into open theism instead.

214. Sánchez, *Pneumatología*, 58.

215. Sánchez, *Pneumatología*, 59.

216. Sánchez, *Teología*, 11.

217. Sánchez, *Teología*, 20.

218. Sánchez, *Teología*, 21–22.

219. Sánchez, *Teología*, 31.

for example, is thought of as a curse, but work is given for humanity's good by the Creator:

> It cannot be reduced to a curse. It is divine vocation that makes humans 'masks of God' in the world, collaborators with the Creator in matters which concern the neighbor, the instruments of His care and provision in the world. . . . From this perspective, the purpose of the human being in the world that God has created and preserves is but to cultivate, care for, responsibly use for the good of the neighbor and the world that which the Creator has given us.[220]

In his account of the sanctified life, Sánchez describes what he calls a dramatic model of sanctification, where he argues that the devil interacts with the church and each Christian in ways which are mirrored in Jesus' own life and ministry.[221] Particularly, Sánchez notes this interaction in the events of the desert temptation and the garden of Gethsemane. Jesus is baptized and the Holy Spirit, who rests upon him, then sends him into the desert to be tempted. But, Sánchez contends, this leading of the Spirit is not for the purpose of trying to make Jesus fall into sin. Rather, the Spirit's role is "to join him in his fight against the evil spirit he will face with the Word, 'the sword of the Spirit.'"[222] The presence of the Spirit, says Sánchez, is with Jesus throughout the attacks of the devil.

Because the same Holy Spirit whom Jesus bears in his life is the Spirit whom Jesus gives to the church, the same struggle is mirrored in the Christian life. Further, if Christians share in the suffering of Christ, they also share in the glory of God gained by Christ for us in his victory over evil.[223] Sánchez observes that just as Jesus is obedient to the Father in the desert when Israel was not, so Jesus is mediator for the Christian before the Father and journeys with the Christian by his Spirit in times of temptation.[224] Sánchez observes such a contrast also between the fall of Adam and Eve in Eden and Jesus' faithfulness to God in Gethsemane.[225]

He builds on this dramatic model in his later book *Sculptor Spirit*, where Sánchez observes that the drama of the devil's attacks against the

---

220. Sánchez, *Teología*, 27–28.
221. Sánchez, *Teología*, 103.
222. Sánchez, *Teología*, 103.
223. Sánchez, *Teología*, 104.
224. Sánchez, *Teología*, 106.
225. Sánchez, *Teología*, 106–8.

Christian are ones with which Christ sympathizes, having himself been tempted. But this also means that as the Spirit walked with Jesus during his temptation, the same Spirit walks with us during our temptations.[226] Further, Sánchez notes God's use of his people in community to support one another during difficult times of temptation, finding support in the fellow saints and their prayers.[227]

Sánchez sets up a strong pneumatic model of the Spirit's presence and advocacy for the Christian in the face of demonic temptation, echoing Kleinig and Luther. He uses both theologians as he reflects on the implications of the work of Luther, as discussed by Kleinig, regarding the work of Satan in the Christian life.[228] The dramatic tension between the saint and sinner is played out as a conflict between the Holy Spirit and the devil.[229]

In addition to the dramatic model, Sánchez argues for a eucharistic model of the Christian life which links the biblical notion of spiritual sacrifice with the Christian's participation in the Lord's Supper (Eucharist), and its implications for describing life with the neighbor. As the Spirit conforms one to Christ, who offered himself as a fragrant offering to God, the Spirit leads the Christian to give his life "as a fragrant offering to the Father in service toward the neighbor, witnessing to Christ through their prayers and sacrifices for the needy."[230] Following Luther, Sánchez links this to the life of the church in the Lord's Supper, where participation in the Supper is communion with Christ and all the saints, and through which each member both receives from and gives to the brother or sister in need.[231] Such gifts extend to all neighbors as works of thanksgiving to God for what is given in the Lord's Supper to us.[232] "The same Spirit with which Jesus was anointed to be our Servant at His baptism also anoints us in our baptism to sacrifice for others."[233] The dramatic, or pneumatic, form of Sánchez's framework presupposes that the

226. Sánchez, *Sculptor Spirit*, 90.
227. Sánchez, *Sculptor Spirit*, 104–5, 112–14.
228. Sánchez, *Teología*, 114.
229. Sánchez, *Teología*, 120. "Si bien es cierto que el bautismo nos introduce al conflict, también lo es que éste nos libera de la tiranía y dictadura del diablo en nuestras vidas. Las dos realidades deben mantenerse en tensión."
230. Sánchez, *Teología*, 127.
231. Sánchez, *Teología*, 135.
232. Sánchez, *Teología*, 137.
233. Sánchez, *Teología*, 140.

saint is a repentant sinner with the Spirit's presence in his or her battle against temptation. Thus being helped, the Christian has room to focus on the social, eucharistic aspect, the needs of the neighbor, in response to God's salvation through Christ.[234]

An Analysis of Sánchez's Views

The work that Sánchez has done regarding pneumatological facets of theology is helpful for building a framework for spiritual warfare. In his efforts to recognize the usefulness of reading the narratives of Jesus in a Spirit-oriented manner, he intimates not only the Trinitarian ramifications of adding a Spirit-Christology component to a Logos-Christology, but also what that means for this age of the church wherein God is still acting through certain means for his purposes. The risen Christ who bears the Spirit is enthroned and from the Father receives the Spirit to send into the world. The Spirit comes to the church by the word of God written and proclaimed so that she may die and live with Christ in his struggle against the devil and in his sacrifice for the neighbor.

Sánchez recognizes that the work of the evil spirits affects the life of the Christian not only personally but also socially with the neighbor. Whereas Sánchez uses two different models (the dramatic and the eucharistic [or sacrificial])[235] to address the pneumatic and social emphases seen in the Western research on spiritual warfare, he also unites these dimensions within the broader pneumatological framework of a Spirit Christology. He notes, for example, that "the life experiences and spiritual issues described in each of these models [of life in the Spirit] often intersect in everyday life. To face his demons, a man struggling with habitual temptation seeks a community of accountability with others who share similar burdens, and in their mutual encouragement they become gifts to one another (dramatic and sacrificial)."[236] By grounding the pneumatic and social trajectories of the Christian life in the economy of salvation, Sánchez, unlike Wingren or Kleinig, offers a creedal Trinitarian

---

234. Sánchez, *Teología*, 144.

235. Sánchez uses the terms "eucharistic" and "sacrificial" to refer to the same social or neighbor-oriented model of life in the Spirit. He has preferred the term "sacrificial" in *Sculptor Spirit*, where he also expands this idea of community to hospitality toward those marginalized, a socially-oriented model of sanctification. See Sánchez, *Sculptor Spirit*, 115–68.

236. Sánchez, *Sculptor Spirit*, 238.

basis for discussing spiritual warfare as a defining dimension of life in the Spirit of Christ. A Lutheran account of spiritual warfare will integrate the pneumatic and social aspects of the Christian life in the Spirit onto one horizon, seeing both aspects as two sides of the same coin.

6

The Antifragile Approach

A Confessional Lutheran Approach to Spiritual Warfare

Antifragility: An Overview of a New Approach

To this point, we have assessed current spiritual warfare proposals in the West from a Lutheran perspective. The four approaches—dismissive, social, pneumatic, and bifurcated—were each found to be inadequate. In light of these unsatisfactory proposals, the remainder of this work will attempt to answer the question posed in the first chapter, "What is a confessional Lutheran approach to spiritual warfare?" The answer proposed will be quite different from the above approaches in a few crucial ways. First, a proper understanding recognizes that an account of spiritual warfare must encompass both the natural and the supernatural elements at play in the dynamic of its narrative. Wink is right to point to broken social systems as a source of evil, but wrong to dismiss the supernatural and Scripture. Wagner is right to point to the reality of the fallen angels which bear negatively upon the natural world but neglects direct, concrete concepts of social forces and actions. The bifurcated approach acknowledges both the natural and supernatural elements, speaking of each of the powers in some way but never cohesively.

Second, because of their partial systems, the conclusions drawn become erroneous or at least inconsistent. Both the social and pneumatic approaches end up with a God who depends upon human endeavors for success. The bifurcated approach has a disconnect between related points which is never resolved. The result is an uneven collection of views in which God seems to lack the power to properly care for his people, creating notions that the fight against the demonic and evil rests on the shoulders of the Christian.

Third, because the other approaches are partial and, at best, inconsistent, they are missing the fundamental dynamic at work within Scripture regarding spiritual warfare. Where the above approaches argue for how the church is to wage war against the demonic forces or oppressive regimes, the remainder of this work argues these anthropocentric approaches are misguided.

The work of properly answering the above question began in chapter 1 where spiritual warfare was defined as "the fallen powers of creation railing against the reign of Christ." This definition reorients the nature of spiritual warfare, moving the center of action away from humanity. Instead, the focus becomes God's sovereign activity and the reactive actions of the fallen powers. In other words, spiritual warfare takes on a theocentric aspect rather than an anthropocentric one. Spiritual warfare, properly speaking, is not being fought by the Christian or the church at all because the work of Christ in overcoming sin, death, and the devil is already completed. Rather, the issue is that those fallen powers, standing at odds with God's will, attempt to refuse acknowledgement of the soteriological work of Jesus and the resulting authority he has attained in his risen and ascended exaltation. This understanding of the fallen powers is the first part of what I call the *antifragile* approach. The examination of the fallen powers and their attempt at warfare against Christ is followed by the second part, how God not only preserves but strengthens his people in the midst of being assailed by those powers.

The term *antifragile* is taken from Nassim Nicolas Taleb, an economics philosopher who was looking for a term to describe natural systems which were not damaged by adversity (*fragile*), nor were unchanged by adversity (*robust*), but needed adverse environments or situations to improve (*antifragile*). This concept explores how some subjects and systems are improved by adverse effects directed upon them.[1] The fallen powers intend to use chaos and evil to deny Christ's reign. God, however, is more creative than those powers and does not just try to minimize the damage (fragility), nor preserve the Christian through the storms of life (robust), but weaves order and good out of the bad and deepens faith (antifragility). God takes fragile sinners and makes them antifragile saints.

---

1. Taleb, *Antifragile*, 31–40. This is the fourth part of his *Incerto* series, which also includes *Fooled by Randomness*, *The Black Swan*, and *The Bed of Procrustes*.

This reorientation is not only more biblically consistent than the other approaches but also speaks to how this warfare affects and interacts with humanity. A proper account of spiritual warfare recognizes that the Holy Spirit acts by means of word, sacrament, and prayer to preserve and even strengthen the regenerated Christian in faith against the warfare of the demonic, the world, and the sinful nature (the sword of the Spirit). He also works through the Christian by means of vocation to bring God's recreative acts upon the neighbor (masks of God). In other words, the Christian identity is not only created, shaped, and maintained by the Holy Spirit, but also encouraged by that same Spirit to enact that identity in love toward the neighbor and, in the midst of it all, the Christian identity and faith in God and his promises is actually deepened despite the machinations of the fallen powers.

Such a reorientation allows for a reconsideration of the fallen powers themselves. The sinful nature is no longer just the antagonist to our new nature in Christ that causes us misery and struggle in temptation and guilt. Rather, the sinful nature is rebelling against the authority of Christ to send the Holy Spirit to create in a person a new nature. The sinful nature not only seeks to deny the Spirit's authority to enact that new identity but also seeks to deny Christ's authority for daily life. To enact this denial of Christ's authority, the sinful nature seeks to wrest the self from that authority by acting contrary to God's will and seeking its own narrative apart from Christ. It seeks to rid the self of that new, imputed nature in Christ by the Holy Spirit. But the Holy Spirit constantly acts to preserve the new nature despite the attempts of the sinful nature. As will be noted, the Lutheran tradition speaks at length of the issues with the sinful nature.

The fallen world is similar to the sinful nature but writ large as collectives of sinful persons. The world strives against the reign of Christ over it and enacts this denial by pursuing narratives that are opposed to the nature and ethics of such a reign. These worldly collectives seek to undermine the collective which God gathers, the church, to delegitimize it so it can then keep individuals out of or remove them from the godly collective by denying the reality of the possibility of a new identity in Christ. Additionally, as collectives attempt to deny Christ's authority, they seek to fill the vacuum with their own assertions of power and vie with each other to fill such voids. This understanding of the sinful nature and the fallen world encompasses social justice, persecution, and care for the other by rooting these problems in concepts of divine authority and human identity. Despite these attempts at denying Christ's authority, the Holy Spirit consistently acts to preserve and strengthen his church and the individual Christians who comprise it. The Lutheran tradition regardng the world appears less prevalent than on the sinful nature because discussion of it is often derived as an extended concept of the sinful nature.

Satan and the fallen angels have a different motive than the sinful nature and the fallen world, and of the fallen powers will receive the lengthiest treatment below because little formal work has been done in Lutheran circles on this subject. As supernatural beings who know the reality of God and heaven, the goal of the fallen angels is not a denial of the reality of the authority of Christ. Rather, it will be shown that the motivation of the demonic is spite toward God. The fallen angels have an unabating hate for God but cannot directly contend with him. Therefore, they attempt to hurt God indirectly by destroying what he loves. Because God considers humanity the pinnacle of his beloved creation, the fallen angels seek to maximize the number of individuals who will refuse faith in Christ in order to spite God. They work in tandem with the other fallen powers, encouraging and enabling their denial of Christ's authority in any way they perceive furthers their end to wrest humans from Christ. This demonic work may be subtle or may involve overt actions on their part, but like the other fallen powers, it is an unrelenting work against God using humanity as an instrument. This reorientation recognizes not only the reality of demonic entities, but it also puts them into proper perspective as creatures also under the rule of Christ. This approach also highlights that these creatures are not merely agents of chaos or general evil, but have a goal which directs all of their work and ties their actions intimately with the other fallen powers.

Once the situation of Christ and the fallen powers is properly oriented, the implications for Christians can be assessed. The antifragile approach recognizes the fallen powers which engage in warfare but focuses on God's action upon and through the Christian wherein God acts despite the fallen powers, even using the efforts of the fallen powers to refine and increase the faith of the individual. God does not merely allow a broken Christian to survive this life with a semblance of faith intact, nor does he simply preserve the Christian in faith from conversion to death or the last day. Rather, God uses the machinations of the fallen powers to increase the faith of persons as they endure the daily challenges of life.

Rightly understanding the fallen powers, and the relation between them and God, allows us to understand where humanity fits into spiritual warfare. The focus is no longer on humanity against the fallen powers but on God preserving and increasing faith in Christians and their resulting response to this of remembering and enacting their imputed, gifted, new identity toward the world around them. Here, we find God at work despite the efforts of the fallen powers. This assessment of God's action upon and for the Christian will highlight two aspects, the work of the Holy Spirit through the word, which is his sword, and his actions behind the scenes in the world as Christians become his masks.

First, the Holy Spirit shapes the identity of the Christian by his sword, the word of God. Here, the themes of law and gospel, repentance and forgiveness, and God's direction through prayer and scriptural meditation are shown to create, preserve, and strengthen the Christian in faith and wisdom. The Holy Spirit also uses his sword to guide and shape proper Christian perspective on life with the neighbor. The daily life of every person is unique and is full of unique interactions with others. The Spirit uses his sword to guide the framework for the Christian's proper action in whatever milieu is encountered. This enacted identity of the Christian includes a dynamic of receptivity from God and the Christian response to the greater cultural and societal situation in which the Christian is immersed. By that sword, the Spirit additionally reminds Christians of God's perspective on all neighbors. God directs the Christian so that not only proper actions are carried out toward neighbors for their temporal needs, but God also uses the Christian to address their spiritual needs. He does this by encouraging and acting upon the prayers of the Christian and also when the Christian bears witness to the neighbor through which the Spirit enacts his declarative and transformational word upon them. Kleinig, Wingren, Sánchez, and Luther are all helpful contributors toward this personal aspect of spiritual warfare.

Second, in the right orientation that is created by the Spirit through the word of God, the Christian is turned toward daily work and social interaction. God uses these actions as opportunities under which to act in a hidden manner to bring his good into the world. The Holy Spirit encourages the Christian to enact her daily work and life with integrity. This action by the Christian is not only for the needs of the individual neighbor but can be directed toward the needs of larger collectives, including providing a right perspective on issues of social justice.

Further, as others work on behalf of the individual, she is able to see God's love and blessings upon her as others faithfully enact their Christian love on her behalf, and her faith is strengthened through the mask of God for her through the neighbor. Any conflict which emerges between the Christian and the fallen powers via the greater world is used by God to drive the Christian back to prayer and Scripture, to further shape and deepen identity, strengthening the Christian's faith. Thus, there is a social dynamic to the spiritual well-being of God's people and the world as God nurtures the faith of Christians by other Christians in mutual loving action and through whom God acts upon the world in acts of love, charity, and acting as the conscience of the state. Wingren, Wink, Sánchez, and Luther will be instrumental in shaping a narrative of the Christian in the world.

The separation of the sword and the mask in this work is in order to highlight these aspects of God's overall work in relation to the attacks of the fallen powers. In reality, the sword and the mask interplay as two integrated parts of God's action in the world. The Spirit uses both sword and mask in tandem to enact the will of the Father in the salvation won and given by the Son. Examples of this tandem nature include how the Spirit uses the law in its third use, as Lutherans describe it, to address the scope of possible loving actions so that as the Christian works, even though all of his actions are tainted with sin, God still enacts his love on the neighbor within these moments. Also, this includes situations of overt demonic activity in harassment and possession, wherein the sword of the Spirit overlaps with God's action through the Christian as one uses word and prayer to bring the presence of Christ to bear on the situation.

Finally, the sword and mask enacted both through and upon the individual and the awareness of what it means to be God's child are further embedded and deepened with an increase in the recognition of the imputed identity as the primary way to understand the self instead of by the sinful nature. These actions under which God enacts his will, by their nature, thwart the work and will of the fallen powers, though they ceaselessly rail against his will and work.

The fallen powers seek to cause a person to reject salvation through Jesus and reject the regenerated nature that the Holy Spirit creates. However, that Spirit not only shapes our identities in Christ but causes us to enact that identity in a world that seeks to deny it. Despite the machinations of the fallen angels distinct from, and in tandem with, the other fallen powers, the Spirit acts to deepen our identities in Christ. As he reigns, God not only preserves but strengthens a people for himself despite the efforts of the fallen powers.

God the Son Reigns Over the Fallen Powers

Concerning God's reign over the created order, the social approach to spiritual warfare depicts a Christ who is an example of advocacy for social justice. However, it does not consider his reign in heaven as significant to enacting warfare on domination systems. The pneumatic approach consistently speaks of Christ's reign as contingent in a subtle dualism, where the victory has been assured but God cannot overcome the fallen angels himself and is dependent upon the church to concretize the victory. Therefore, the church is engaged in spiritual warfare to take back the world for Jesus. The bifurcated approach also acknowledges the reign of Christ, but it separates out the devil from the events of life and the world, and so divorces spiritual evils from temporal ones. In light of this variance in perspective regarding Christ's reign, a look that reign in terms of spiritual warfare is needed. The above approaches each leave a question that needs to be answered: Does Christ reign now? If so, to what extent? How does this pertain to a proper approach to spiritual warfare?

This section asserts the traditional understanding that Christ reigns over all the created order. Because his reign is over all things, natural and supernatural, it has ramifications for a proper understanding of the relationship between God, the fallen powers, and humanity. This section begins with the reign of Christ as an approach "from above." This differs in perspective from the other spiritual warfare approaches, which start with the problems of the world and seek answers "from below." When starting "from below," the framework for all approaches has been to seek how God reacts to the evil of the world and the demons, leading to an anthropocentric practice of spiritual warfare. By starting "from above," with a theocentric outlook, this work will show that rather than God reacting to the actions of fallen powers beyond his control, it is the fallen powers which are reacting to Christ's reign in an attempt to undo what they might of its reality. The real enemy of the fallen powers is not the Christian, but Christ. However, this is still pertinent for the Christian's daily life because the identity of the Christian becomes the target of the fallen powers in their work against God.

The Nature of Christ's Reign in the New Testament

The New Testament states unequivocally that Jesus Christ, in his resurrection and ascension into heaven, has assumed kingship of all of creation. John records the words of Jesus, about to enter Gethsemane, declaring he has overcome the world (John 16:18). In his following prayer, Jesus states the Father has given to him "authority over all flesh" and in that authority to give eternal life to all of God's people (John 17:2). In Matthew, Jesus tells the Sanhedrin that they will see him, the Son of Man, "seated at the right hand of Power and coming on the clouds of heaven" (Matt 26:64; also Mark 14:62; 16:19; and Luke 22:69). The response of the high priest, in the next verse, is to tear his robes and declare that Jesus has spoken blasphemy by equating himself with God, using images from Daniel and Psalm 110 to claim his authority.[2] This word from Jesus speaks of a time when he will rule at the right hand of God the Father and also of the Last Day. It does not state the timeframe for either of these events.

However, Matthew also records Jesus' words after his resurrection, when speaking to his disciples, where he says, "All authority in heaven and on earth has been given to me" (Matt 28:18), indicating that with his resurrection, Jesus has been given the authority to reign over all creation. That part of the future of which Jesus spoke to the Sanhedrin is now a reality.[3] Luke later records Peter's words at Pentecost in which the disciple speaks of Jesus at the right hand of God and as the one who pours out the Holy Spirit to the nascent church at Pentecost (Acts 2:32–35). Luke also notes Stephen's vision of Jesus at the right hand of God (Acts 7:55–56).[4]

When Jesus ascends into heaven, John speaks in his revelation of Jesus coming to his throne and ushering in the final age of this world before the last day (Rev 5:6–14). In that depiction, the Lamb, being Jesus, sits at the right hand of the Father and he, with the Father, has "blessing and honor and glory and might forever and ever" (Rev 5:13). Through this vision to John, we are given an account of what happens after the ascension

---

2. Gibbs, *Matthew 21:1—28:20*, 1472–76.

3. Gibbs, *Matthew 21:1—28:20*, 1636–37.

4. "The Son of Man, who now is suffering, will be exalted to the right hand of the Father, for he is crowned as King when he is vindicated by the Father in the resurrection. At the right hand of the power of God, Jesus becomes the judge." Just, *Luke 9:51—24:53*, 887.

of Jesus beyond the natural part of creation. When he ascended, he did so to the right hand of God the Father in all power and authority.[5]

The significance of this assumption of glory and authority by God the Son is not lost on Paul. He speaks of Jesus as seated at God's right hand (Rom 8:34). He elaborates on this in the second chapter of his letter to the Ephesians. There, Paul speaks of Jesus' authority at his ascension by saying Christians have hope in Jesus, whose work was verified by God the Father, who "raised him from the dead and seated him at his right hand in the heavenly places, far above all rule and authority and power and dominion, and above every name that is named, not only in this age but also in the one to come. And he put all things under his feet and gave him as head over all things to the church, which is his body, the fullness of him who fills all in all" (Eph 1:20–23; 4:10). In his letter to the Philippians, he also notes that, upon Jesus, God the Father has "highly exalted him and bestowed upon him the name that is above every name so that at the name of Jesus every knee should bow in heaven and on earth and under the earth, and every tongue confess that Jesus Christ is Lord, to the glory of God the Father" (Phil 2:9–10).[6] Paul speaks further of the glory of the ascended Jesus when he talks to the church in Colossae, saying of Jesus:

> He is the image of the firstborn of all creation. For by him all things were created, in heaven and on earth, visible and invisible, whether thrones or dominions or rulers or authorities—all things were created through him and for him. And he is before all things, and in him all things hold together. And he is the head of the body, the church. He is the beginning, the firstborn from the dead, that in everything he might be preeminent. For in him all the fullness of God was pleased to dwell, and through him to reconcile to himself all things, whether on earth or in heaven, making peace by the blood of his cross. (Col 1:15–20)[7]

---

5. Brighton, in *Revelation*, 139, notes, "The entire destiny of the church, of the human race, and of all history is thus revealed as the scroll is opened—not as a blueprint or a time schedule of human history, but rather as a visionary, prophetic picture of the times from the ascension of Christ to the eschaton. And it is all under the lordship of Jesus Christ, for the glory of God, and for the benefit of his people."

6. "With his ascension this lowly Jesus, the incarnate Son of God in his state of humiliation, was exalted.... This lowly man who was tried by human governments was now exalted above all governments. This lowly man who was mortal was now exalted above death. This lowly man who was tempted by Satan was now exalted over Satan and all angels and rulers of darkness." Raabe, "Christ's Ascension and Session," 74.

7. Deterding writes, "The apostle's statement that Christ is before all things (Col 1:17) is to be understood in terms of both time (our Lord existed prior to the creation)

He further speaks of Jesus as having "all rule and authority" (Col 2:10) and that God, through Jesus, "disarmed the rulers and authorities and put them to open shame by triumphing over them in him" (Col 2:15).

Likewise, among the general epistles, the author to the Hebrews points out Christ's rule in his introductory words (Heb 1:1–4). Peter also speaks of Christ, in his ascension, as being "at the right hand of God, with angels, authorities, and powers having been subjected to him" (1 Pet 3:22).

From this brief survey of New Testament references, Jesus is depicted as having all authority over creation. The image of Jesus sitting at the right hand of God the Father is the main picture given to portray that he has all aspects of creation in subjection to himself. There is no question that the writers of the New Testament understood Jesus' words during his ministry concerning his glory and reign as coming to fruition with his resurrection and ascension. This fruition, but not absolute fulfillment as will occur at the eschaton, is the current state and will remain so until the last day. The reign of Christ over all creation is a reality. He has the power and authority to bring a final end to the fallen powers and to death, but has chosen to wait. This view of the reign of Jesus is consistent with the Lutheran tradition.[8]

---

and pre-eminence (Christ has authority over all the creation). The whole universe is said to have its existence in Christ." Deterding, *Colossians*, 57.

8. The pneumatic approach argues Jesus' reign is contingent. Its primary reference for this position is Paul's first letter to the church in Corinth (1 Cor 15:22–26). There, Paul refers to the return of Jesus on the last day, on which Jesus delivers the world over to the Father "after destroying every rule and authority and power. For he must rule until he has put all his enemies under his feet. The last enemy to be destroyed is death" (1 Cor 15:25–26). In reference to these sayings, the argument made is that Jesus does not yet have all things under his authority because the devil and the fallen angels still hold much of the world under their sway such that Jesus has no power to act in those places. Wagner explicitly uses these words of Paul to argue this point (Wagner, *Confronting the Powers*, 64–65, 121–25); also Wagner and Greenwood, "Strategic-Level Deliverance Model," 179.

The context of the verse calls this interpretation into question. The very next verse from Paul states, "For God has put all things in subjection under his feet" (1 Cor 15:27). So which is it, then? Are all things subject to Christ or not? In their immediate context (1 Cor 15:20–28), these verses (vv. 25–27) are speaking about the nature of the Last Day, on which Jesus will put an end to all the fallen powers and to death itself. This does not mean that these powers are not now in subjection under him, only that he has not yet brought about the fullness of his judgment against those powers. This crucial difference in understanding Paul's argument puts these verses properly in line with the context of the chapter. The larger context of the whole of chapter 15 is Paul's discussion of the ramifications of Jesus' resurrection as the firstfruits of the resurrection of the

The Lutheran Confessions and Tradition on the Reign of Christ: Jesus Christ Reigns in the Spirit in Accordance with the Will of the Father

Lutheran tradition is in harmony with the heritage of the historic church in stating that Christ has authority over all created things to rule and reign without exception. The three traditional ecumenical creeds all speak of Jesus at the "right hand of God the Father," reflecting the above statements by Jesus and Paul.[9] On that rule, the Augsburg Confession notes Jesus "'sitting at the right hand of God' in order to rule and reign forever over all creatures, so that through the Holy Spirit he may make holy, purify, strengthen, and comfort all who believe in him, also distribute to them life and various gifts and benefits, and shield and protect them against the devil and sin."[10] The Formula of Concord notes that Jesus is Lord, Creator, and Redeemer,[11] and Almighty God.[12] He is the right hand of God with all majesty, power, and might over all things[13] and is able to exercise it everywhere,[14] being immanent in and transcendent over all created things.[15]

---

dead and the reality of the future resurrection. If Christ is resurrected and all things are subject to him, then the Christian is certain that the present enemies, who are the enemies of Christ, are subject to him also. Because those enemies are subject to the Lord, the Christian is also victorious over them and the resurrection is as certain for God's people as it was for Jesus. This greater context further harmonizes this passage with Paul's other letters and with the rest of Scripture, in contrast to the interpretation of the pneumatic approach.

9. On the image of the right hand of God, Chemnitz writes in the Solid Declaration, "Jesus ascended far above all the heavens, truly fills all things, and now rules everywhere, from one sea to the other and to the end of the world, not only as God but also as a human being. As the prophets prophesy and the apostles testify [Pss 8:2, 7; 93:1; Zech 9:19; Mark 16:19–20], he worked everywhere with them and has confirmed their message through the signs that accompanied it. Indeed, this did not take place in an earthly manner but, as Dr. Luther explains, according to the mode of the right hand of God. It is not some specific spot in heaven, as the Sacramentarians propose without basis in the Holy Scripture. Instead, it is nothing other than the almighty power of God, which fills heaven and earth," FC SD VIII, 27–28 in Kolb and Wengert, *Book of Concord*, 621. See also: Pieper, *Christian Dogmatics*, 2:329.

10. CA III, 4–5 in Kolb and Wengert, *Book of Concord*, 38.
11. FC SD VII, 44 in Kolb and Wengert, *Book of Concord*, 600.
12. FC SD VII, 89 in Kolb and Wengert, *Book of Concord*, 608.
13. FC SD VIII, 12 in Kolb and Wengert, *Book of Concord*, 658.
14. FC SD VII, 95 in Kolb and Wengert, *Book of Concord*, 609.
15. FC SD VII, 101 in Kolb and Wengert, *Book of Concord*, 610.

As Pieper notes, "Christ, the Redeemer, also exercises dominion over all the world and the whole universe. Scripture stresses the universal character of the dominion of Christ. . . . Scripture exempts no territory in the universe from the dominion of Christ; the *officium Christi regium* extends over all relations and situations in the universe."[16] One of the ramifications of this is noted in *The Bondage of the Will (De servo arbitrio)*, where Luther speaks to a consequence of God's absolute reign, in which "God foreknows nothing contingently, but that he foresees and purposes all things by his immutable, eternal, and infallible will."[17]

In every way, Christ does rule over all things now, but the created order has not yet experienced the full eschaton of Christ's return. This inaugurated eschaton is the age in which Christ reigns, but does so in a mediated way. The issue of the *manner* of Christ's reign over this age becomes important for the consideration of spiritual warfare. The remainder of this section will summarize the way in which Jesus reigns as it relates to spiritual warfare. This section does not intend to cover all the dynamics of God's reign in Christ nor to cover the *why* he reigns in this way, which concerns theodicy. The issue for our purpose is to simply examine his reign as it is revealed to his church with regard to spiritual warfare.

The Narrative of Christ's Reign Regarding Spiritual Warfare

In the quote above, the Augsburg Confession describes Christ's reign by making special note of the Holy Spirit as the one through whom Christ exercises the powers of his reign. Specifically, the keeping of Christians in faith, the giving of his gifts to them, and protection from the fallen angels and sin in its various facets. These aspects deserve a closer look from a Lutheran perspective.

As examined earlier,[18] Sánchez highlights the interconnected nature between the reign of Jesus and the enactment of the fruits of that reign by the Holy Spirit in accordance with the will of the Father. Christ's reign is a continuation of the Trinitarian economy of salvation into this age of the church. As regards the world in general, Jesus reigns with power, but as it pertains to the church, he reigns through grace given by

16. Pieper, *Christian Dogmatics*, 2:385.
17. *LW* 33:37.
18. See chapter 5.

the Spirit. Luther describes the full picture of Christ's reign over all things and, within this, over the church in a special way by the Spirit when he argues in *The Bondage of the Will*:

> For what we assert and contend for is this, that when God operates without regard to the grace of the Spirit, he works all in all, even in the ungodly inasmuch as he alone moves, actuates, and carries along by the motion of his omnipotence all things, even as he alone has created them, and this motion the creatures can neither avoid nor alter, but they necessarily follow and obey it, each according to its capacity as given it by God; and thus all things, even the ungodly, cooperate with God. Then, when he acts by the Spirit of grace in those whom he has justified, that is in his Kingdom, he actuates and moves them in a similar way, and they, inasmuch as they are his new creation, follow and cooperate, or rather, as Paul says, they are led [Rom 8:14].[19]

Lutherans speak about this distinction between Christ ruling over creation in general, and humanity in particular, and his rule over the church as a distinction between Christ's rule by the worldly government and through the spiritual government in his earthly kingdom.[20] The spiritual government is one of grace, delineated by the work of the Holy Spirit in which he plants into the person faith in Jesus and his saving work. This saving faith is regenerative for the person, who is turned from being at enmity with the Father to being described as God's child on account of Christ. The Spirit compels and encourages the Christian into acts of love for the neighbor, and God works in a hidden way, despite the sin tainting the human work, to bring his good and will into the world for the neighbor. In this way, faith imbues these acts with a different nature than the works of the world. These acts are not synergistic nor salvific in character for the Christian; rather, they are in godly service toward the neighbor as a fruit of faith.

Luther speaks of the Trinitarian economy of salvation, this cooperative effort of the Father's will, Christ's reign, and the Spirit's actions in the Confessions. In the Large Catechism, Luther notes, "we could never come to recognize the Father's favor and grace were it not for the Lord Christ, who is a mirror of the Father's heart. . . . But neither could we know anything of Christ, had it not been revealed by the Holy Spirit."[21]

---

19. *LW* 33:242.
20. This was discussed by Wingren in chapter 5.
21. LC II, 65 in Kolb and Wengert, *Book of Concord*, 440.

He also summarizes this work of the Holy Spirit in connecting humanity to Christ when he says of the Spirit's work, "I believe that by my own understanding or strength I cannot believe in Jesus Christ my Lord or come to him, but instead the Holy Spirit has called me through the gospel, enlightened me with his gifts, made me holy and kept me in the true faith, just as he calls, gathers, enlightens, and makes holy the whole Christian church on earth and keep it with Jesus Christ in the one common, true faith."[22]

These passages show that while Christ does reign over all things, he chooses to give the gifts he earned for the world through the Holy Spirit. Outside of the church that the Spirit makes under Christ, the world has the capacity to resist the gift of grace offered to it, and Christ suffers that rejection. As Fagerberg summarizes, while Jesus does reign absolutely, "outside of the Christian context the worship of God is generally perverted. Although God guides and upholds the created world, men do not acknowledge Him."[23] Faith in the salvific work of Christ is not coerced; God allows rejection of his gifts. It is in this lack of coercion and allowance of rejection that the fallen powers find room to enact their spiritual warfare as resistance and denial of Christ's reign.

The resistance to the reign of Christ is categorized by the Confessions into the three fallen powers of the flesh, the world, and the devil.[24] Jesus reigns over all things, even if all things, at this time, do not acknowledge it and are allowed to persist in this attitude. This is not the portrait of God produced by the social approach, which assumes God is indifferent or apathetic toward human evil. This also differs from the pneumatic approach, with territory left to be won for Jesus by his church. In contrast to both of these, the Lutheran approach recognizes the unequivocal statements that Jesus reigns completely over all of the created order—over all of the natural and supernatural elements of this creation—and yet suffers the fallen powers to work in denial of his reign. This understanding of Christ's reign moves the focus of spiritual warfare from an anthropocentric center to a theocentric and Trinitarian one.

---

22. SC "Apostles' Creed," 6 in Kolb and Wengert, *Book of Concord*, 355–56.

23. Fagerberg, *New Look at the Lutheran Confessions*, 115.

24. For example, in his explanation of the Third Petition of the Lord's Prayer, Luther comments on God's work of breaking and hindering "every evil scheme and will—as are present in the will of the devil, the world, and our flesh," SC "Lord's Prayer," 11 in Kolb and Wengert, *Book of Concord*, 357.

The Antifragile Approach, Part One: The Fallen Powers and Their Targets

Jesus Christ reigns over all things, yet there are still evil forces in the world. The next two sections offer a deeper examination of the antifragile approach toward the conundrum of spiritual warfare. Spiritual warfare defined as the fallen powers railing against the reign of Christ allows for a two-part explanation of spiritual warfare. First, the nature of and actions of the fallen powers in their work to deny the reign of Christ. Second, a description of how God acts despite these attempts by the fallen powers to war with him. In this first part, the three fallen powers are scrutinized according to their natures, their motivations, and their works. This is followed by the explanation of how their work is in tandem with one another and the implications of that for the Christian life. The second part will feature God's response to these powers and their works, and how God acts in and through the Christian to not only refute the works of these powers, but to strengthen the Christian despite persistent evils.

The Fallen Sinful Nature: Warfare Against Christ and the Imputed Regenerate Identity

The Lutheran tradition is strong in its understanding and description of the conflict between the sinful nature and the imputed nature. However, here this teaching will be reframed as a part of spiritual warfare. The sinful nature, with which all are born, conflicts with the new nature which the Holy Spirit generates in a person by faith in Jesus. To relate the terminology of these two aspects of being in the following exploration, the state of being sinful is referred to as *unregenerate*, and the new state created in faith is referred to as *regenerate*. However, as noted below, both states paradoxically, simultaneously, and fully comprise the being of a Christian in this life.

The Origin and Definition of the Unregenerate Nature

Adam and Eve were created in a state of righteousness before God, in the image of God (Gen 1:2-27).[25] In this *iustitia originalis*,[26] not only were all their actions right before God, but at their foundation "a wisdom and righteousness that would grasp God and reflect God was implanted in humankind, that is, humankind received gifts like the knowledge of God, fear of God, trust in God and the like."[27] It was in this original righteousness that, as Fagerberg puts it, man's "intellect and will were so directed towards God that he was able to live in a manner consistent with God's expectations."[28]

The first sin, perpetrated by Adam and Eve, was doubt in God and his words of promise. The serpent poses the question of God's wording, then contradicts it.[29] Eve, and Adam with her, sees the fruit in light of the serpent's words and accepts those words (Gen 3:6). As Kolb notes, we often think of the root of sin as disobedience. But when Adam and Eve sinned, it began with the doubting of God's word to them concerning the fruit of the tree of the knowledge of good and evil.[30] This led to a replacing of God's wisdom with a person's own desire.[31] In the fall of man, humanity moves from an original righteousness into a state of

---

25. Additionally, it is only after creating man and woman and blessing them that he looks at the entirety of creation and recognizes it as "very good" (Gen 1:31).

26. This is Melanchthon's term for the status of man before the Fall (e.g., Ap II, 15–23 in Kolb and Wengert, *Book of Concord*, 114–15). For a discussion of his use of the term in contrast to the Roman Catholic use, see Fagerberg, *New Look at the Lutheran Confessions*, 129–33. Pieper uses the complementary term *in statu integritatis*, a state of integrity before God. Pieper, *Christian Dogmatics*, 1:515.

27. Ap II, 18 in Kolb and Wengert, *Book of Concord*, 115.

28. Fagerberg, *New Look at the Lutheran Confessions*, 132. Also, the image of God "consisted in much more than in his possession of intellect and will, in his personality; it consisted in the right disposition of his intellect and will, in his knowledge of God and the will to do only God's will." Pieper, *Christian Dogmatics*, 1:516–17.

29. The serpent questions God's words: "He said to the woman, 'Did God actually say, 'You shall not eat of any tree in the garden'?" (Gen 3:1). Then, he contradicts God's words, saying, "You will not surely die. For God knows that when you eat of it your eyes will be opened, and you will be like God, knowing good and evil" (Gen 1:4–5).

30. Kolb, *Christian Faith*, 91.

31. "The corruption or depravity is absolute or total in the vertical relationship. There sinners have lost it all. They cannot turn to God on their own. Their will automatically and instinctively chooses the alternative—any alternative—to their Creator, Yahweh." Kolb, *Christian Faith*, 93.

sinfulness.[32] This is marked in Genesis with the two humans trying to hide from God (Gen 3:8), followed by their blame of others rather than repentance (Gen 3:12–13).[33]

This state of sinfulness is carried from Adam and Eve to every person[34] born in a natural manner.[35] This state is a loss of righteousness before God, not only becoming accountable for our sins unto God through the law (Rom 3:19–20), but also having a stance against him.[36] Therefore the sinful state is *unregenerate*, having lost its righteousness, unable to regain it and, moreover, does not want to regain it.

The Lutheran Confessions consistently speak of the unregenerate person at odds with God in this way. In the Small Catechism of 1529, Martin Luther writes of the unregenerate person "by my own understanding or strength I cannot believe in Jesus Christ my Lord or come to him."[37] In the Augsburg Confession of the next year, Philip Melanchthon gives a more technical picture of original sin and how it defines the unregenerate person, stating that from the fall of Adam, "all human beings who are propagated according to nature are born with sin, that is, without fear of God, without trust in God, and with concupiscence. And they teach that this disease or original fault is truly sin, which even now damns and brings eternal death to those who are not born again."[38] Be-

---

32. Sin is a thorough corruption of human nature, but not the definition of human nature. See, e.g.: FC Ep I, 2–10 in Kolb and Wengert, *Book of Concord*, 488–89; and FC SD I, 5–14 in Kolb and Wengert, *Book of Concord*, 533–34.

33. Sin committed in interaction with others, as seen in the blaming here, is part of the category of fallen power of the sinful world, which is examined in the next section.

34. Paul writes, "Therefore, just as sin came into the world through one man, and death through sin, and so death spread to all men because all sinned. . . . Therefore, as one trespass led to condemnation for all men, so one act of righteousness leads to justification and life for all men. For as by the one man's disobedience the many were made sinners, so by the one man's obedience the many will be made righteous" (Rom 5:12, 18–19). See also 1 Cor 15:22.

35. The term "natural manner" means by biological means in contrast to the immaculate conception of Jesus.

36. "For the mind that is set on the flesh is hostile to God, for it does not submit to God's law; indeed, it cannot" (Rom 8:7). This hostility to God is shown, for example, in the scene of the plagues of God's wrath on sinful humanity in Revelation, where instead of repenting of their sins and turning to God when they are shown such consequences, "People gnawed their tongues in anguish and cursed the God of heaven for their pain and sores. They did not repent of their deeds" (Rev 16:10–11).

37. SC "Apostles' Creed," 6 in Kolb and Wengert, *Book of Concord*, 355.

38. CA II, 1–2 in Kolb and Wengert, *Book of Concord*, 36–39.

cause of disagreement from the Roman Catholic opponents at Augsburg, Melanchthon further expounds on this teaching in the Apology to the Augsburg Confession of 1531, stating:

> We deny to those conceived and born according to the course of nature not only the act of fearing and trusting God, but also the ability or gifts needed to produce such fear and trust. For we say that those who have been born in this way have concupiscence and are unable to produce true fear and trust in God . . . in this sense the Latin text denies the ability of human nature (that is, the gift and power needed to produce fear and faith in God), and it also denies to adults the act of producing it. So when we use the word "concupiscence," we understand not only its acts or fruits, but the continual tendency of our nature.[39]

The move from *iustitias originalis* to *in statu peccatur* in the event of the Fall breaks humanity's relationship with God. No person is able to keep the first table of the Decalogue. The self attempts to replace God. The unregenerate is *homo incurvatus in se*, the individual curved back onto one's self to find what to trust, to love, and to fear.[40] As Luther says, "to have a god is nothing else than to trust and believe in that one with your whole heart . . . If your faith and trust are right, then your God is the true one. Conversely, where your trust is false and wrong, there you do not have the true God."[41] The unregenerate state not only tempts the self to sin toward the neighbor, but because of our inability to fear and trust God it also consists of "being ignorant of God, despising God, lacking fear and confidence in God, hating the judgment of God, fleeing this judging God, being angry with God, despairing of his grace, and placing confidence in temporal things."[42] This is the state of all persons without intervention.

The Origin of the Regenerate State of the New Identity

Regeneration of a person as a gift given by God through faith in Christ is the cornerstone of the Christian faith. The Confessions echo the

---

39. Ap II, 3 in Kolb and Wengert, *Book of Concord*, 112.

40. Luther uses this term in his lecture on Romans from 1515–16; in Luther, *Lectures on Romans*, LW 25:345.

41. LC, I, 2–3 in Kolb and Wengert, *Book of Concord*, 386.

42. Ap II, 8 in Kolb and Wengert, *Book of Concord*, 113.

emphasis from Scripture that salvation from such a state cannot come in any other form than Jesus[43] interceding by means of his incarnate life, death, and resurrection so that a person may receive restoration before God the Father and the blessings which come with such restoration. A main emphasis of the Confessions is the gift of salvation in Christ apart from the works of man. For example, Melanchthon speaks of one receiving forgiveness of sins, a state of righteousness before God, and eternal life not from being good, but "out of grace for Christ's sake through faith when we believe that Christ has suffered for us."[44]

Luther speaks of this reality of Christ's work for man's regeneration before God. In the Small Catechism, he notes in his explanation of the Second Article of the Apostles Creed, "he has purchased and freed me from all sins, from death, and from the power of devil, not with gold or silver but with his holy, precious blood and with his innocent suffering and death. He has done all this in order that I may belong to him, live under him in his kingdom, and serve him."[45] This belonging to God in Christ is referred to by Paul as adoption by God as his children (Gal 4:4-6).

This salvation and adoption must be imputed since the unregenerate person cannot go to God, nor wants to do so (Rom 5:14-19; 2 Cor 5:19-21). Luther speaks thoroughly of the Holy Spirit's part of bringing persons into faith and keeping them there, noting that when the salvation of Christ intervenes, the Holy Spirit uses God's word to bring faith in Jesus to the unregenerate person and to preserve them in that faith.[46] He later argues if the unregenerate person could love God or do good works which pleased God, then salvation could be gained without Christ, and Christ would have died in vain.[47] This work of the Holy Spirit to create faith in Christ within a person is referred to by Melanchthon as regeneration,[48] and so this new person in Christ may be referred to as *regenerate*. An understanding of self as God's child by the imputed

---

43. This is the central point of Scripture, e.g., Gen 3:15; John 3:16-17; Rom 3:21-28; Eph 2:8-10; 1 Pet 3:21.

44. CA IV, 1–3 in Kolb and Wengert, *Book of Concord*, 58–60.

45. SC "Apostles' Creed," 4 in Kolb and Wengert, *Book of Concord*, 355.

46. SC "Apostles' Creed," 6 in Kolb and Wengert, *Book of Concord*, 355–56.

47. SA III.I, 1–3, 11 in Kolb and Wengert, *Book of Concord*, 310–11. See also Ap IV, 12 in Kolb and Wengert, *Book of Concord*, 122.

48. Ap IV, 72 in Kolb and Wengert, *Book of Concord*, 132.

righteousness of Christ becomes the Christian identity.[49] This is how God perceives the Christian in light of Christ's actions, and it is to be the perspective of the Christian; even though one is yet completely a sinner due to the fall, one is also, in Christ, completely a saint. It is the saint, the regenerate nature, that is the eternal nature of a person, if one does not reject that imputed gift.

The production and maintenance of the regenerated nature is received by the Christian from God. There is no work a person can do to claim this gift for the self. The Holy Spirit acts to bring conversion to the sinner through baptism, where God's words (God's triune name) are linked to the water and bring faith, or later in life through God's words spoken, read, and preached, which compel one by faith to baptism. But God's use of his words in the Christian life does not end at conversion. Rather, God uses his word to maintain and strengthen the regenerate nature in a person during this life. This is required because the person who has been regenerated also retains the unregenerate nature.

The Unregenerate and Regenerate in Paradox—The Sinful Nature at War Against Christ and Christian Identity

The unregenerate nature has no interest in recognizing salvation through Jesus Christ or the victory and reign of Christ over all things. It is set against anything which will thrust the self from the center of authority and perspective. The regenerate nature, though, is made right with God and turned again toward God through faith in Christ Jesus. Thus, a paradox is created. Through faith in Jesus Christ a right relationship with God is established by God toward the Christian, and yet in this life the unregenerate nature is neither completely destroyed nor removed. Since Christ paid the consequence for all sins in his death on the cross, all is forgiven and reconciled with God concerning both actual sins and original sin, but the reality of the unregenerate person remains. Therefore, in this life on earth the unregenerate, sinful person remains in conjunction with the regenerate, sainted identity in Jesus.[50] Yet they are not two per-

---

49. SC "The Lord's Prayer," 2 in Kolb and Wengert, *Book of Concord*, 336. See also, LC III, 32, 37–44, in Kolb and Wengert, *Book of Concord*, 444–45.

50. "Through Baptism (Rom 6:1–12) believers are united with Christ in his vicarious death for their sin, and also with his new life of freedom (after his sacrifice on the cross) from sin and its curse of death. In this remarkable union, the believer lives out the parallel with Christ by crucifying the sinful flesh with its works, putting it

sons, but a single person. As Luther later states in his commentary on Galatians (1535), the Christian is "righteous and a sinner at the same time, holy and profane, an enemy of God and a child of God."[51] The Christian is simultaneously saint and sinner, both regenerate and unregenerate. Althaus, citing Luther, notes, "'In myself outside of Christ, I am a sinner; in Christ outside of myself, I am not a sinner.' This double character remains through all of life. Both are always true of me at one and the same time. This is the great paradox of Christian existence. Neither reason nor legalistic thinking can understand the contradiction involved in the fact that one and the same man is at one and the same time both a righteous man and a sinner."[52]

In terms of spiritual warfare, the unregenerate nature constantly tries to undermine the identity of the regenerate nature in Christ as a denial of Christ's authority over it. The unregenerate nature, in trying to deny Christ' authority, daily antagonizes the regenerate nature. In his Large Catechism, Luther notes how the unregenerate nature "goes to work and lures us daily into unchastity, laziness, gluttony and drunkenness, greed and deceit, into acts of fraud and deception against our neighbor—in short, into all kinds of evil lusts that by nature cling to us."[53]

To frame this in a slightly different manner in regard to spiritual warfare, the unregenerate nature is not idle because of the imputation of Christ's righteousness upon a person. Rather, it struggles against this new nature because the regenerate nature has appeared and is antithetical to it. The regenerate nature is called upon to fear, love, and trust in God. The unregenerate nature desires to fear, love, and trust in self or anything other than God. The unregenerate nature refuses to acknowledge, and actively tries to undo, if possible, the regenerate nature and its foundational faith in Jesus Christ.[54] The unregenerate nature is in spiritual warfare against the reign of Christ and the Spirit's regeneration of the Christian.

continually to death by the sanctifying power of Christ's Spirit (Rom 8:13; Gal 5:24–24 [sic]). Although the corruption of the Adamic flesh continues (Rom 6:13–18; 7:14–25; Eph 4:22–23; Heb 12:1), Christians look forward to the time when they will experience the union with the Savior in its fullness without the devastation of carnal corruption." Nafzger, *Confessing the Gospel*, 308.

51. Luther, *Lectures on Galatians (1535)*, LW 26:232. In the Latin, "Sic homo Christianus simil iustus et peccator, Sanctus, prophanus, inimicus et filius Dei est." WA 40:368.

52. Althaus, *Theology of Martin Luther*, cited from WA 38:205.

53. LC III, 102 in Kolb and Wengert, *Book of Concord*, 453–54.

54. SC "Lord's Prayer," 18 in Kolb and Wengert, *Book of Concord*, 358.

This warfare is a matter of life and death for the unregenerate nature, for it will be eradicated if the regenerate nature remains upon death or the last day. Therefore, in spiritual warfare, the unregenerate nature is constantly fighting against the will of God for the identity of the self. There is no neutral aspect to this. The unregenerate nature does not fight against God's will merely by denying that will, but it must fill the vacuum with something which is against God's will. It will not only refuse to fear, love, and trust in God, but will actively fear, love, and trust in whatever is not God in order to suppress God's will in the person. The goal is to eventually snuff out the Holy Spirit's presence and action in the person such that self-identification with being regenerate in Christ is rejected along with faith in the promises of God in Jesus. The direness of such a situation is expressed by the author to the Hebrews when he says "For it is impossible, in the case of those who have once been enlightened, who have tasted the heavenly gift, and have shared in the Holy Spirit, and have tasted the goodness of the word of God and the powers of the age to come, and then have fallen away, to restore them again to repentance, since they are crucifying once again the Son of God to their own harm and hold him up to contempt" (Heb 6:4–6).[55]

Despite the persistent efforts of the unregenerate nature, God is not struggling to keep purchase for the regenerate nature in the self. The Holy Spirit has already brought the fruits of Christ's victory to bear for the Christian. The regeneration is full and real.[56] Rather, it is the unregenerate nature that is already on the defensive, trying by any means available to thrust off this imputed righteousness that has given the regenerate nature to the Christian. Because the imputation is given and not earned, because the Christian is passive in righteousness before God, it is God's action that must be repudiated by the unregenerate nature, which it attempts by every means possible.

---

55. This is the blaspheming of the Holy Spirit of which Jesus speaks in Matt 12:22–32. To blaspheme the Holy Spirit is to renounce the regenerative claim he makes on the person when he places faith in Christ within the person. This rejection of being God's child in Christ is one way to understand the unforgivable sin. "The regenerated children of God need to be lovingly admonished not to enter into actions in which the power of original sin gains mastery in their hearts with the result that impenitent defiance takes place (Rom 6:11–13, 17; Gal 5:19–21; cf. Joel 2:13)." (Nafzger, *Confessing the Faith*, 303).

56. The implications of this for the Christian life will be examined in the second part of the Antifragile approach.

While the reality of both the unregenerate and regenerate natures needs to be acknowledged to properly understand this perspective on spiritual warfare in which the unregenerate nature wages war against regeneration in Christ, our primary way to identify the Christian self should not be in this manner. Rather, The Christian should see the self primarily in light of how God perceives us as his adopted children by faith in his Son. It is the unregenerate nature trying to undo what has been done by God in the Christian, railing at Christ's work, which defines this aspect of the warfare taking place.

The Fallen World: Warfare Against Christ, the Church, and Competing Collectives

This section will briefly review a Lutheran theology concerning the nature of the fallen world and how it rails against Christ's rule. Here, the world is used as a term for the unregenerate collectives of sinful humanity. The fallen world is antagonistic toward the authority of Christ, the regeneration given by the Spirit, and the gospel proclaimed by the church. In addition, the various collectives in the world constantly attempt to exert their own authority in defiance of Christ and one another, creating the oppressive power structures prevalent throughout history.

A Definition of "World" as a Fallen Power

The term "world" has several theological attributes. Biblically, the term is used when speaking of the creation at large and of the care of it, often synonymous with "earth." (1 Sam 2:8; 2 Sam 22:16; 1 Chr 16:30; Job 34:13; Ps 18:15; Prov 8:26; Jer 51:15). Another way it is used is to express its positive connotation as the object of redemption. Typically, this is understood as all the peoples of the world instead of all of the earth or all of creation, though these are sometimes also meant by this term (Ps 89:9; Isa 27:6). "World" is also used when speaking of missiology, going into the world with the gospel of Christ to its peoples. Matthew, for example, records Jesus using the term in this manner when he says that Christians are "the light of the world" (Matt 5:14).

The above definitions have either a neutral or a positive connotation to them. None of them express any instance of antagonism toward God or humanity. But the Bible also commonly uses the term with a negative connotation as having enmity toward God, his plans, and his people. It is most often associated with the collective sinfulness of groups of persons and their collective rebellion against God (e.g., Pss 9:8; 17:14; Isa 13:11; 14:17; 23:17; 24:4; 26:9; Jer 25:26; Lam 4:12; Matt 13:22; 13:38; 18:7; Mark 4:19; John 1:10; 15:19; 17:14; 1 Cor 7:31; Gal 6:14; Col 2:20; Jas 4:4; 1 John 2:15; 4:5).

Because each person has a sinful nature, that nature will inherently collide with the natures of other persons in some way. The self-interest of the individual is in competition with the self-interest of another, but there is also common ground that is made of common interests and goals, despite selfishness. The same is true for persons in groups together, whether their common ground is political, economic, racial, concerning interests or hobbies, or any of the myriads of things persons use as factors in gravitating toward one another; the collectives look to self-interest in interaction with other collectives. In other words, groups of persons do not become less sinful as a collective. Rather, they are a collective of sinners who are still sinful. Since such social systems are created by and populated by persons with fallen natures, they will be collectively fallen in their implementation and their interaction with other systems and persons. Even though they are, on the surface, competing and creating misery, they are still acting together against God's will. In this sense, the antagonism of competing groups is a cooperative work of the world in spiritual warfare against the will and rule of God.

As this plays out in life, the collective which finds common ground against another group will find itself in competition with that opposition concerning the legitimacy of its own position and authority. This ties to the negative theological notions of "the other,"[57] and leads to antagonism toward any other group which appears to threaten any perceived positive traits of the person's group.

These groups are found on every level of social interaction, including an individual interacting with another individual, one person in contact with some size of collective, and collectives interacting with other collectives. On each level, the interactions are, at their core, comprised of sinful individuals. Therefore, for our purposes the definition of the fallen world is *the interaction of sinful persons on any systemic social level.*

---

57. Nahi Alon and Haim Omer argue that when "a highly negative view of the other evolves . . . a vicious cycle arises in which both sides become more and more entrenched in their negative positions." Alon and Omer, *Psychology of Demonization*, 1.

This notion of a collective of sinners of any size as a component group of the fallen world is an important distinction to make because Wink's social approach and Wingren's take on vocation focus on large problematic systems. Wingren writes about vocation in terms of the two worldly governments of the church and the state and talks about how the vocations in those governments are often confused by the devil's work to twist them and abused by persons and people groups.[58] Wink focuses on the demonic and benevolent natures of political and business systems in relation to those who they have the power to oppress.[59] With both authors, their examinations speak of the world in terms of the broad strokes of nations and conglomerates.

They do not spend much time or ink on the understanding that these entities are *corporate*, meaning the body exerting power over others is not just a series of enacted policies, but a group of persons who have excused and, in their own minds, legitimized the actions taken upon their victims. A collective of any size is, ultimately, still made of individuals. This recognition takes the concepts of Wingren and Wink down the strata of society to recognize their reality at every social level. What they see and examine in nations and conglomerates is also true of a mere plurality of individuals,[60] including, for example, abuse in families and bullying in classrooms. One has to keep both the larger picture and the smaller picture in balanced view. There is not sweeping change for people groups without challenging the power brokers of the community, but justice, however one defines it, is hard to quantify or carry out apart from a concrete neighbor.[61]

The Fallen World in Spiritual Warfare

The collectives of the fallen world will be in competition, on some level, with other collectives. This competition acknowledges many of the evils and ills of the world. In terms of spiritual warfare, however, we see not only the general vying of collective interests, but also the particular case

---

58. Wingren, *Luther on Vocation*, 79.

59. Wink, *Engaging the Powers*, 49.

60. This is not excluding concepts of "mob mentality," but that the oppressive and sinful nature of large systems is a just a larger public stage for the same issues that happen on more intimate, often private, levels.

61. Sánchez, "Human Face of Justice," 117.

The Antifragile Approach

of the fallen world at war against the reign of Christ. As a result, any outside collective onto which Christ might exert ethical or spiritual authority will react with denial and persecution of anything which represents his voice and presence, namely, the church, the gospel, and the individual Christian.

The confrontation of the world with the reign of Christ is described in the Confessions as a collective that is dismissive and antagonistic toward God and his will. Luther points out in his Large Catechism that the "world is evil and full of misery,"[62] that it is dismissive and abusive of God's name[63] and his gifts,[64] attacks the Christian faith,[65] makes for itself any god but the true God,[66] and joins in with the devil and the flesh in its work.[67] Likewise, Melanchthon writes that the world persecutes the gospel and Christian truth,[68] trusting in its own works and false gods.[69]

The fallen world assaults the church from without, but there is also an assault from within. Because the church on earth is also comprised of persons still struggling with the sinful nature, the nature of the fallen world is also found in its own communities and gatherings. For example, Sánchez speaks to issues of separation and unity involved in the label "Hispanic" in North and South American culture and within the Lutheran church.[70] The problems within the church created by collectives of the fallen world is the reason why Paul speaks so strongly against the factions of Corinth, why Wingren talks about confusion of vocation within the spiritual government as well as the worldly government, and why Wink is critical of the Roman Catholic Church and its moments in history of silence in the face of Latin American dictatorships. As the classic hymn *The Church's One Foundation* states in its third verse, "with a scornful wonder, the world sees her oppressed, by schisms rent asunder, by heresies distressed."[71] The fallen world outside of the church seeks to

---

62. LC I, 183 in Kolb and Wengert, *Book of Concord*, 411.
63. LC, I, 58, and III, 49 in Kolb and Wengert, *Book of Concord*, 393, 446.
64. LC, II, 21 in Kolb and Wengert, *Book of Concord*, 433.
65. LC V, 23 in Kolb and Wengert, *Book of Concord*, 469.
66. LC I, 17 in Kolb and Wengert, *Book of Concord*, 388.
67. LC III, 62 in Kolb and Wengert, *Book of Concord*, 448.
68. Ap XX, 6–8 in Kolb and Wengert, *Book of Concord*, 236.
69. Ap IV, 205–06 in Kolb and Wengert, *Book of Concord*, 151.
70. Sánchez, "Hispanic is Not What You Think," 232–34.
71. Commission on Worship of The Lutheran Church—Missouri Synod, *Lutheran Service Book*, 644.

oppress her voice of ethics and her voice of hope in Christ. The fallen world inside the church seeks to corrupt and pervert God's truth for the ends of its various collectives, as Wingren notes, and to the detriment of its work and voice in the world, as Wink points out.

Despite the fallen world's tendencies toward xenophobia and the confusion intrinsic to sin, allowing for the fallen world to be acknowledged at every strata of human interaction also means something for its redemption. When God announces that he loves the world and that through Christ he brings the gift of redemption to the world, this is a gift offered to every person with a love not only for individual persons but for humanity; there is no "other" in Christ. This will be a focus in the second part of the presentation of the antifragile approach, below.

The fallen world sees the reign of Christ as a threat to its autonomy and the legitimacy of its authority, spiritually and temporally. The fallen world is both outside the church and within the church, and they often mirror each other just as non-Christians and Christians, as individuals, have the same litany of sins perpetrated by their sinful natures. The sinful nature and the fallen world are based in the fall of humanity into sin. The third power, however, stands outside of humanity while still influencing it.

The Fallen Angels: Warfare Against Creation to Spite God

The third, and final, fallen power to examine is the fallen angels. This power is the most difficult to discern because it is the one whose origins are supernatural and so not susceptible to careful human observation. However, Scripture does have much to say regarding the narrative of the fallen angels. Care will be taken to prevent overextending from what Scripture says into speculation. The result may, at first, seem to lack comprehensiveness since God only reveals the work of the fallen angels insofar as it intersects with the salvation narrative. But as we rightly approach Scripture and this narrative of demons, all we need to understand them becomes apparent.

The narrative of the fallen angels can be broken up into three stages which correspond with the biblical narrative of salvation. The first stage is from creation to Jesus as recorded in the Old Testament. Though the amount of data is not extensive, the narrative highlights Satan accusing and testing both God and mankind. This addition of God as a target of Satan is overlooked in the literature, which only focuses on humanity as the target for the devil. By this omission, they are making a critical oversight.[72] The second stage is the life and ministry of Jesus, in which Satan, again, is accusing and testing God in the temptations of Jesus. It also includes the possession and harassment of persons by demons. Here, the real nature of the fallen angels' warfare against God gains clarity. This stage culminates in the death of the Christ. The third stage begins with the resurrection and ascension of Jesus, resulting in a permanent loss of place for the fallen angels. That loss of place creates the situation as it still stands in our current age. Today, the fallen angels rail against Christ's authority out of spite, trying to destroy as much of what God loves as they can while there is time left for them to do so.

The Fallen Angels from Creation to Jesus

As noted above with the sinful nature, the narrative of creation given in the first three chapters of Genesis recalls not only how God made all things good, but also how humanity broke that goodness asunder. Satan,[73] who is equated with the serpent of the event of the Fall (Gen 3:1; Rev 12:9), is in the garden of Eden enticing both Eve and Adam into doubting the word of God concerning the Tree of the Knowledge of Good and Evil. The serpent is already working against God's will at this point, indicating he is already antagonistic towards God. This is not the fall from heaven in which there was a war resulting in his permanent banishment from that place (Rev 12:7–12); that event has not yet occurred.[74] Rather, this

---

72. It is this oversight which accounts for the erroneous claims that the theology of the Old Testament regarding Satan is fundamentally different from the revelations given in the New Testament.

73. Even this term is the subject of much debate. Meaning "adversary" or "opponent" (BDB 966), this Hebrew word was used, in one sense, of any being in an adversarial relationship with another, including angels toward men (Num 22:22, 32) and men against other men (1 Sam 29:4; 2 Sam 19:22; 1 Kgs 5:4; 11:14, 23, 25; Ps 109:6). It is also used of a supernatural being that is in opposition both to God's will and to humanity, which is discussed below.

74. The lack of discussion in Scripture regarding the initial fall of Satan and his fellows has not stopped speculation, from which theories abound. Main theories include a pre-Adamic creation that fell into a chaos that God cannot quite overcome and from which entities remain who persist as threats to God and his will. Proponents of this view include: Boyd, *God at War*, 100–113, Barnhouse, *Invisible War*, 22–27; and Lovett, *Dealing With the Devil*, 17. Another theory is that the events of Revelation 12 occur before the fall, though the context of the passage clearly puts it at Christ's ascension. Advocates for the early war view include Larson, *Larson's Book of Spiritual*

is an event of which there is no explicit account in Scripture. For an uncertain reason,[75] Satan and other angels turned against God soon after their creation and they sought to corrupt the rest of creation, particularly humanity. Satan then tempted Adam and Eve to deny God's will. By being a key participant in the fall of humanity into sin through the twisting of God's words, and the fall's consequence of death, Satan confirms both of Jesus' condemnations against him, that he was a liar and a murderer from the beginning (John 8:44).

If our contemplation of Satan's role in the fall of creation stops with his part in undoing humanity's relationship to God, a crucial aspect of this moment is lost. Satan is not just trying to cause humanity to fall into sin, but in this action he is attempting also to antagonize God. That which was "very good" in God's eyes at the end of his creative act was marred by sin. By the days of Noah, we are told "The LORD saw that the wickedness of man was great in the earth, and that every intention of the thoughts of his heart was only evil continually. And the LORD was sorry that he had made man on the earth, and it grieved him to his heart" (Gen 6:5–6). The fall into sin of humanity, and subsequently all of the creation, was grievous for God, and Satan played a central part in the originations of that grief.

In this stage in history, Satan is still able to speak to God before his throne in heaven. In Job 1:6–19, Satan appears before God's throne with purpose.[76] First, in response to Satan's comment that he has wandered

---

Warfare, 45–47 and Kreeft, *Angels (and Demons)*, 116–20. A third view is that the demons are kicked out of different heavens but still inhabit others. This is based upon Paul's note of a "third heaven" (2 Cor 12:2), from which it is assumed there are others in which the demons dwelled and still dwell even after being removed from God's immediate presence. Advocates of this view include Prince, *Spiritual Warfare*, 9–13; and Basham, *Deliver Us From Evil*, 217–19. Agreeing with this work, on this point: Unger, *Biblical Demonology*, 42–55.

75. The most popular tradition holds that Satan was one of the archangels and in pride wanted to take God's place. This is based on prophecies concerning enemy kings from Isa 14:12–20 and Ezek 28:11–19 which are assumed to also be about Satan and his angels. Some holding the Ezekiel and Isaiah view: Barnhouse, *Invisible War*, 22–27; McCulley, *House Swept Clean*, 42–44; Lindsell, *World, the Flesh, and the Devil*, 27; Lovett, *Dealing with the Devil*, 17–18; and Kreeft, *Angels (and Demons)*, 116–19. Examples of those rejecting the Isaiah and Ezekiel view: Fernando, *Message of Spiritual Warfare*, 26; Boyd, *God at War*, 157–62; and Page, *Powers of Evil*, 38–42. Dennis McCallum argues against Isaiah but for Ezekiel (McCallum, *Satan and His Kingdom*, 20–25). The arguments he makes concerning these prophecies referring to Satan are interesting but unconvincing.

76. For the purpose of this narrative, I have passed over the discussion of the

the earth, God declares that Job is "a blameless and upright man, who fears God and turns away from evil" (Job 1:8). Satan's reply is that Job only loves God because God continues to provide him with an abundance of blessings. Satan then challenges God by arguing that a removal of Job's material, social, and familial blessings will cause Job to lose faith in God and so cease to be upright (Job 1:9–12).

Significant for this narrative is recognizing what Satan is challenging here. At the core, Satan is not testing Job's faith but God's truth. God has stated unequivocally that Job is blameless and upright, an absolute and declarative statement. Satan argues that Job's state is contingent on blessings, and therefore God's statements are also contingent. By insisting on the testing of Job, Satan is actually testing the veracity and trustworthiness of God's word, which holds true despite the deprivation of all blessings and the temptation to heresy provided by Job's friends in the ensuing debate. In the end, God's word holds true despite the works of Satan.

Later in the Old Testament comes Zechariah's vision of Joshua, the high priest. Satan is accusing Joshua on account of the man's sins. This is an accusation not only of Joshua, but against God for the choice of high priest, the mediator of the sacrifices to God on behalf of the people. Satan is rebuked on account of God's forgiveness of Joshua's sins and he is restored in the vision as a proper high priest (Zech 3:1–10). Here again, Satan is the accuser of a person before God but it is God who is indirectly challenged.[77]

The third and final instance of Satan in the Old Testament is by the chronicler in reference to David ordering that the census be taken (1 Chr 21:1). There, Satan incites David to take the census. Of further interest for this account is the parallel in 2 Sam 24:1 which says, "Again, the anger of the LORD was kindled against Israel, and he incited David against them, saying, 'Go, number Israel and Judah.'" While some scholars argue that the writer of the books of Samuel had a morally ambiguous view of Yahweh,[78] Boyd is right when he says that the two authors are merely approaching the event from differing views. The chronicler is looking at the instrument of provocation and the writer of Samuel at the reason for

---

identification of the "sons of God" here.

77. Page, *Powers of Evil*, 32–33.
78. For example: Page, *Powers of Evil*, 35.

provoking David.[79] Between the two perspectives, Satan can be seen as doing God's work, wittingly or otherwise, by which God's will is brought about.[80]

From the other accounts of the Old Testament, there are other spirits at work than God's loyal angels and Satan. For some, their identity is opaque.[81] There are spirits that are used by God to bring about problems in the lives of those who have rejected him (Judg 9:23, 56–57; 1 Sam 15:26–29; 16:14–23; 1 Kgs 22:14–40). There are the "princes" of Persia and Greece from Daniel's vision (Dan 10:12–14, 20–21), which sound like antagonistic opposing angels to Michael and the angel who came to Daniel.[82]

For others, their identities are clearly in connection with idolatry. The gods of the nations are spoken of as demonic in nature (Deut 32:17; Ps 106:36–37).[83] Isaiah speaks of God punishing "the host of heaven" and the kings of the earth on the last day, which does not refer to his holy angels, but to ones who have fallen (Isa 24:21–22). On the earth, there are also mentioned beings whose name has been translated variously

---

79. Boyd speculates, "The Lord was burning with anger toward Israel on a number of counts, and Satan was (as usual?) looking for any opportunity he could to incite David to rebel against God and thereby bring the nation of Israel under God's judgment. God wants to judge Israel; Satan wants Israel judged. Thus God allows Satan to motivate David to carry out an act that is going to result in Israel's judgment. From one perspective it was Satan who incited judgment, but from a broader perspective it was God himself." Boyd, *God at War*, 154.

80. McCarter, *II Samuel*, 512–14.

81. There are some terms that are not considered here due to their questionable acceptance as a reference to a being. This includes Lilith, an unclear reference from Isa 34:14, and Belial, which can just be translated "wickedness" (2 Sam 22:5; 2 Cor 6:15–16). Also, the idea that Azazel is a demon rather than just a title for the rejected goat from Israel's atonement. On Azazel, see the discussion in De La Torre and Hernández, *Quest for the Historical Satan*, 60.

82. There is no other reference in the Old Testament with these descriptions. It appears, since the term "prince" is used for Michael as well as the antagonists, that it is a likely reference to fallen angels. Regardless, as noted in chapter 4, the importance of this text is greatly exaggerated by the pneumatic approach. The angel bringing the vision to Daniel is giving an explanation for the timing of his arrival; this is not an apology. It is more accurate to say that the angel had a job to do before his assignment to come to Daniel. That assignment took time, including the three weeks which overlapped with Daniel's prayer. This delay did not prevent the angel from doing God's work for Daniel.

83. This is especially evident in the LXX where the translation concerning these entities is *daimonion*.

as "satyrs" in the King James Version or "goat demons" in the English Standard Version, to which the people of God are expressly forbidden to sacrifice (Lev 17:3), a command which Jeroboam ignores (2 Chr 11:15). Isaiah relates these beings with desolation (Isa 13:12; 34:14) as part of his oracles against Babylon and Edom, who are cursed by God.[84]

The common thread of the work of the demons is to draw their worshippers into further sins on the pretense of gaining favor or fending off punishment from them as gods. These fallen angels have set themselves in opposition to God and to his will in order to draw persons and nations away from him. They are associated by Isaiah with being where God's hand of blessing is removed.

A picture emerges from the Old Testament accounts. Satan explicitly challenges God's will and attempts to test both God and humanity. The fallen angels work to lead humanity astray so that they would fear, love, and trust in idols rather than God, and thus further damage what God loves. The demons appear to have some ability to affect human life, but it is dependent upon the boundaries God has set for their actions. Satan and the demons encourage the sinful nature to rebel against God. The collectives of nations and religions are drawn to rejection of God in favor of self-interest and idolatry.

Judging by the extent of idolatry which occurs between Adam and Noah such that the flood event occurs, the immediate re-emergence of idolatry again among the nations, and the severe apostasy of Israel itself, one might conclude that the power of the fallen angels ran largely unchecked in the Old Testament era. However, God's absolute authority as Creator of all things is never questioned in the Old Testament, nor is his ability to constrain and have rule over the fallen angels. Also, God's instruction regarding the demons is consistent: the people of God have him as their only God (Deut 6:4). They are to reject all other gods, fearing, loving, and trusting in him only. For his hidden reasons, God's methodology of reigning in the Old Testament allows Satan and the demons to work against his own purposes.

In this stage of history, Satan and other fallen angels try to work against God's will and against humanity. Satan has the ability, at this point, to stand before God in accusation of him and of all peoples. Two

---

84. It is unclear from the passages if there is a literal connection to desolate, cursed places and the goat demons as entities of such places, or if it is just imagery concerning the fate of those who would commit idolatry to the goat demons, that they would become desolate lands.

additional observations are now appropriate. First, when the Old Testament speaks of the demonic, it does so as personal forces, not merely as negative powers, structures, or symbols. Second, there is not a single narrative or instruction from God for humans to war against fallen angels. The closest event to this notion is the revelation to Daniel regarding the interval of time in which his prayers were answered. But even there, the angel speaks no mandate or suggestion of action to Daniel regarding those entities. He merely speaks of them to illustrate the reason for the interim between prayer and response. God's people in the Old Testament were to trust in God and his promises, both of temporal care and the eternal promise of salvation. They were called to live as God's people, with great detail about moral, civil, and ceremonial laws. Any mention of striving against demonic powers is absent; there is only a call to reject their idolatrous personages.

The Fallen Angels During the Time of Jesus' Ministry

When Jesus begins his public ministry, a more explicit dynamic emerges on top of what was built in the Old Testament.[85] This section will look first at the interactions with demons recorded in the Gospel accounts and then what Jesus taught concerning them during his ministry. The account of Jesus' temptation by Satan in the wilderness (Matt 4:1–11; Mark 1:12–13; Luke 4:1–13) is the first event in which Jesus shows his ability to be victorious over Satan's power and schemes.[86] Jesus is able to withstand

---

85. A popular school of thought posits that the demonology of the New Testament differs from the Old Testament because Judaism brought in the cosmology of the various religions of their neighbors and conquerors, or that because of the oppression, particularly in the Intertestamental period, the theology changed as views on theodicy changed. I believe that, like so much of the Old Testament, it is simply a limited revelation which is opened up by Jesus. For the evolution of the theology of Satan and the demons, see, for example: Finlay, *Demons!*, 11–18, and De La Torre and Hernández, *Quest for the Historical Satan*, 62–73. For the Judaistic evolution of theodicy, see Brown, *God of This Age*, 21–60; Page, *Powers of Evil*, 87–88; Becker, "Anmerkungen zur Dämonologie," 169–85; and Boyd, *God at War*, 172–80.

86. This event is more than Jesus as exemplar of how to resist the devil using Scripture. "Given the dominant Christology in this Matthean context, it is difficult to conclude that the evangelist wants his audience to view Jesus primarily as a moral example . . . given Jesus' identity as Son of God in the place of the failed, fallen, sinful nation in both 3:13–17 and 4:1–11, the primary message of 4:1–11 must be that *Jesus is Victor over Satan on behalf of the nation and ultimately on behalf of all people.*" Gibbs, *Matthew 1:1—11:1*, 198 (emphasis original).

the temptations presented by addressing the devil's comments with the proper use of Scripture, trusting in the Father. Matthew's account uses three names for Jesus' antagonist in this episode: devil (Matt 4:1, 5, 8, 11), tempter (Matt 4:3), and Satan (Matt 4:10). This episode ties all three of these names together, and with the use of Satan here, ties him to the Old Testament personage of the same name.

Though Jesus overcame the devil's temptations in the desert, Satan and the fallen angels continue to play a significant role in the Gospel accounts. As Jesus goes about his ministry, he has several occasions on which he exorcises demons from persons, alongside his works of teaching and healing. The reaction of the crowds to these miracles is amazement. But they are not amazed at the reality of demons, the possibility of possession, or that exorcism is possible.[87] Rather, they are amazed that Jesus casts them out by virtue of his own authority (Matt 12:22–23; Luke 4:36–37).[88]

The exorcisms of Jesus clearly show that fallen angels are able to possess persons and that Jesus has the authority to exorcise them. Most of the accounts are general statements of Jesus exorcising demons (e.g., Matt 4:24; 8:16; 15:22; Mark 7:26–30; Luke 4:41). Other accounts speak of a particular person being possessed, such as Mary Magdalene (Mark 16:9; Luke 8:2) and, in some way, Judas (John 13:2, 27). There are two narratives in the Synoptics which lay out a more detailed account of Jesus' exorcistic work. First, the event in the region of the Gadarenes (Matt 8:28–34; Mark 5:1–20; Luke 8:26–40) and, second, a boy whom a demon convulses (Matt 17:16–21; Mark 9:14–28; Luke 9:37–43).[89]

The exorcism events recorded in the Gospel accounts tell about the abilities of the fallen angels regarding a person who is possessed. The demons can create and sustain various disabilities (e.g., Matt 9:32–33; 12:22; 17:14–15), move persons, even exercising drastic strength (Matt 17:28; Luke 8:29), and speak through the person being possessed (Matt 8:29, 31; Mark 1:23–24, 34; Luke 4:33–34, 41).

87. Clearly in Scripture and outside of it there were faithful Jewish persons performing exorcisms. For example, when the Pharisees accuse Jesus of exorcising by Beelzebub, part of his response includes asking by whom their own Jewish exorcists cast out demons (Matt 12:27; Luke 11:19).

88. In his study of parallel exorcistic practices of the ancient Middle East, Graham Twelftree noted that Jesus "used the emphatic 'I,' for which I can find no parallel in any other incantation or exorcism story in the ancient world." Twelftree, *In the Name of Jesus*, 48. See also Bell, *Deliver Us From Evil*, 73–77.

89. These two events will be examined more closely at the end of the chapter.

In addition to learning some of the abilities of the demons regarding possession, we also see some of their traits toward Jesus. They know exactly who he is and what he is capable of, including enacting God's judgment upon them (Matt 8:29; Mark 1:24). But even then, they use this information to try to work against Jesus. Jesus rebukes them for saying his titles, commanding them to silence so they do not corrupt the understanding of those watching the exorcism. Without the lens of the cross and the empty tomb, the crowds would not properly understand his authority to judge the demons or understand the titles "Holy One of God" or "Son of God," just as the disciples misunderstood what it meant for Jesus to be the Christ before his death and resurrection. The demons acknowledge who Jesus is but still try to taint his ministry.[90]

Significantly, every demonic encounter described in the Gospels involves the demoniac crossing into the path of Jesus and his disciples. Either the demoniac himself wanders into the path of Jesus or is brought to him, or his disciples, by other persons. There is no instance of Jesus or the disciples seeking out persons with demons in order to bring about an exorcism. There is no instance of them ever speaking about or enacting a deliverance ministry. The exorcistic confrontations are always in the greater context of confirming Jesus' teachings and authority as part of his greater salvation ministry. These acts confirm the truth of his claims; they are a part of his ministerial work, but they are not the primary purpose of it. That purpose is to call persons to repentance in order to be ready when the kingdom of heaven comes through his impending death and resurrection.

In addition to interactions with Satan and the demons, the gospels also record what Jesus taught about the fallen angels. They are called "demons," "unclean spirits," and "evil spirits" by Jesus and the gospel writers.[91] Jesus describes Satan as "the father of lies" and a murderer when

---

90. Little is written concerning the significance of the demons' words to Jesus. The literature that does talk about it almost exclusively focuses on Jesus asking the name of the demons in the Gadarene event. This is used as encouragement for the exorcist to also ask the name of the demon in order to use that name in the banishment process, though there is no biblical evidence for such talk with the demonic being beneficial. This is included not only in the literature of the pneumatic approach but in the *Rituale Romanum* of Roman Catholic exorcism. On the Roman rite's use of speaking with demons, see Amorth, *Exorcist Tells His Story*, 93–96 and Rodewyk, *Possessed by Satan*, 101–19.

91. For example, Luke records Jesus' exorcism of the demon at the Capernaum synagogue, referring to the entity as "the spirit of an unclean demon" (Luke 4:33), as

talking with the Pharisees (John 8:44). He is also depicted in the Parable of the Sower as stealing away God's truth from the heart of a person to keep them away from faith in Jesus (Matt 13:19). Presumably, these character traits also generally apply to the other fallen angels with Satan.

In addition to their lying and murderous natures, Jesus also teaches that Satan is a kind of ruler over the world. These passages are used in the pneumatic approach to postulate the need to take back the world from Satan for Jesus. However, to take this idea in this manner is inconsistent with the other clear teachings of Scripture concerning Christ's reign, as shown above. Jesus speaks of Satan as ruling over the world because the world acts in alignment with the desires of the demons. All three fallen powers are antagonistic to God's will, but Satan and the fallen angels are first among those powers. This is why Jesus says that the Pharisees who oppose him are really children of the devil rather than children of God (John 8:44).[92] In his parable about a field of wheat and weeds, those who reject Jesus are spoken of as sown by the devil (Matt 13:38–39) and work to choke out the wheat. In the context of Jesus saying he has authority over the demonic, he also illustrates the devil's ability to rule the other fallen powers in terms of the strong man protecting his goods until one even stronger takes them from him (Matt 12:29; Mark 3:27; Luke 11:21–22). Jesus shows in these passages that Satan is still under God's dominion but is the first among the fallen powers of the world.

The final teaching of Jesus on the demons' power concerns repossession. He teaches the disciples what happens behind the scenes after an exorcism. The demon "passes through waterless places" for a time, but when able it will try to return to the person it possessed. If the spiritual life of the person is not filled with something better, if the person continues to reject the Holy Spirit and Jesus, the demon will return, bringing more demons with it, and the person's situation becomes worse than before (Matt 12:43–45; Luke 11:24–26).

Despite these fearsome abilities, direction is also offered by Jesus. Jesus prays for the disciples and all faithful persons that God preserve

---

a "demon" (Luke 4:45), and as an "unclean spirit" (Luke 4:46), explicitly connecting these terms.

92. Jesus does not say they are merely slaves to their sinful natures or living as part of the fallen world. He says they are children of the devil. There is a precedence of power among the fallen powers in Jesus' choice of statements that should cause all Christians to pause in their consideration of the demons in relation to the fallen powers.

them (John 17:15) and encourages them to pray for their own safety against the evil foe (Matt 6:13).[93] Jesus notes that when he performs exorcisms, the Holy Spirit is present and acting, the finger of God to enact the dispossession (Matt 12:28; Luke 11:20). This can occur, Jesus teaches, because someone, that is, himself, is stronger than the strong man of the world (Matt 12:29; Luke 11:22), and he has overcome the devil and the world (John 16:11, 33). Jesus concretely enacts this prayer of overcoming the devil with Peter when the devil demands "to sift Peter like wheat" (Luke 22:31–32). Jesus says that he has prayed for Peter and immediately follows this fact with instructions for Peter once he is restored. Jesus is already so sure of Peter's restoration that post-event instructions are presented to Peter before the event has even started!

Jesus also teaches about the future of the fallen angels. Proleptically, he sees Satan fall from heaven "like lightning" (Luke 10:17). Hell and the lake of eternal fire were made for the fallen angels (Matt 25:41). Jesus is the one who will judge them by virtue of his victory via his death, resurrection, and ascension (Luke 10:18; John 14:30; 16:4–11).

The gospels present a substantial amount of information regarding the nature of the fallen angels as well as their relationship with humanity and with God at the time of Jesus' ministry. Satan and the fallen angels were focused on destroying humanity's relationship with God, persisting in defiance of God's will. They tempted persons into sin and possessed persons. They continued in their attempts to tempt God as well, as seen with Jesus in the wilderness. The demons clearly recognized Jesus and his authority but sought to disrupt his work even as he was about to exorcise them. They preyed on persons to the point of possessing them, sometimes with multiple spirits attending a single person. Beyond this, they promoted heresy and rejection of God's truths. Because the fallen world and the sinful nature seek to reject God's authority, they have many common aims with the fallen angels and are unwittingly influenced by them. Therefore, it is appropriate to describe Satan, as leader of the fallen angels, as the prince of the world and as a strong man holding sway, though Jesus is greater than Satan.

---

93. Luther writes in his Large Catechism, "In the Greek this petition reads, 'Deliver or preserve us from the Evil One, or the Wicked One.' It seems to be speaking of the devil as the sum of all evil in order that the entire substance of our prayer may be directed against our archenemy." LC 3, 113 in Kolb and Wengert, *Book of Concord*, 455.

The Fallen Angels at Christ's Resurrection and Ascension

As noted above, during his ministry Jesus observed the devil fall from heaven like lightning and spoke of Satan as judged. In the small record we have of Jesus' words after his resurrection and before his ascension, only the long ending of Mark mentions demons, where Jesus points to exorcism as a sign the disciples will perform which points to the veracity of their gospel proclamation (Mark 16:17).

On the ephemeral side of the biblical account, Revelation gives a glimpse of the significant shift the ascension and reign of Christ brings regarding the place of the fallen angels. The twelfth chapter, properly read, speaks briefly of Satan's attempt to stop Jesus' work of salvation on earth (Rev 12:4). Jesus, however, is successful and ascends to God's throne (Rev 12:5). It is only at this point that full war breaks out in heaven (Rev 12:7). The catalyst is the ascension of Jesus with all power and authority to save and to rule. As the loud voice from heaven points out, the role of Satan as accuser of the brothers, who relentlessly accused humanity before God's throne, is over (Rev 12:10). Jesus is victorious despite all of the machinations of the devil to prevent his salvific work. Because the blood of Jesus covers over all of the sins of humanity, there is no place for accusation of faithful persons before God's throne anymore. This defeat of Satan is in the redemption of humanity and of creation through the crucified and resurrected Christ, who ascends to reign.

The main act of Satan depicted in the Old Testament was that of accuser of God and humanity. But Jesus is the one who has become the end of the sacrificial system, fulfilling all of the Law for the sake of the world. As the author to the Hebrews notes, Jesus has become both the final sacrifice for sin and the permanent high priest before God, who mediates for the Christian before the Father (Heb 10:19–21). Jesus has all authority in heaven and on earth and reigns over all creation, both maker and redeemer of his creation. The result is that Jesus has removed this weapon of Satan. The Christian can no longer be accused before God by Satan. Jesus has removed that possibility.

This fulfillment of God's love for his creation is what sparks the violent rebellion of the fallen angels. Losing this war, the demons are thrown from heaven for good (Rev 12:10). The ones who reap the fruits of Jesus' victory are those "who conquered in the blood of the Lamb and by the word of their testimony" (Rev 12:11). However, the judgment of the demons to the lake of fire does not occur. Rather, there is one more age of interim before the final judgment. The observing angel, therefore, speaks a warning to the world, that the devil is on the earth and in great wrath at God for his defeat (Rev 12:12).

This moment, from the perspective of spiritual warfare, is not only a removal of Satan's ability to accuse humanity before God, but it is also the end of his ability to antagonize God by accusing us. His ability to accuse God is gone. This loss of stratagem causes Satan and the fallen angels to react with open war against God. The main path by which Satan worked against God and humanity is closed by Jesus. Yet, as we also learn from Revelation, because Satan cannot get at God, he redoubles his efforts to hurt God indirectly by destroying what God loves, which is humanity and the creation (Rev 12:17).

The Current Situation until Judgment Day—The Power of Spite

The New Testament beyond the gospel accounts gives some clues to the work and patterns of the fallen angels in their exile from heaven following Christ's ascension. John says that a fruit of Jesus' work is the destruction of the works of the devil (1 John 3:8). The author to the Hebrews elaborates on this idea when he notes that the devil's ability to use death and sin against Christians is lost because of Jesus' work (Heb 2:14–15). Where the devil once could debate with God over the worthiness of humans to be counted as righteous and to receive eternal life, Jesus overcame that ability with his full atonement for sin and his resurrection from death.

One might expect that once Jesus achieved this victory for humanity and creation, and the fallen angels became not only fallen in nature but also in place, they might give up or repent. But Scripture indicates this is not the case. As noted above, John's revelation shows the fallen angels turn their aggression against God's people. The purpose for this is also indicated. Satan and the fallen angels hate God. They cannot get at God, but if they destroy what God loves, then they can still hurt him indirectly. This is an all-consuming hatred for God, as much of the rest of John's revelation shows. It is a hatred that cannot win but seeks merely to hurt and harm its target in any way possible while there is yet time to do so. This is *spite*, unabated. Such spite should not be underestimated because regarding persons and creation, it is impersonal. The fallen angels only have interest in persons and creation insofar as they continue to be a means to act maliciously against God's will and nature. All genocides

The Antifragile Approach

stem of depersonalization of the other, and this one is no different. John Milton tried to create a sympathetic Satan in *Paradise Lost*, but the fallen angels are more akin to James Cameron's original *Terminator*. Indifferent to the life they destroy, they mechanistically, methodically, and relentlessly destroy humanity and creation in their goal of hurting God as much as possible before their final judgment.

To achieve their goal, the demons attempt to maximize the number of persons who reject Christ. Peter uses the well-known image of Satan as the roaring lion seeking whom he can devour, looking to bring persons in opposition to God, warning them to stand firm in faith (1 Pet 5:6–10). To pursue this goal, the devil depends on the same techniques he has used throughout the ages, including temptation to sin, persecution, heresy, and idolatry.

The Fallen Powers in Tandem

It was noted in chapter 2 that in the greater Western culture the devil is mainly connected to temptation toward sin for the purpose of getting someone to make the wrong choice. In the bifurcated approach in chapter 5, there was an emphasis on temptation as a real obstacle of faith but divorced from other parts of the Christian life. While these points are valid, we have shown that the stakes for the fallen angels are much higher than merely tempting in order to produce sin. Their goal is, if possible, to produce and maintain unbelief in Christ's salvific work in order to cause God to suffer the loss of a person. Therefore, all of the temptations, in all their variety, have a direction and a goal. The devil goads and uses the unregenerate natures and the fallen world to work with him toward his goal. Since they share the common purpose of defying God, the first two powers work in tandem with the third to bring about a rejection of God's authority and of the regenerate nature. John, therefore, rightly says "whoever makes a practice of sinning is of the devil" (1 John 3:8), because in defying God's will by holding not to Christ and his forgiveness but instead holding unrepentantly to sin, the person is doing the will of Satan. This is why God tells us to be wary of temptation (e.g., Matt 6:13; 26:41; Mark 14:38; Luke 22:40, 46; Heb 3:8) and Luther says,

> There are so many hindrances and attacks of the devil and the world that we often grow weary and faint and at times even stumble. . . . The devil is a furious enemy; when he sees that we

resist him and attack the old creature, and when he cannot rout us by force, he sneaks and skulks about at every turn, trying all kinds of tricks, and does not stop until he has finally worn us out so that we either renounce our faith or lose heart and become indifferent or impatient.[94]

The devil's work in temptation starts subtle but, like a driving swing in golf where a small inaccuracy at the tee creates a large impact over the distance, the quiet work of the devil can result in great apostasy and great suffering in the world. This is why Paul warns the Ephesians against something as seemingly insignificant as holding onto their anger as an opportunity for the devil (Eph 4:26–27) and he warns Timothy against putting persons new to faith in leadership since they may not yet be prepared for the subtleties of the devil's work (1 Tim 3:6–7). The small things can become large enough to affect faith and salvation if left unchecked. The fallen angels constantly probe persons for ways to drive a larger wedge between them and salvation in Jesus Christ.

Temptation is the seedbed Satan then uses to sow and to encourage heresy, idolatry, and persecution that are performed by the sinful nature and the fallen world. This is why Luther can say that even the Fourth Petition of the Lord's Prayer is a prayer against the devil:

> But especially is this petition directed against our chief enemy, the devil, whose whole purpose and desire it is to take away or interfere with all we have received from God. He is not satisfied to obstruct and overthrow the spiritual order, by deceiving souls with his lies and bring them under his power, but he also prevents and impedes the establishment of any kind of government or honorable and peaceful relations on earth. This is why he causes so much contention, murder, sedition, and war, why he sends storms and hail to destroy crops and cattle, why he poisons the air, etc. In short, it pains him that anyone should receive even a mouthful of bread from God and eat it in peace.[95]

Because the world and the unregenerate nature are also seeking to avoid recognizing the authority of Jesus, the devil is able to recruit these

---

94. LC V, 23, 26 in Kolb and Wengert, *Book of Concord*, 469. See also LC III, 87 in Kolb and Wengert, *Book of Concord*, 452.

95. LC.III, 80–81 in Kolb and Wengert, *Book of Concord*, 451. See also Luther's *The Bondage of the Will*, where he observes that Satan "holds captive to his will all who are not snatched away from him by the Spirit of Christ." *LW* 33:287.

powers for his purposes.[96] This is why Scripture speaks of the world as ruled by the evil one, even though Jesus definitively reigns (John 12:31; 2 Cor 4:4). Luther says in *The Bondage of the Will* that there is no neutral ground for the individual or the collective of the world between God and the devil. Every person is serving one or the other:

> If we are under the god of this world, away from the work and Spirit of the one true God, we are held captive to his will, as Paul says to Timothy, so that we cannot will anything but what he wills. For he is that strong man armed, who guards his own palace in such a way that those whom he possesses are at peace, so as to prevent them from stirring up any thought or feeling against him. . . . But if a Stronger One comes who overcomes him and takes us as his spoil, then through his Spirit we are again slaves and captives—though this is royal freedom—so that we readily will and do what he wills. Thus the human is placed between the two like a beast of burden. If God rides it, it wills and goes where God wills. . . . If Satan rides it, it wills and goes where Satan wills.[97]

The pneumatic approach is missing the point when it claims that Christians have to retake or reclaim the world from Satan's rule. In Scripture, Satan's rule is not in lieu of Christ's rule, but the powers which seek to reject Christ's rule will follow a power which seeks the same end. However, the unregenerate nature and the fallen world are seeking only a means to an end in this life, that is, to reject Christ's authority over them in these days. The fallen angels seek this also, but for the purpose that this rejection continues unto death and leads to damnation. The result is

---

96. Several chapters of Revelation depict this situation. As Brighton notes, "the beast [of the sea] represents and symbolizes every human authority and everything of the human nature that the dragon can corrupt and control and use in his warfare against the woman (the church) and her seed (individual Christians) . . . the beast from the earth represents religious tyranny. In brief, the first beast can be called the 'political beast,' while the second is the 'religious beast.'" Brighton, *Revelation*, 352, 358.

97. *LW* 33:65. In the Latin: "Si sub Deo huins saeculi sumus, sine opere et spiritu Dei veri, captivi tenemur ad ipsius voluntatem, ut Paulus ad Timotheon dicit, ut non possimus velle, nisi quod ipse velit. Ipse enim fortis est ille armatus, qui atrium suum sie servat, ut in pace siut quos possidet, ne ullum motum ant sensum contra eum concitent. . . . Si autem fortior superveniat et illo victo nos rapiat in spolium suum, rursus per spiritum eius servi et captivi sumus (quae tamen regia libertas est), ut velimus et faciamus lubentes quae ipse velit. Sic humana voluntas in medio posita est, cen inmentum, si insederit Deus, vult et vadit, quo vult Deus. . . . Si insederit Satan, vult et vadit, quo vult Satan." *WA* 18:635.

that the greed and selfishness by which the first two powers seek to reject Christ become their own destruction, to the spiteful satisfaction of the third power.

The Lutheran Confessions keep the Scriptural balance in, on the one hand, saying that Satan is the prince of the world and ruler over the sinful nature and fallen world but, on the other hand, listing out all three fallen powers to emphasize that they are still all culpable for evil and its actions, that all three fallen powers are usually working in tandem.[98]

Not only does the devil seek to destroy the eternity of persons, but he also seeks misery for humanity in the process. The fallen angels seek to pit persons and groups against one another in order to ferment hatred of the other and to inflict misery. Misery of what God loves is seen in the desire to tempt Adam and Eve to doubt God. It is in the wanton idolatry that is so often associated with the great evils of nations against others and in the oppression of peoples, as declaimed by the Old Testament prophets. It is in the friction created between Job and his wife and friends. The misery is evident in the stories of the demonized and possessed persons in the gospel accounts. That desire is on display in the depiction of the political and religious factions under Satan's sway in John's revelation. However, though the fallen angels seek and encourage such wanton destruction in creation and humanity, the reality remains that it is the other two fallen powers which enact most of the work themselves as they join in tandem with the fallen angels.

The three powers each seek to defy God's will on their own but at the same time encourage one another's defiance of God in their common interest to reject the authority of Jesus. The individual promotes and participates in groups which encourage the particular sins of interest or perceived advantage. The collectives seek to legitimize themselves at the expense of other competing groups by growing their numbers of participants. Individuals then point back to the collective for legitimization. Satan encourages all of this and is encouraged by the willing participation

---

98. For example, from the catechisms: SC "Lord's Prayer," 11, 18 in Kolb and Wengert, *Book of Concord*, 357–58; Also, LC Preface, 10 in Kolb and Wengert, *Book of Concord*, 381; and LC III, 2, 101 in Kolb and Wengert, *Book of Concord*, 440, 453. As Althaus notes of Luther's view: "Each of these three powers seduces men to sin and holds them captive in it; all three are opposed to God, to his word, and to faith. The effect of these powers on us cannot be completely differentiated. . . . Though the three powers are still quite distinct, all three concepts represent that unified will which surrounds us on every side and is opposed to God." Althaus, *Theology of Martin Luther*, 161.

in his work, in his intended misery of humanity. This participation of humans in the goals of the fallen angels ranges on the spectrum from ignorance to willing possession. All three of these powers intertwine in intention and action in such a way that we should recognize the three powers as all being a part of the evils of the world. Recognizing this tandem action of the fallen powers allows for a robust acknowledgement of spiritual warfare that the other approaches lack.

For example, for the social approach, a reference to fallen angels in light of egregious human evil is seen as an evasion of responsibility, the proverbial remark that "the devil made me do it." Wink insists on this when he recalls two moments of German reflection regarding World War II. The first cites an account by Gordon Rupp about Karl Barth, that during a postwar discussion among theologians about demonic influence during the war, Barth commented in frustration, "Why all this talk about demons? Why not just admit we have been political idiots?"[99] The second is at a similar meeting where a German pastor said, "You cannot understand what has happened in Germany unless you understand that we were possessed by demonic powers. I do not say this to excuse ourselves, because *we let ourselves be possessed*." To these quotes, Wink comments, "In a sense both statements are correct. The problem with both of them, however, is that they treat demons as if they were disincarnate spiritual beings in the air, rather than *the actual spirituality of Nazism*. The demonic was inseparable from its political forms."[100]

Wink is exactly wrong in his interpretation of these moments. Both comments are correct, but not for the reason Wink asserts. Barth, in his frustration, points straight to the culpability of the sinful world as the collective of unregenerate persons, that is, the fallen collective of Nazism. This is true, but it reduces the focus to political waywardness when Nazism was so much more profoundly evil in its actions and goals than being "political idiots." The German pastor in the second quote is not excusing the acts of those who participated in Nazi activities, but he is pointing out that there was more going on than a collective of persons in defiance of God's will, something beyond Wink's scope. The Nazi actions had something beyond the persons, even beyond the collective, that was driving their intensity and their depravity, the impersonal slaughter reflecting the attitude of the fallen angels toward humanity. They readily

---

99. Wink, *Unmasking the Powers*, 54.
100. Wink, *Unmasking the Powers*, 54 (emphases original).

cooperated with that demonic encouragement. Both quotes are correct in their recognition of the magnitude of harm and destruction each of the fallen powers can create. The social approach asserts that a personal demonic reality would allow the other two fallen powers to deny culpability. This is a straw man since such an attempt to defer blame would merely be a further exercise of the unregenerate nature trying to deny its sinful actions. Wink is correct in pointing out how such an attempt at victimization is itself destructive, but that does not mean the reality of the fallen angels needs to be denied. Rather, it means that all three powers must be taken seriously on their own as well as in tandem. Both the individual and the collective must be made aware of the unseen nefarious influence at work or else, if unchecked, be cajoled into horrors.

Additionally, this tandem view of the antifragile approach acknowledges the reality the pneumatic approach tries to address. That view would dismiss Barth's point and latch onto the second narrative and the mention of demonic forces, focusing on that issue as the main point of the pastor's quote. But that falls into the trap which Wink is trying to avoid, which is victimization of the perpetrator, that somehow Nazism would not have been a problem, or existed, without the fallen angels, which is incorrect. Rather, one can acknowledge both the culpability of the actor and the hidden forces which support, promote, and even celebrate such evil acts.

The antifragile approach to the fallen powers also allows Wink's broad narrative regarding social policies and institutions to be understood in the same sphere as Boyd's initial argument in his theodicy book *God at War* when he regards a singular act of evil. There, also using an event in World War II, Boyd speaks of the evil of particular Nazi soldiers who, for fun, blind a Jewish girl. Boyd comments, "Radical evil of this sort cannot be captured in abstract definitions. Indeed, 'abstractions . . . *distract* us from that immediate reality [of evil] and reduces evil to a statistic' as Jeffrey Burton Russell suggests."[101] This is a legitimate criticism of the pneumatic approach, where spiritual warfare is only about removing demonic influence from a region and not about concrete evils. It is also a criticism of the social approach, which speaks of broad issues regarding human systems and is in danger of depersonalization of the oppressor and the oppressed.[102]

---

101. Boyd, *God at War*, 34 (emphasis original).

102. This is one of Russell's points in his exploration of depictions of evil, that when evil is abstracted, it suffers depersonalization: "Six million Jews exterminated by

The antifragile approach, however, recognizes all three fallen powers at war against the reign of Christ, making room for personal, concrete evil to also be recognized. The unregenerate nature, in the midst of interaction with others and enticed by the devil can, little by little, be brought into a worldview where such individual acts of atrocious evil are seen as valid. As persons gather to encourage each other in these aberrant views, the fallen angels continue to encourage those views and actions, both individually and collectively. In this way, every person, a fallen power in one's self, is culpable and accountable. Every collective of persons in interaction with the world is held culpable and accountable. The fallen angels who urge all of these evils on with determination are recognized and held culpable and accountable as well. In the reality of life in this fallen creation, the powers working in tandem are so all-encompassing and persistent in their sins that no one comes out unscathed or unaccused or unaccountable for adding evils into the world. Such evils are a war against the reign of Christ, his will, and his authority. Their temporal fruit is, on every social level, terror, misery, oppression, and destruction.

The Antifragile Approach, Part Two: The Sword of the Spirit and the Mask of God Shape, Enact, and Deepen Christian Identity Despite the Fallen Powers

The first part of the antifragile approach to spiritual warfare recognized that the fallen powers are constantly at work and affect every part of life. What, then, is to be done? One might expect the second part of such a study to examine the manner in which God and his church react to these schemes of the fallen powers in order to curb or minimize their effects on the Christian and the church. This is the view of the subject which forms the direction of the other approaches to spiritual warfare examined earlier in this dissertation. The social justice approach seeks earthly justice against oppressive systems. The pneumatic approach seeks to win the world from Satan for Jesus. The bifurcated approach treats the devil as a separate problem from the sinful nature and the fallen world and treats them all from a stance of resisting their works in a reactionary manner.

However, the idea that God is merely reacting to evil is a misguided understanding because it puts God in a reactionary position, responding

---

the Nazis become an abstraction. It is the suffering of one Jew that you understand, and your powers to extrapolate beyond are limited" Russell, *Devil*, 21.

to the craftiness of sinful humanity or to the devil's wiles. To speak of how God reacts to the devils and sin is to put the fallen powers at advantage over God, leaning toward a kind of subtle dualism or open theism. This is untrue. Rather, Scripture clearly shows that God not only reigns but does so from a position of omnipotence and omniscience, as reviewed above. A different approach to spiritual warfare concepts is required.

An Overview of the Sword and Mask as God's Tools

We have defined spiritual warfare as the powers of the fallen creation railing against the reign of Christ because, for all of their destructive power, they are the ones who are reacting to a larger reality than themselves. The victory of Christ is already fulfilled. The fallen powers are already conquered. However, Christ, in his own inscrutable wisdom, has not yet brought about the final end to this age and enacted final judgment upon the fallen powers. This is not because he is unable do to so but because he desires to wait, acting through the means he chooses to enact his will in this age. Among those means are his working through the word of God and working behind the scenes in the Christian's life. This approach allows for an understanding of spiritual warfare which is theocentric rather than anthropocentric and yet still pertains to the daily life of the Christian in the world.

As noted before, the Holy Spirit acts not only by means of word, sacrament, and prayer (all together comprising the sword of the Spirit) to preserve, and even strengthen, the regenerated Christian in faith against the warfare of the demonic, the world, and the sinful nature, but also works through the Christian by means of vocation and Christian love (the masks of God) to bring God's recreative acts upon the neighbor. This antifragile approach contends that, despite the work of the fallen powers, God works to not only sustain the Christian and the church, but redirects even the works of those fallen powers, in a hidden way, to deepen faith and to draw others to himself by his word and his acts of mercy in the midst of their evils. These two tools of God, the sword of the Spirit and the masks of God, are used by God to shape, enact, and deepen the faith of every Christian and to call others to himself. It is God's use of these tools to which the fallen powers react, attempting to thwart their effects.

The rest of this section will explore each of the tools in turn. After defining the sword of the Spirit based on its context in Ephesians, the first part examines how the Holy Spirit uses the sword of the word of God not only to create and maintain Christian faith and identity, but also to deepen it despite the work of the fallen powers. Here, life in the Spirit regarding the word and the individual in light of the fallen powers will be looked at first, followed by the public, social context of the Spirit's sword in daily Christian life. It will be shown that in the face of the sinful nature's efforts to deny Christ's reign, the Spirit uses the word of God to direct the Christian to a life of repentance and forgiveness, thus preventing the sinful nature from gaining a hold over the Christian. The Spirit's sword is also used to encourage the prayer life of the person both in petitions for the self against the temptations and disturbances of the fallen angels and the world and in intercession for the needs of the neighbor. Life in the Spirit also compels the Christian to speak God's words into their relationships and the world, whereby the Spirit enacts his work on the other, including as the conscience of the state and culture as well as instances of overt demonic activity. By this word of truth proclaimed by Christians and the larger church, the reminder of Christ's rule, and his presence, is brought to bear upon the fallen world and the demons.

The second part begins by defining the concept of the mask of God as Luther describes it. It will then examine how the Spirit compels Christian love in its reflection of Christ's love in the midst of the fallen powers. Life in the Spirit regarding the enactment of the regenerate nature is put in terms of the Lutheran third use of the law and the dynamic between God's hidden work and Christian actions. It will also look at the Christian not only as enactor of loving acts, but the dynamic at play in the reception of such acts from others. It will be shown that, in the face of the world and the sinful nature, the Christian is called to acts of love for the other. By enacting Christian love in and beyond vocational roles, God is acting to bring real love and good into the world, which by its nature thwarts the will of the fallen powers. The Christian enacts God's love in terms of God's ethical perspective, not those of the cultural milieu, for the sake of the neighbor, in and beyond vocational roles. This includes enactment of forms of social justice. It also includes the speech acts of the Christian using God's word. Within the church, Christians speak and act God's love toward one another in the bonds of faith, including the divine service and the sacraments as well as speaking and sharing God's truths with one another. Outside of the church, the Christian joins actions of Christian love with truth to power, acting as the conscience of the collectives of the world and calling it to redemption in the one who truly reigns over it.

Like separating out the sinner and the saint in a person, the separation of these tools from each other is, on an enacted level, a false separation. They are pulled apart here so that they can be examined more closely. Therefore, in the discussion of each, there will necessarily be an overlap of some concepts.

The Sword of the Spirit

Defining the Spirit's Sword

In Eph 6:10–20, Paul is creating a comparison between armor and the life of faith.[103] In his letter to the church in Ephesus, he has reminded them they are "sealed with the promised Holy Spirit, who is the guarantee of our inheritance until we acquire possession of it" (Eph 1:14). He then explains to them that faith in Christ, and the benefits that come with it, is given as a gift from God (Eph 2:8–9)[104] which results in acting in accordance with God's will (Eph 2:10).[105] The Christian is not a singularity in this gift and life, but is united with all other Christians, both Jew and Gentile (Eph 2:11—3:13). He then tells them about life in the Spirit, in this identity they have been given, both individually and corporately, when he says, "according to the riches of his glory he may grant you to be strengthened with power through the Spirit in your inner being, so that Christ may dwell in your hearts through faith—that you, being rooted and grounded in love, may have strength to comprehend, with all the saints, what is the breadth and length and height and depth, and to know the love of Christ that surpasses knowledge, that you may be filled with all the fullness of God" (Eph 3:16–19). Paul is commending them to remember who they are, who the Spirit has made them to be. But, it is also a gift that is lived out.

---

103. This comparison does not mean that the Christian is a literal soldier any more than when Paul talks about the church as an olive tree (Rom 11:24), Jesus as the head of the church, his body (Eph 4:15–16), or Jesus and the church as a married couple (Eph 5:27). Those are readily understood as metaphor and image; there are aspects of the image which get across the points Paul is making. This is true of his depiction of the armor of God. Paul is saying that there are forces which assail the Christian under whose attack the Christian should not falter but stand. He is using an image that relates.

104. Thielman, *Ephesians*, 142–43; Winger, *Ephesians*, 297.

105. Thielman, *Ephesians*, 146–47;

The Antifragile Approach

In this identity, he commends them to live in unity of purpose amid the diversity of gifts given them so that the church may be built on God's truth and wisdom and enact those gifts with love for one another (Eph 4:1-16).[106] He contrasts this gifted new life with the old life outside of faith in Christ (Eph 4:17—5:21), including examples of roles in daily life of marriage (Eph 5:22-33), children and parents (Eph 6:1-4), and slaves and masters (Eph 6:5-9).

Finally, Paul notes that while the Christian no longer sees life or acts in it like the old sinful nature before a person was saved or like the world without Christ, there is another enemy that works behind the scenes in all of this against whom the Christian also stands, but does so "strong in the Lord and the strength of his might" (Eph 6:10). If the Christian is being assailed by something unseen, the "spiritual forces of evil in the heavenly places" (Eph 6:12), then the only hope is in the promises of God, in remembering who we have been made to be and living in that identity, as the rest of the letter has emphasized.

In this imagery, Paul makes comparisons between various parts of armor and the gifts God gives to his people, the gifts of truth, righteousness, the gospel of peace, faith, and salvation (Eph 6:14-17a).[107] Then, he says in Eph 6:17b-18 to also take up, "the sword of the Spirit, which is the word of God, praying at all times in the Spirit, with all prayer and supplication." Of the parts of the armor that Paul mentions, it is only the sword as word and prayer that Paul explicitly connects to the Holy Spirit. This is the only part of the armor metaphor which could imply the action of the Christian, the other parts of the armor are gifts passively received that come with the imputed regenerate nature. But Paul explicitly connects the sword to the Holy Spirit, highlighting who is really doing the work with that sword. The Christian wields it but does so in the faith given and preserved by the Spirit and at his direction and behest. The word of God is external to the person, and prayer is not automatic. The Spirit compels the Christian by faith toward both. Though using God's word and prayer are actions of the Christian, the efficacy of them is rooted in the Holy Spirit's work.[108]

106. Thielman, *Ephesians*, 286–88.

107. All of these pieces are understood as defensive armor, but not always as gifts. As gifts: Stoeckhardt, *Commentary on Ephesians*, 259; Winger, *Ephesians*, 748–53. As armor stressed as all actively used by the Christian, see Arnold, *Ephesians: Power and Magic*, 109–23; and Wink, *Naming the Powers*, 85–88.

108. For a discussion of the term for this sword in the Greek and the debate about

The sword of the Spirit is, just as Paul says, the word of God and prayer.[109] The image of the sword of the Spirit represents the reality that the Holy Spirit acts through the word of God to bring about God's will (Isa 55:10–12). An in-depth theology of the word is beyond the scope of this work. Rather, this part will focus on some of the ways in which the Holy Spirit uses the word of God to bring the authority and blessings of Christ's reign to bear in the life of the Christian and the greater church in contrast to the efforts of the fallen powers.

The Spirit's Sword as Law and Gospel

As noted above when examining the first fallen power of the sinful nature, the Holy Spirit uses his sword to create faith in the individual. That gift includes the imputation of righteousness on a person, wherein one is no longer only a sinner but now also a saint. This regeneration before God by the Spirit should be foremost in the Christian's understanding of identity, without forgetting that the sinful nature remains and is acting against Christ's reign over the self and against the new, imputed righteousness. Before becoming a Christian, a person is a part of the fallen powers. It is when the gospel and faith in Christ arrive that the person, the new Christian, finds himself beset by the fallen powers.[110] But, as Lu-

---

it as an offensive or defensive weapon, see for example, Winger, *Ephesians*, 718–21. At the end of his review, he notes that the genitive phrase "of the Spirit" is unique in the list because it is qualitative, indicating the source of its effectiveness, rather than being appositional like the descriptions of the other the pieces of armor. See also Thielman, *Ephesians*, 429. This is in contrast to Wink, who equated the sword with the Latin *gladius*, and saw it as an indication of offensive battle tactics. Wink, *Naming the Powers*, 86.

109. There is some controversy over whether or not Paul means for prayer to be a part of the image of the sword. Winger, for example, argues against prayer being a part of this motif, but does so from a position of prayer as a separate piece of armor, not as included in Paul's idea of the sword of the Spirit, even though the section on prayer is grammatically tied to the sword of the Spirit. In the end, it appears he says this to avoid the idea of prayer as a synergistic form of work by the Christian, as used by the pneumatic approach. (Winger, *Ephesians*, 727–28).

110. This does not mean the fallen powers are at rest with the non-Christian. The self-serving nature of the first two and the spite of the third compel misery and woe throughout the world. But the Christian becomes a particular target. See part 2 of the antifragile approach on the fallen powers for more discussion of this topic.

ther quipped, "When the devil harasses us, then we know ourselves to be in good shape!"[111]

Luther can speak in this manner because he rightly recognizes what is going on. The fallen powers are real, and they are a mighty force that does not rest or parley. However, on the Christian's side is Jesus Christ, the one who has won the battle and "holds the field forever."[112] The imputed identity is a partaker of this sure defense. The Holy Spirit bears forth the fruit of that victory in the life of the Christian through the word of God, if the Christian, yet with a sinful nature, will partake of the offered gifts from God by that word. Luther emphasizes the centrality of the sword of the Spirit being a part of the Christian life in his longer preface to his Large Catechism, where, considering a lack of attention to God's word and teaching, he states:

> God solemnly enjoins us in Deuteronomy 6[:7–8] that we should meditate on his precepts while sitting, walking, standing, lying down, and rising, and should keep them as an ever-present emblem and sign before our eyes and on our hands. God certainly does not require and command this so solemnly without reason. He knows our danger and need; he knows the constant and furious attacks and assaults of the devil. Therefore, he wishes to warn, equip, and protect us with his good "armor" against their "flaming arrows," and with a good antidote against their evil infection and poison. Oh, what mad, senseless fools we are! We must ever live and dwell in the midst of such mighty enemies like the devils, and yet we would despise our weapons and armor, too lazy to examine them or give them a thought![113]

As we receive from God by his word, it affects our prayers and how we perceive the world. Within Scripture itself, prayer is emphasized and demonstrated. It contains prayers of the exemplars of the faith such as Moses, David, and Jesus, and the Lord's Prayer is given to us from Jesus. The word of God and prayer are interrelated for God's people. Kleinig notes that a life of receptivity from God intertwines life in the word and the life of prayer that corresponds to it.[114] Kleinig based this on Luther's

---

111. In Oberman, *Luther: Man between God and the Devil*, 106.
112. From the fourth verse of "A Mighty Fortress is Our God" in *LSB*, 656–57.
113. LC Preface, 14 in Kolb and Wengert, *Book of Concord*, 382.
114. Kleinig, *Grace Upon Grace*, 45.

Preface to the Wittenberg Edition of His German Writings,[115] where Luther speaks of the connection between a life of prayer (*oratio*), meditation on God's word (*meditatio*), and the daily struggles with and assaults of the fallen powers (*tentatio*). There, Luther speaks of David and the Psalms, particularly Psalm 119, where David constantly prays to God for instruction, but in the same psalm also speaks of God instructing him.[116]

As the word of God is read, recalled, heard by the Christian, or spoken by others to the Christian, the Spirit is at work.[117] One such way the Spirit uses this sword is to wield it as both law and gospel in the life of the Christian. In the classic Lutheran understanding of the three uses of the Law, the first two uses of it are manifest for curbing the amount of evil enacted by persons as well as for the indictment of sin upon the individual in self-examination.[118] The first use of the law strikes the conscience as an aid in limiting the egregiousness of sinful thoughts and actions. The second use of the law confronts persons with their sins, both the reality of their sinful, unregenerate natures that taint everything with sin, as well as the actual sins perpetrated.

Because the unregenerate and regenerate natures are, anthropocentrically, inseparable, the Christian recognizes the reality of his sins without room for a separation of the two natures in some form of split personality. The Christian even repents of what appear to be good works because original sin mars everything. Through the law revealed by God's word and by the conscience, the Christian is brought to a position of sorrow over sin. In contrast, the unregenerate nature might feel guilt or shame in conscience for evils done, and in this sense God's law applies to all persons, but the unregenerate nature does not acknowledge the gulf

---

115. Luther, "Preface to the Wittenberg Edition of Luther's German Writings," *LW* 34:283–87.

116. *LW* 34:285–86.

117. This is why memorizing Scripture is a good practice; the sword of the Spirit cannot be any closer than in one's mind.

118. The three uses of the law, as Andreae writes in the Epitome of the Formula of Concord, "The law has been given to people for three reasons: first, that through it external discipline may be maintained against the unruly and the disobedient; second, that people may be led through it to a recognition of their sins; third, after they have been reborn—since nevertheless the flesh still clings to them—that precisely because of the flesh they may have a sure guide, according to which they can orient and conduct their entire life." FC Ep VI, 1 in Kolb and Wengert, *Book of Concord*, 502.

between the self and God or the authority of Jesus over it, and so finds no need for forgiveness from God or reconciliation with him.[119]

The Spirit, through the law in its first two functions, highlights how a Christian is acting in opposition to God's will and their imputed identity in Christ. This work of the Spirit, the conviction of sin and the call to repentance by its nature, thwarts the efforts of the sinful nature and the fallen powers.

The Holy Spirit uses this moment to point the person to Jesus Christ with an urge to repentance but that is not the end of his work. For the Christian, the Holy Spirit brings not only a sorrow over sins, but the desire to turn away from those sins in accordance with one's identity in Christ. It compels the person to pray in supplication for forgiveness and the power to live more closely in accord with the new nature God gives. Such repentance brought on by the Spirit allows room for another function of the Spirit's sword, the gospel, to act. The gospel bestows the intended gifts for maintaining the regenerate nature by proclaiming to Christians the benefits of Christ's salvific work for them, particularly the forgiveness of sins given by God on account of Jesus. The gospel proclaimed to the Christian also causes remembrance of the person's identity in Christ, turning focus from the sin to the Savior. The Spirit, therefore, uses his sword to remind the Christian of the imputed identity and all the gifts which come with it in connection with Christ's salvific actions, and brings those gifts to bear in the Christian's life.

Because both the unregenerate nature and the imputed nature are continually present and inseparable in the life of the Christian, the move toward repentance and, through it, to assurance of Christ's forgiveness is ongoing. This cycle of repentance and forgiveness is both unique to the Christian and a perpetual part of the Christian's life on earth.

As Kleinig notes, this work of the word of God upon Christians is all done by the Spirit.[120] The person receives the Spirit's work through

---

119. Luther says in *Bondage of the Will*: "Scripture, however, represents man as one who is not only bound, wretched, captive, sick, and dead, but in addition to his other miseries is afflicted, through the agency of Satan his prince, with this misery of blindness, so that he believes himself to be free, happy, unfettered, able, well, and alive. For Satan knows that if men were aware of their misery, he would not be able to retain a single one of them in his kingdom, because God could not but at once pity and succour them in their acknowledged and crying wretchedness. . . . Accordingly, it is Satan's work to prevent men from recognizing their plight and to keep them presuming they can do everything they are told." *LW* 33:130.

120. This was discussed in chapter 5.

the word of God according to what the individual needs from that word for their lives, be it law or gospel. Faith and the imputed nature are not because of any inherent righteousness in the person, or in one's efforts to reach for God, or one's attempts to attain a pleasing status before God. Rather, the Spirit acts through the word to bring about faith and also brings about this Christian cycle wherein the individual is constantly made aware of sin for the purposes of enacting forgiveness on the Christian and returning the person's focus to God's manifest love for him in Jesus Christ.

This is where Luther's concept of receptivity, highlighted by Kleinig, becomes important. In contrast to the social approach, where the Christian has an unending obligation to self-reflection for the purpose of humility related to social justice, or the pneumatic approach, where a person strives to be in a right relationship with God via one's self-purification, the antifragile approach recognizes the proper focus of the Christian concerning the self finds its beginning and end with Christ, who both stands in judgment over sin and has died for all of the sins of the world. In the midst of the constant attempts by the fallen powers to sabotage the cycle of repentance and forgiveness, the Spirit compels the Christian, as a child of God, with the gift of his sword back to a life centered on supplicative prayer for the self and on God's word.

In reaction to this cyclical effort of the Holy Spirit by his sword upon the individual, the fallen powers attempt to disrupt the cycle of repentance and forgiveness. On one hand, they try to keep the Christian in the realm of the law, by such acts as tempting the Christian to indulge in sins, to promote suffering over the guilt and shame of past sins without turning to Christ with those sins, and to focus on sin to the point of despair of God's love due to such sins. On the other hand, the fallen powers also attempt to disrupt the cycle by corrupting the understanding of the gospel and forgiveness. They do this in various ways, including downplaying the significance of sin before God and the need for forgiveness, twisting the understanding of forgiveness such that sin no longer appears significant, or by the turning the gospel message into another set of laws rather than forgiveness. By corruption of the understanding of God's word, the fallen powers attempt to disrupt what God is already doing in the Christian life, like Jesus spoke about in the Parables of the Sower (Matt 13:1–9, 18–23). This assault on the cycle of repentance and forgiveness is a reaction by them to Christ's reign and the Spirit's continued work.

The Spirit's Sword Amidst the Anfechtungen

In the face of these temptations, the Spirit continues to call the Christian back to contemplation of the word of God and to prayer over the present struggles. But the cycle of repentance and forgiveness that perpetually marks the Christian life is not a kind of vicious cycle, ever retreading the same terrain. Through this process, the Holy Spirit is not only maintaining the faith against the wiles of the sinful nature and the other fallen powers but also using their efforts to strengthen the Christian's faith and deepen his identity in Christ. Despite Kleinig's focus on the individual conscience as the battleground of spiritual warfare,[121] there are more problems in the Christian life stemming from the fallen powers than the disruption of the cycle of repentance and forgiveness and a good conscience. The world persecutes faith and the devil tempts and goads the world on in its depravity and destruction, and the nature of the fallen world itself brings harm and difficulties. Luther shows that even these things are accounted for by God through the Spirit's sword. Reflecting on the relationship between meditating on Scripture, prayers to God, and suffering the assaults of the fallen powers, Luther introduces the concept of *tentatio* by observing:

> As soon as God's Word takes root and grows in you, the devil will harry you, and make a real doctor of you, and by his assaults will teach you to seek and love God's Word. I myself . . . am deeply indebted to my papists that through the devil's raging they have beaten, oppressed, and distressed me so much. That is to say, they have made a fairly good theologian of me, which I would not have become otherwise.[122]

When Luther says that the devil creates theologians by his assaults (in his example, by means of his persecutors), he is not saying that the devil does good, or that being persecuted is, in itself, good, or that temptation to sin is a positive occurrence. Rather, to clarify, he further says, "thirdly, there is *tentatio*, *Anfechtung*. This is the touchstone which teaches you not only to know and understand, but also to experience how right, how true, how sweet, how lovely, how mighty, how comforting God's Word is, wisdom beyond all wisdom."[123]

---

121. Kleinig, *Grace Upon Grace*, 223.
122. *LW* 34:287.
123. *LW* 34:286–87.

Here, he clearly calls the assaults of the fallen powers the *tentatio* and the *Anfechtung*. They cause struggles for humanity, they are an assault upon the church and the Christian. Yet, as Sánchez says, the works of the devil backfire upon him.[124] Luther not only looked at the receptivity of faith and spirituality, as Kleinig highlights,[125] but also discusses the idea that the Holy Spirit uses the works of the devil as a touchpoint for his greater work of increasing faith in the Christian.[126] Luther declares that these assaults become moments of clarity of faith for the Christian as God is working, even moments where the Christian finds the joys of faith and an increase in wisdom. Specifically, these assaults are used by God to turn Christians back to his word of law and gospel and give them the experience of the rightness and truth of his word. There is more going on in this perspective than the Spirit keeping faith alive in the face of the devil's attacks. The Spirit uses the crucible of *tentatio* to drive the Christian back to Christ with a greater sense of identity in the Savior. Luther is using words which describe growth, teaching, and an increase of wisdom and faith that is created as the Spirit leads the Christian through the turmoil of the fallen powers. In *The Freedom of a Christian* (1520), Luther writes of the perspective on the *tentatio* that the Spirit creates in the Christian by means of the word of God, observing, "What man is there whose heart, upon hearing these things, will not rejoice in its depth . . . Who would have the power to harm or frighten such a heart? If the knowledge of sin or the fear of death should break in upon it, it is ready to hope in the Lord. It does not grow afraid when it hears tidings of evil. It is not disturbed when it sees its enemies. This is so because it believes that the righteousness of Christ is its own and that its sin is not its own, but Christ's, and that all sin is swallowed up by the righteousness of Christ."[127] The imputed righteousness of Christ grants a new perspective on suffering and evil such that it points the Christian back to Christ.

In *Sculptor Spirit*, Sánchez writes of the Christian life in the Spirit in this world as a share in suffering the devil's attacks. He notes that just as Jesus was beset by the devil with temptations in the wilderness, so

---

124. Sánchez, *Pneumatología*, 59.

125. Kleinig, *Grace Upon Grace*, 12–16.

126. As noted in chapter 5, Kleinig comments on this counter-productivity of the devil's work at the beginning of his work (Kleinig, *Grace Upon Grace*, 20–22), but he leaves that idea in favor of Christian action when he discusses spiritual warfare.

127. Luther, "Freedom of a Christian (1520)," *LW* 31:357.

The Antifragile Approach

the Christian should also expect to be the object of the devil's attacks.[128] However, like Luther, he also notes how God turns these attacks on their head. God uses the devil's attacks on Christians, he says, "as a form of training so that they might grow strong and healthy to withstand further attacks, make it out alive, and finally share in God's righteousness and peace." He concludes by noting, "Through struggle and testing, the Spirit forms the saints to be Christlike, making them vigilant, strong, and resilient in the face of spiritual attacks, and shaping them to anchor their lives in the Word of God and prayer as they journey through life."[129]

This life journey has its times in deserts of trial and temptation, much like that of the Israelites in the Old Testament and of Jesus at the start of his ministry. Sánchez observes that these deserts don't have to come in the form of temptation toward some hedonistic gratification. Rather, referencing Bonhoeffer's *Creation and Fall*, he points out that temptations to walk away from Christ often come through a protracted situation, such as poverty or illness like cancer or depression. In the face of the long slog of such suffering, we are tempted to demand a sign from God (in the form of resolution to the problem) and, when it does not occur, think that God has forgotten us and then, in turn, to forget God ourselves.[130] Sánchez concludes his thoughts on temptation and suffering by noting that God is with us, turning the devil's attacks into events by which he produces resilience in his people, and that the Holy Spirit "leads those under attack to prayer, the Word of God, and the community of saints for comfort, protection, and guidance."[131] Sánchez speaks of a gifted "resilience" to the Christian, but it is really an increase in resiliency and a growth that he is describing. The person is caused to cling to Jesus more tightly and is drawn closer to him. This is not just resilience. It is the development of antifragility.

Another observation of Sánchez in the above quote notes that the Holy Spirit leads troubled Christians to the community of saints, pointing them to the communal life of Christians in God's word. The Holy Spirit's work by his sword is not done in a vacuum of an isolated Christian life, it is lived out in a social context. The Holy Spirit acts by the sword through Christians toward each other in the informal daily walk in

---

128. Sánchez, *Sculptor Spirit*, 93.
129. Sánchez, *Sculptor Spirit*, 95.
130. Sánchez, *Sculptor Spirit*, 110, 112–13.
131. Sánchez, *Sculptor Spirit*, 113.

which the "mutual conversation and consolation of the brethren"[132] takes place, and in the formal settings of the divine service and the sacraments.

The Communal Aspect of the Sword of the Spirit

This proclamatory word is also used by God through the Christian in the church as Christians use the word of God to model with each other a life of repentance and forgiveness. The Spirit also uses Christians in the world to speak as the conscience of the world and to speak the gospel truth into it. Wagner separated the word spoken to other persons from spiritual warfare, limiting the word to spoken commands against the demonic entities or words of deliverance power to remove demons from persons, even Christians, who feel like they have a demonic influence upon them. Wink, in contrast, used the proclamatory word in spiritual warfare as a call of truth to power. The bifurcated approach typically divorces the word spoken and proclaimed from issues of spiritual warfare. In the antifragile approach, however, when the fallen powers are rightly understood the need for God's word to be recognized, spoken, discussed, and applied to communal life together takes on an urgent significance.

The informal, daily, communal life in the Spirit is one that is built, as Kleinig notes, around the common life of receptivity from that Spirit through his sword. But the Spirit brings that sword to bear through the proclamatory acts of Christians toward one another, wherein that cycle of repentance and forgiveness detailed above is not only found to be between the individual and God, but between persons. The proclamation of one Christian to another of repentance for wrongs done, and words of forgiveness upon the wrongdoer, acknowledges the common identity they have in Christ. The Spirit's sword calls each of them in love to model the cycle God makes with them for one another, and reassures them, in words from one to another, that they are not defined by the fallen powers but instead by God in Christ. Counterintuitively, this act of mutual repentance and forgiveness concerning sin toward each other is used by the Spirit to increase bonds between the persons as they are made to recognize and enact their mutual identities in Christ.

The Christian, and the church, is called beyond those bonds to also interact with the world. Christians are called to proclaim the same truths of God's law into the culture and world. This is what Wink is trying to

---

132. SA III, 4 in Kolb and Wengert, *Book of Concord*, 319.

emphasize in speaking truth to power, to shame the domination systems by publicly pointing out their sins. But it is not enough to break a problem; the created void must be filled with something better. Therefore, the Christian, and the church, is called upon in the Spirit to also speak the hope of Christ into the world. It is the Spirit's sword that affects true change.[133] The Spirit acts through the word as it is used in the life of Christians and the world in this informal manner, but it also acts in a formal way for God's people in the divine service and the sacraments.

The people of God are compelled by faith to gather to receive God's gifts in the divine service.[134] There, God's word is given through the liturgy and the hymns, and there the "gospel is taught purely and the sacraments are administered rightly."[135] As the preaching and sacraments are carried out by the pastor, the Holy Spirit acts through these forms of the word to create and increase faith.[136] The law and gospel are preached and the Spirit uses those words of the preacher to act in the lives of the hearers.[137] The elements of the liturgy, the hymnody, and the prayers draw on Scripture to bring God's truths to the persons who hear, sing, pray, and confess their faith. As God gathers his people in this place, he gathers them to enact his word together. As a group, the congregation not only receives, each individually, the gifts of Jesus for faith and life, but they also enact that life together in the liturgy, including repentance and forgiveness on a communal level in the confession and absolution. This reinforces their identity as God's children, together regenerated in the salvation of Jesus. The sword of the Spirit in the liturgy acts as the service is tied to the word of God. This thwarts the devil and the fallen powers by centering the Christian constantly on Christ and his gifts. That centering is not only in the liturgy, but the sacraments the church connects to that liturgy.

---

133. Forde, *Theology Is for Proclamation*, 66–68.

134. "Here we see the origin of Luther's word for worship, *Gottesdienst*—God serving the world with His gifts of forgiveness, life, and salvation through Word and Sacrament . . . the liturgy is where God is present in Christ to save us from sin, death, and the devil." Just, *Heaven on Earth*, 23.

135. CA VII, 1 in Kolb and Wengert, *Book of Concord*, 43.

136. CA V, 2–3 in Kolb and Wengert, *Book of Concord*, 41.

137. "Preaching is nothing less than mortal combat for the conscience. The theology of the cross reveals to the hearer the full horror of the situation in which he finds himself when his conscience is attacked or tempted, and then delivers that conscience safely to faith in Christ." Toso, "Luther's Theology of the Cross," 77.

In Luther's Small Catechism, he describes baptism as "water enclosed in God's command and connected with God's Word"[138] which "brings forgiveness of sin, redeems from death and the devil, and gives eternal salvation to all who believe it."[139] Though this is enacted by the pastor or, in an emergency, another Christian, what is accomplished is not by the water or the pastor,[140] but the word of God, with which "it is a baptism, that is, a grace-filled water of life and a 'bath of the new birth in the Holy Spirit.'"[141] Baptism is a point at which the Holy Spirit uses his sword to carve the Christian out from the domain of the devil through regeneration and inserts the person into the God's kingdom in Christ. But baptism's benefits do not end there because it is a concrete event to which the Christian can look for confidence in the promises of God. Any Christian who is tempted to doubt God's love or care of them can turn to their remembrance of this event, or have others tell them about this event, to clear the conscience regarding salvation. This connection to the regenerate identity is such a strong anchor that Luther admonished his readers that Baptism "signifies that the old creature in us with all sins and evil desires is to be drowned and die through daily contrition and repentance, and on the other hand that daily a new person is to come forth and rise up to live before God in righteousness and purity forever."[142] In remembrance of the God's word of promise in baptism, the Christian is reminded of that identity given in Christ and acts in that identity by "drowning" the old nature in the promise of God, participating in the cycle produced by the sword of the Spirit that marks the Christian life.

This sounds triumphant, but Luther understood the significance of baptism as it pertains to spiritual warfare. In his *Baptismal Booklet* regarding further instruction about baptism and the rite he used for the sacrament, Luther notes, "you have to realize that it is no joke at all to take action against the devil and not only to drive him away from the little child but also to hang around the child's neck such a mighty, lifelong enemy."[143] Luther used this concept to stress the importance of raising the

138. SC "Baptism," 2 in Kolb and Wengert, *Book of Concord*, 359.

139. SC "Baptism," 6 in Kolb and Wengert, *Book of Concord*, 359.

140. Water and a pastor or other person is necessary for a baptism to happen, but the efficacy of the baptism itself lies in the word of God combined with the water, as Christ mandated (Matt 28:19).

141. SC "Baptism," 10 in Kolb and Wengert, *Book of Concord*, 359.

142. SC "Baptism," 12 in Kolb and Wengert, *Book of Concord*, 360.

143. SC "Baptismal Booklet," 3 in Kolb and Wengert, *Book of Concord*, 372.

The Antifragile Approach

child in the faith and that the parents say prayers for the child so that the child would grow up to resist the wiles of the devil.[144] Luther links this action of the word with prayer, as connected to word and sacrament, such that the priest, parents, and godparents (and for most baptisms today, the congregation) are, by prayers for the child "setting themselves against the devil with all their strength, and demonstrating that they take seriously what is no joke to the devil."[145] Luther's given rite in the booklet includes an exorcism of the child[146] (twice),[147] as well as the sponsors' renunciation of the devil,[148] because of this understanding that baptism was an event in which the child was moved from the kingdom of Satan to the kingdom of God; a true, regenerative, rebirth.[149]

In baptism, not only is a person regenerated and targeted by the fallen powers, but Luther notes how that word and prayer become communal as the pastor, the parents and sponsor, and other witnesses pledge Christian love and aid for the new Christian. The liturgy and baptism become communal acts of the Spirit's sword. This is also true of the Lord's Supper.

As early as 1519, Luther was making the connection of these sacraments in terms of the strengthening of faith it gave to the Christian, now such a target for Satan. In *The Blessed Sacrament of the Holy and True Body of Christ, and the Brotherhoods*, Luther notes that since the devil, the world, and our own flesh constantly hound the Christian, "we need the strength, support and the help of Christ and the saints" through the Supper.[150] He then points out that faith in the true presence of Christ is fought against strenuously by the devil and the sinful nature, trying to

---

144. SC "Baptismal Booklet," 3 in Kolb and Wengert, *Book of Concord*, 372.
145. SC "Baptismal Booklet," 7 in Kolb and Wengert, *Book of Concord*, 373.
146. SC "Baptismal Booklet," 11 in Kolb and Wengert, *Book of Concord*, 373.
147. SC "Baptismal Booklet," 15 in Kolb and Wengert, *Book of Concord*, 374.
148. SC "Baptismal Booklet," 20–22 in Kolb and Wengert, *Book of Concord*, 374–75.
149. SC "Baptismal Booklet," 30 in Kolb and Wengert, *Book of Concord*, 375. For an interesting account of the unique take of Luther's view of Baptism and the Spirit's work against the devil, see Burreson, "Saving Flood," 123–46.
150. Luther, "Blessed Sacrament," *LW* 35:55. One can see that Luther still held to the saints in heaven having some weight concerning earthly affairs at this point. But what he says of Christ is accurate.

cause denial of the reality of Jesus himself given[151] for the Christian to eat and drink.

Here again, in the Supper, the Christian finds the concrete consolation of salvation. As Luther declares in his Large Catechism when talking of the Supper and its connection to Jesus' words,

> With this Word you can strengthen your conscience and declare, "Let a hundred thousand devils, with all the fanatics, come forward." . . . Still I know that all the spirits and scholars put together have less wisdom than the divine Majesty has in his littlest finger. Here is Christ's word: "Take, eat, this is my body." "Drink of this, all of you, this is the New Testament in my blood."[152]

This food of God, Christ himself for his people, nourishes the new creature, giving strength in the midst of the attacks of the fallen powers.[153]

Luther emphasizes the importance of the Supper when he talks about those who claim they do not need it, noting first the attacks of the sinful nature which attempts to forget the Supper and its importance. Luther observes that the less a person feels the need for the sacrament, the more reason they need to go because they have become numb to that nature.[154] He then goes on to talk about the sacrament's relevance to life against the fallen world in a characteristic fashion:

> Look around you and see whether you are also in the world. If you do not know, ask your neighbors about it. If you are in the world, do not think that there will be any lack of sins and needs. Just begin to act as if you want to become upright and cling to the gospel, and see whether you will not acquire enemies who harm, wrong, and injure you and give you cause to sin and do wrong.[155]

He finishes by noting that the devil is also active against the Christian, "a murderer who begrudges you every hour of your life."[156] He speaks of the fallen powers in this way so to encourage the Christian to

---

151. *LW* 35:60.
152. LC V, 12–13, in Kolb and Wengert, *Book of Concord*, 468.
153. LC V, 23–27, in Kolb and Wengert, *Book of Concord*, 469.
154. LC V, 76–78, in Kolb and Wengert, *Book of Concord*, 475.
155. LC V, 79 in Kolb and Wengert, *Book of Concord*, 475.
156. LC V, 82 in Kolb and Wengert, *Book of Concord*, 475.

see just how constant the danger is and how important the Supper is for the growth of the regenerate nature and the Christian life.[157]

Like baptism and the rest of the divine service, there is a communal act of the use of the sword of the Spirit in the Supper. As the congregation gathers together to receive Christ to themselves, they come as one body to receive this gift of body and blood in the word of God. The Holy Spirit ties the bonds of Christians not only more closely to Jesus as he gives himself in this meal, but to each other by a communal participation in the Lord.[158]

The Holy Spirit is constantly acting through the word, in all of its variety, on behalf of the Christian. The fallen powers assail these actions and the Christian in an effort to nullify the Spirit's work by his sword. But the Holy Spirit does not stop working, calling Christians to Christ and to remembrance of who they are in him. He compels the Christian to prayer in response to the word and daily life. He gathers the people of God together to communally share in the word and the gifts of Christ given through word and sacrament in the divine service.

It may seem that Luther, and the antifragile approach, vacillate between sounding as if the fallen powers are overwhelming and creating an image that the Christian has great confidence in the face of the fallen powers. This is because of the nature of this warfare. On the one hand, the Christian alone, faced with the fallen powers, would soon give way, abandon faith in Christ, and resume life in the devil's thrall. But on the other hand, God's action through the word of God has the power to not only sustain the Christian in the face of the fallen powers, but also is the main means by which God shapes and deepens this Christian faith. Luther is so emphatic about the word and sacraments being an indelible part of the Christian life because the sword of the Spirit is the Christian's lifeline in Christ in the midst of the fallen powers. God in his wisdom, though, does not only keep the Christian by the sword of his Spirit, but seeks to involve the Christian in his good work in the world. This was already encountered in the divine service and the sacraments, but it is also found beyond the devotional room and the walls of the church in the daily life and situations of the Christian. There, the Christian finds more than just the *tentatio*. He also finds the opportunity to enact his vocation

---

157. LC V, 83–84 in Kolb and Wengert, *Book of Concord*, 475.
158. Just, *Heaven on Earth*, 232.

and Christian love as God continues his purpose of redemptive love in a world in desperate need of these very things.

The Masks of God

Martin Luther's Concept of a Mask of God

The move from self-understanding to attention toward the neighbor is emphasized by Luther's propositions in his *The Freedom of a Christian*, where he notes: "A Christian is a perfectly free lord of all, subject to none. A Christian is a perfectly dutiful servant of all, subject to all."[159] Toward that end, the Christian

> does not live for himself alone in this mortal body to work for it alone, but he lives also for all men on earth; rather, he lives only for others and not for himself. . . . [He] needs none of these things for his righteousness and salvation. Therefore, he should be guided in all his works by this thought and contemplate this one thing alone, that he may serve and benefit others in all that he does, considering nothing except the need and the advantage of his neighbor.[160]

The idea of Luther's that Christians are God's masks is not used by Luther in a literal or Pelagian (or semi-Pelagian) manner. In his Lectures on Deuteronomy, Luther speaks of God's masks, the *larvae Dei*, in his way:

> Even if God creates, nourishes, preserves, and governs all the sons of men, nevertheless he does not want any to be idle but gives them members with which they should bear, cherish, and govern one another, whereby God is given the occasion for creating, nourishing, and ruling. Thus the power of God hidden under the human activity is seen by faith to do all things; and the unbelieving, who see only the work of man and do not know the power of God, are deceived. So here, too, they [the men of Reuben, Gad, and Manasseh] are ordered to use arms, and yet they are forbidden to trust in arms. In the work of God they proceed with their own powers, and yet they are not presumptuous with their own power. What, then, are human powers, where faith and the Word reign, except masks of God, as it were, under which he hides and does his wonders, while

---

159. *LW* 31:344.
160. *LW* 31:364–65.

through their weakness he stirs up the proud, brave, wise, and holy against himself? And where they have collided, he soon gets rid of them, triumphs over them, and makes a show of them openly. Blessed is he whose members and arms thus serve God. Yes, if someone knows that the power and wisdom of God are of such a sort, he trusts wholly, not in the mask of God but in the Word behind the mask; and he can and does perform wonders, yes, everything, in the Lord.[161]

Here, Luther points out that the work of the person who has faith is used by God to enact his will. God chooses to act this way through persons, behind the scenes, using the efforts of men to bring his action to bear on the world. Though all the works of every person, even Christians, are still tainted by the sinful nature, God himself works and creates true good. The non-Christian and nature[162] are also masks of God, but the works God does through them are different than the ones he does through the Christian. Wingren talked about this in terms of "stations" and "vocation" saying that all persons have stations but only Christians have vocations.[163] Luther prefers to talk about the distinction in terms of faith, saying, for example:

> If I had a choice, I would select the most sordid and most rustic work of a Christian peasant or maid in preference to all the victories and triumphs of Alexander the Great, Julius Caesar, etc. Why? Because God is here, and the devil is there. This is the essential difference. The material of the works is the same, but the distinguishing characteristics and the difference are infinitely diverse.... Leah and Rachel were maids of this kind. They pastured the flocks of their father, drove them to the water, and milked the cows and goats. These works were pleasing to God. But Hannibal, Alexander, Scipio, and Cicero do not please God. ... Faith and the Word make their works important and give them the greatest worth.[164]

---

161. Luther, *Lectures on Deuteronomy*, LW 9:40–41.

162. Luther notes, "Hannibal thinks that he is conquering the Romans by reason of the great courage and the extraordinary diligence he possesses ... But these are "masks." They are only things we see. But God's control, by which governments are either strengthened or overturned, we do not see." Luther, *Lectures on Genesis, Chapters 6–14*, LW 2:343.

163. Wingren, *Luther on Vocation*, 2.

164. Luther, *Lectures on Genesis, Chapters 26–30*, LW 5:270. See also *The Bondage of the Will*, where Luther observes, "there is no middle kingdom between the Kingdom of God and the Kingdom of Satan, which are mutually and perpetually in conflict with

As God is reigning and in charge, he has regard for the works he does through the Christian and considers them to be pleasing, but the works done by the non-Christian, even if they are great in the eyes of men, are still sinful works before God, even though he still draws good from them.

Luther emphasizes that the works of Christians are the tools by which God is enacting his will toward whom the Christian encounters. Because God's action is hidden by the Christian's earthly work, the Christian is a mask of God, the perception of reality hiding a greater person, purpose, and action in the midst of the mundane. Under this Christian work, God accomplishes his truly good and perfect work. Knowing this, the Christian is encouraged to do the work given in the day simply because it is work for God, regardless of its exoticness or mundanity. As Paul says, "we are his workmanship, created in Christ Jesus for good works, which God prepared beforehand, that we should walk in them" (Eph 2:10). The Christian acts simply because it is the work of the day that is given by God and, as such, is imbued with a heavenly purpose. This interconnectedness between God's love for the world and Christian action is summed up by Luther when he concludes, "a Christian lives not in himself, but in Christ and in his neighbor. Otherwise, he is not a Christian. He lives in Christ through faith, in the neighbor through love. By faith he is caught up beyond himself into God. By love he descends beneath himself into his neighbor."[165] Therefore, whether a great person or a small person by the world's eyes, every Christian's daily work gains a sense of heavenly splendor because God is acting behind the scenes not only guiding the Christian to real acts of love for the neighbor, but also bringing true good into the world through that mask.

The Scope of God's Masks in Christian Love and Vocation

The mask of God as a concept is a more general understanding than the concept of vocation. Benjamin Mayes points out Luther's distinction between offices explicitly defined in Scripture and the other choices we

---

each other. These are facts which prove that the loftiest virtues of the heathen, the best things of the philosophers, the most excellent things in men, which in the eyes of the world certainly appear to be, as they are said to be, honorable and good, are nonetheless in the sight of God truly flesh and subservient to the kingdom of Satan; that is to say, they are impious and sacrilegious and on all counts bad." *LW* 33:227.

165. *LW* 31:371.

The Antifragile Approach

make about our lives that are done with the guidance of Scripture, but not with its mandate. He points out Luther's highlight of three religious institutes: the church, the family, and the civil government.[166] These have specific callings and functions according to God's word. These stations, or vocations, fall under the larger umbrella of Christian love, which Luther defines as those actions "in which one serves not only the three orders, but also serves every needy person in general with all kinds of benevolent deeds."[167] This greater order of Christian love is the domain of God's masks.

The distinction between Luther's understanding of biblical vocation and general Christian love is an important corrective from the popular view espoused by Wingren. He argued that all Christian works were vocation. But this led to his understanding of each person's set of holy vocations as each unique and not able to be imitated. Because of their uniqueness, the law of God did not apply to these actions but only a law of love which involved spontaneous acts of love prompted in the moment by the Holy Spirit.[168] The fundamental flaw with this approach is that it disregards the continued presence of the fallen powers. In the middle section of his book, he talks about the devil confusing the vocations of the church and the state and the persons who make up those stations. This is then expanded to every walk of life. According to this analysis, Wingren concludes that careful, prayerful discernment of the Holy Spirit's direction is needed to be sure that one is doing what is really needed in that moment and not being confused by the devil.

Wingren ends up separating the sword of the Spirit from daily life. He omits the *meditatio* from the discernment in the midst of *tentatio*. Without the external sword of the Spirit of Scripture and the truths of God, one is left to the fallen human reason, the impulsivity of emotion, and the fallen powers in an attempt to discern what is truly good in that moment. Wingren ignores those issues and argues instead for an inner calling and direction by the Holy Spirit, which leads toward the pneumatic approach regarding an inner *rhema* from God.

Instead, Luther speaks of vocations in terms of specific stations in life where Scripture speaks to them. The rest of life's decisions about career choices and other paths are left to the discretion of the Christian as

---

166. Mayes, "Luther on Vocation and Baptism," 57.
167. Mayes, "Luther on Vocation and Baptism," 57.
168. Also see chapter 5 for a critique of Wingren's approach.

bound by God's moral laws and mandates. Wingren had no use for the Lutheran third use of the law, but that aspect of the sword of the Spirit has a close intersection with the masks of God because it provides for the scope and bounds of Christian love that are needed in this age since the fallen powers still exist and wreak havoc and chaos in and around the Christian life.

The sword of the Spirit brings the Christian into repentance and forgiveness by means of the first two uses of the law and through the gospel. As the Christian is re-centered on Christ, he also grows in wisdom and understanding and more tightly clings to his Savior. As a result, his lens on the world is changed to a godly perspective. The Spirit now uses his sword to guide the Christian in his daily actions, in the third use of the law. The law here allows for the illumination of the Christian as a reminder of the range of acceptable actions for particular situations. This is needed since the fallen nature still clouds a person's judgment and reason.[169] This use of the law does not have to do with salvation, in which the Christian is passive, but with the contemplation of and concern for the neighbor which is a compulsion of the Holy Spirit. This prompting of the Spirit through the guidance of the word of God leads to action for the neighbor in their need.[170]

In his essay *The Human Face of Justice*, Sánchez writes, "the law of God, as we know it from the Decalogue, points us to the that of justice—that is to say, its content, what you must do nor not do as God demands. But the law of God does not point us to the how of justice—that is to say, to its lived forms or expressions, which are indeed manifold and depend on our particular contexts of service where actual neighbors are cared for."[171] This guidance makes Luther's view of Christian love a reality in that such actions are not limited only to works that the world sees as pious or to works of social justice. Rather, any and all things which the Christian is brought to think, speak, and act upon have parameters set by that external word of God. The guide provides the lens by which the Christian sees the actions to take in love for the neighbor, the sword of the Spirit informs and guides God's people acting as his masks.

For example, in speaking of the scriptural vocations, Luther was emphatic about the dignity of and need for vocational integrity. In a sermon

---

169. FC SD VI, 17–18 in Kolb and Wengert, *Book of Concord*, 590.

170. For more on Luther's distinction between passive and active righteousness, see Kolb and Arand, *Genius of Luther's Theology*, 21–126.

171. Sánchez, "Human Face of Justice," 118.

from November of 1530, just after returning to Wittenberg after the days of the Diet of Augsburg, Luther preached on Eph 6:10–17, particularly verses 10–12. In the sermon,[172] he relates daily vocation to the sword of the Spirit. After reminding the congregation that he had already talked about the specific stations outlined by Paul previously in Ephesians, he reminds the hearers that "we do not fight with flesh and blood, therefore, it is not enough that one preach to Christians what they should believe and do, but one must also warn them about those who are against them so that they do not lose faith."[173]

He explicitly speaks of all three fallen powers,[174] but his focus is on the devil urging the sinful nature to abandon the daily vocational office given to it. He says,

> It is not enough to know what you should believe or do, but you must also see how you stay [in your state], that the devil does not say the word to you and by a foolish mouth rid you of your office. Also, your own flesh makes you unruly and disobedient. That is why I say: See that the devil does not provide for you a foolish mouth for your rotten flesh. That is why Paul wants to say: "You know how you should believe and what you have to do, just watch that you are awake and do not forget, because you will have those who will tempt you."[175]

He uses confusion of roles in marriage and the roles between serfs and masters (from earlier in Ephesians) as examples of how Christians can be tempted to refuse and reject their vocational roles.[176] No matter what a Christian's class or station in life, as the Spirit urges the Christian to the word of God and then acts through it, the Christian overcomes the temptations of the devil to abandon vocation: "Because we find ourselves tempted who, as usual, have to argue with the devil, the world, and our flesh, a Christian must be one who can not only sit before the devil, as one sits in a strong castle, but he must also strike and overcome him. Some, who listen more [to the word], know how to defend themselves such that they drive the enemies away and go hunting them in the escape."[177] The

---

172. WA 32:141–49. All translations by this author.
173. WA 32:141.
174. WA 32:145.
175. WA 32:143–44.
176. WA 32:142–43.
177. WA 32:147–48.

practical meaning of this image is laid out by Luther toward the end of the sermon when he says, reflecting James's admonition to submit to God and, in that, to resist the devil such that he would flee (Jas 4:7), that in God and the strength of his might, the Christian is able "not only to resist the devil, but also to take away his strength."[178]

There is a powerful truth in this image and explanation of Luther. He succinctly describes how the defense of the Christian becomes, without the Christian's effort, the thwarting of the devil. When the Christian clings to the word of God for guidance in biblical vocations, it necessarily focuses the Christian back onto Christ. The *meditatio* and the *oratio* affect the perspective and actions in the midst of *tentatio*, which is suddenly no longer a threat to faith and life but a cause to cling more tightly to the promises of God. This sermon ties vocational integrity to life in God's external word, contra the conclusions of Wingren. Rather than a complete spontaneity, in the face of the fallen powers the Christian is driven by the Holy Spirit back to Christ, to identity given as child of God, and the proper boundaries such identity and service entail.

Beyond the explicit vocational calls of Scripture, the Christian has great freedom in deciding how to run life and daily interactions, but these are guided by the Spirit in a similar manner to the biblical vocations. The Spirit uses his sword to create the guide and frame for Christian integrity, and Christian love, in the world. The Christian has freedom to choose where to live, what occupation to pursue, who to marry (but no choice in honoring that marriage), and many of the day-to-day aspects of life in this world. As a result, the Christian, in many ways, chooses a social context in which God acts in a hidden way.

The Neighbor in Identity and Relation

Every Christian has a social context. That context may involve few Christians, mostly Christians or, as for most persons in Western culture, a mix of both. God works for the Christian individual by others and through that Christian for others with both the sword of the Spirit and by his masks. As the individual Christian is constantly reoriented toward Christ by the Spirit's sword, he is also, simultaneously, turned toward his neighbors to act. The Spirit causes the Christian to see the neighbor through the lens of God's love, to see neighbor in a new light. As the Christian is

---

178. WA 32:149.

turned by God toward the neighbor, the Spirit uses the law, godly wisdom, and the fruit of the Spirit to help the Christian contextualize the shape of godly, loving action for the other.

Each Christian's context can be considered a unique milieu, meaning, it is true that no person is quite the same as another and their network of persons is also not the same another person's network. Wingren took this to mean that the immediate direction of the Holy Spirit could be the only guidance. But, as we noted above, the word provides the law as a guide, a heuristic that helps the Christian understand the spectrum of acceptable responses to a given situation with a neighbor. But who is that neighbor to whom a Christian may be a mask of God?

This requires an understanding of what is meant by "neighbor." The lawyer in Luke (Luke 10:29) asks who his neighbor is to try to find justification by his own works. He found from Jesus that the neighbor for the beaten man was the one who had mercy on him (Luke 10:37). From this event, the neighbor may be defined as one who has need and crosses a person's path.

There are over seven billion people in the world. No Christian could help them all, and God does not expect one to do so. But for the person with need whose life intersects with the Christian's, there is an opportunity presented for the Christian to act out godly love toward them, and God takes that opportunity to enact his own work as well.

In one regard, it is really that simple. But in other ways, even narrowing down seven billion neighbors to relational ones presents a daunting task because of the fallen powers. Each person in need carries with them their cultural and personal differences which weigh upon the answer to their needs, sometimes even defining those needs. Each person comes with a sinful nature and is affected in various ways by a sinful world and the devil. The neighbor is not always just one person, but often a family, a group of persons, or an entire people. But the neighbor, in a singular or plural understanding, is in some interaction with the Christian (or group of Christians) whom the Spirit compels to action for the need of the other.

The concepts of Christian love and of the neighbor are abstract and flexible, but the mask of God happens in concrete actions with concrete neighbors. There is no real mask of God as an abstraction, it is the moment of God getting earthy as he acts hiddenly in the actual event of enacted Christian love to an actual neighbor.

The Neighbor and God's Mask in Spiritual Warfare

Wink's discussion of the social approach to spiritual warfare had two neighbors: the oppressors and the oppressed. Wagner's examination of spiritual warfare in the pneumatic approach also had two neighbors: those under Christ's rule and those not yet rescued from Satan's rule by Strategic-Level Spiritual Warfare. The bifurcated approach does not see the neighbor in terms of spiritual warfare except those possessed, in occultic groups, or in gross idolatry, and a second group of those who are tempted. In each of these approaches, the neighbors are seen in terms of being "other," dominating or subjugated, satanically oppressed, outside the family of the church, or excessively struggling with sins.

In one sense, the concept of "other" is inescapable; this side of the Last Day, there will always be customs, traditions, mannerisms, and perspectives which alienate others in their unfamiliarity. But from the perspective of Luther's masks of God, we find that the orientation is not the anthropocentric otherness, but is instead oriented in God's love for the world and his desire to redeem it. *In spiritual warfare, by his masks God is either loving the Christian's neighbor more deeply into their redemption or is loving the neighbor toward the gift of redemption.*[179] There is no "other" before God, in the human sense, in this life. God means it when he "desires that all be saved and come to a knowledge of the truth" (1 Tim 2:4).[180]

The fallen powers that drive against the reign of Christ push even against Christian good works because they are expressions of the redemptive reality and authority of God. They seek to suppress and minimize God's opportunities for the Christian to be a mask of God. Here, the understanding that the sword of the Spirit and the masks of God are two sides of one coin regarding God's action through the lens of spiritual

---

179. This is the understanding of the intention of the masks of God concept used for the rest of this work.

180. In "The Human Face of Justice," Sánchez speaks of a model in which the neighbor is seen as "belonging to the world God so loved" and in this redemptive view of justice that care is "a means to get a hearing for the proclamation of the gospel. Justice becomes a form, and perhaps even a preeminent form, of *praeparatio evangelica*. ... Such a model, which sees justice in evangelistic terms, has a neighbor in mind who will only hear the gospel if the church lives the gospel out in the world" (Sánchez, "Human Face of Justice," 123). This is a model "from below" of the Christian's perception of the "why" of action for the neighbor. The proposed definition in this dissertation is instead a lens "from above" of God's view of his acts of love in relation to the machinations of the fallen powers.

warfare is evident. As life in the Spirit brings the Christian identity in Christ to the fore, it also turns the Christian in godly love toward the neighbor which God purposes in relation to his redemptive acts.

In response to God's actions, the fallen powers work to suppress God's work in the individual and to create barriers for God's love toward the other. Both efforts, though, are resolved on the same purpose, which is to deny the reality of Christ's reign in the lives of persons. The reaction of the fallen powers recognizes that divorced from the word of God, the Christian will also be divorced from a right love for the world behind which God participates in the life of the Christian and the neighbor. Going the other way, if the fallen powers can foster a lack of love for the world, it leads to an insular faith that dislocates the word of God and the world, which may be used by the fallen powers to lead persons to dislocate themselves from the Spirit in an abandonment of faith via apathy.

Masks as Enacted Identity and Redemptive Gestures

When the concept of masks of God is looked at through the lens of spiritual warfare, its association with redemption takes center focus.[181] There are blessings in being a mask of God, found in the enactment of the Christian identity.

Sánchez speaks of a Eucharistic model of Christian compassion, where "just as Christ's entire cruciform life in the Spirit may be seen as a living sacrifice and pleasing worship to the Lord for the sake of the world, so also Christians are shaped by the Spirit to be living sacrifices unto the Lord for the sake of the neighbor (Rom 12). Through their faithful witness and good works, Christians spread the aroma of Christ throughout the world."[182] He goes into more detail on this idea in his later book *Sculptor Spirit*, where he similarly depicts a sacrificial model in which life in the Spirit is "an offering to God in thanksgiving for his gifts and for the sake of serving neighbors," but is also a life in which "the Spirit conforms us to Christ in his humiliation or kenosis through discipleship and witness in the world."[183]

---

181. Keep in mind that this is not necessarily the view of the Christian in the daily work of life, but is the act of God in relation to the reaction of the fallen powers.

182. Sánchez, *Receiver, Bearer, and Giver*, 234.

183. Sánchez, *Sculptor Spirit*, 115.

In both paradigms, there is a focus on the growth and participation of the Christian. The Spirit, as he notes, "conforms us to Christ," as the Christian is compelled to action for the neighbor. The Christian sees the self not primarily as a sinner but as a living sacrifice for the sake of the world, and is shaped by the Spirit accordingly. The enactment of the daily work of Christian love entrenches and deepens the imputed identity into the Christian's self-understanding, making the task of the fallen powers more difficult. The Spirit compels acts of love as part of life in him so that the Christian continues to identify with what is repeatedly done and antifragility is fostered.

The life in the Spirit which becomes the mask of God is not just of benefit to the redemption of the acting Christian regarding spiritual warfare. It also bolsters the faith of the fellow Christians who are helped and becomes an exemplar of love and service to the one not yet a Christian. In both cases, the Christian action is the tool by which God shows his love for the neighbor. While it is not possible to cover the myriad of ways God enacts his love in this hidden work of his masks, some brief examples from the perspective of spiritual warfare are in order:

Mercy and Hospitality

Luther upended the church's understanding of the purpose of mercy. On Luther's change to the concept of social welfare, Rosin notes,

> Because the relationship of faith and works was reordered . . . there was nothing to gain by giving, so the temptation to watch out for one's own salvation vanished. Those whose faith was active in love could concentrate instead on the needy. With the self-interest removed, greater emphasis would understandably fall on the needy . . . the focus moves from the given to those in need, and charity is seen as a way to deal with the neighbor's problem in this life rather than as a way to pave one's own path to eternity.[184]

In the Reformation, the purpose of mercy on the poor was no longer to help one with heavenly merits, but simply because the poor person was in need of help. This led to concepts of hospitality. Luther took Abraham as an example and model of hospitality. As one who was a sojourner himself, Abraham could relate to the plights of those who needed assistance

---

184. Rosin, "Bringing Forth Fruit," 131–32.

and gave generously to assist them. Writing about Lutheran concepts of hospitality for today's issues, such as immigration in the United States, Sánchez observed that, while Luther noted the preference toward helping fellow Christians before helping those who are not, he was also adamant about hospitality "towards all kinds of exiles suffering from various catastrophes and hardships. In Luther's language, Christians are called to imitate Abraham by exercising both 'brotherly love' toward the saints and 'general kindness' toward others."[185]

From a general perspective of God's masks, Luther's concepts of mercy and hospitality as addressed above point to a work by Christians that is done because of perceived need and opportunity to aid the neighbor in the midst of their hardship. From a spiritual warfare view, God is acting in different ways. For a Christian upon whom mercy is shown, God acts such that his promise of mercy and care is being enacted, and the Christian's trust in the promises of God is affirmed. For the non-Christian receiving mercy, God acts such that he creates an example of his mercy for all despite the appearance of the worldly situation. He exemplifies that he cares for and loves that person, calling them to himself. In both cases, God is also showing the reality of his love for his creation and his desire to act, in a hidden way, for the redemption of all.

Social Justice

Wink argues that the Powers are made good, yet fallen, but this means they are redeemable.[186] He says, "the Powers are inextricably locked into God's system, whose human face is revealed by Jesus. They are answerable to God. And that means that every subsystem in the world is, in principle, redeemable. Nothing is outside the redemptive care and transforming love of God."[187] To a degree, Wink is correct. But his rejection of the demonic as personal forces and his focus on systems together depersonalize both God and injustice, creating a definition that is difficult to reconcile with the personal reality of evil and of justice.[188]

In contrast, Sánchez argues that any kind of justice has to begin and end with a neighbor in mind. He argues, "We may say that, by giving a

---

185. Sánchez, "Church Is the House of Abraham," 33.
186. Wink, *Powers That Be*, 31.
187. Wink, *Powers That Be*, 33.
188. For more on this, see the conclusions in chapter 3.

human face to justice, the neighbor serves as a critical point of departure for holding accountable individual Christians, congregations acting as corporate citizens in their communities, and Christian social agencies in their theoretical and practical approaches to justice."[189] The neighbor serves as a lens for guidance of works of justice and mercy. There is no justice apart from justice for a particular neighbor.

For social justice, from a perspective of the antifragile approach to spiritual warfare, the fallen powers are seeking to create and inculcate selfish power in the abuser and tragedy in the abused such that the former will ignore God in its own self-absorption and the latter will despair of the reality of God's love. Life in the Spirit prompts the Christian to advocate for the welfare of the neighbor, calling out the one wronging them with the proclamatory truth of God's word. For Wink, this is action against systems. But for Luther's masks, social justice is a reality at every level of interaction in the fallen world. Further, Wink's impersonal systems are, in reality, made of persons who carry out the systemic policies. As the Christian speaks truth to power, the goal is not, in the end, only the relief of the oppressed neighbor, or a turn of policy to benevolence, but also a call to repentance and change of the persons involved in oppression. God acts behind the scenes, in the face of the fallen powers' wanton influence upon the situation, to bring the law and a call to repentance into the lives of the oppressors with the goal that they would shift their understanding of identity away from the power they wield to being a child of God in service toward those in need. God is not just looking to get the entity to change its policies but to redeem the policy makers and enforcers themselves. In other words, there is a greater drive to God's actions behind Christian actions of social justice than temporal reform and relief. He loves both the oppressed and the oppressor and drives, behind the scenes, for the redemption of both.

Not only does the antifragile view of spiritual warfare propose a more personalized reality than Wink, it also acknowledges that, in Luther's view of vocational integrity, the Christians in vocations where systemic problems are taking place have opportunity to speak to change from within the systems themselves. Whether it is problems in church, state, or home, the Christian not only has the Decalogue's guidance but also mandates from God as to the place and purpose of these offices and the vocations within them. Life in the Spirit compels the Christian to

---

189. Sánchez, "Human Face of Justice," 117.

reflect on the adherence to God's mandates to these offices and to advocate for the adjustment of them in order to align with God's stated purpose for them. Where from outside these states, the Decalogue and Christian freedom allow and guide Christian love to be enacted for the neighbor in need of social justice, the Christian also has even more guidance toward the ethic of those states which govern these key areas of life. God both guides the Christian to action and also uses the Christian as a mask of the law and a call to repentance in and beyond vocational orders, with the goal of forgiveness and regeneration for the perceived enemy as well as freedom and peace and restoration for the oppressed.

Intercession

On the connection of prayer and service, Sánchez observes, "In the rush to go to work for the neighbor, a spirituality of justice cannot forget the need for prayer. . . . As the Spirit shapes us into the likeness of Jesus, we learn to work for the needy even as we pray for the needy."[190] He is pointing out that prayer and work go hand in hand, hearkening back to Luther's central place for *oratio* in the midst of our neighbor's *tentatio*, and that, even though a Christian can only be a personal neighbor for a small number of persons and groups, he is able to serve many more in prayer.[191]

When seen from the lens of the antifragile approach to spiritual warfare, the line of sword and mask is quickly blurred. In the previous section on the sword of the Spirit, supplicative prayer for the self was examined as part of the cycle of repentance and forgiveness. Here, the same process of conversation with God occurs, also prompted by the word and circumstance, but now it is with an eye for the neighbor rather than the self. Moreover, there is not only the facet of intercessory prayer concerning those beyond the Christian's reach or as an indelible part of life in the Spirit or the power of God confirmed in clearly answered prayers for the neighbor, but it is also the place where the Christian joins the neighbor in confronting the hiddenness of God. Where the rest of the above discussion of Christians as masks of God has been noting God's

---

190. Sánchez, "Human Face of Justice," 127.

191. "We are thus encouraged to pray for neighbors who not fit into our vocations as well as for those brothers and sisters who serve them more directly." Sánchez, "Human Face of Justice," 127.

positive action toward redemption through acts of mercy and advocacy, intercessory prayer is God's mask, on the one hand, wherein he works on the one praying by forcing the acknowledgment that God is God and the Christian is standing at the great divide between the divine and the creature. But, on the other hand, he also works on the ones being prayed for, bringing consolation in the midst of their desert through the solidarity of empathy of the one praying yet without any innate power to concretely give aid.

Luther talks about how in the face of the hiddenness of God, the Christian goes to Christ for comfort, where Jesus and his mercy as mediator is revealed. The Christian clings to the promises of God in the face of God's apparent distance, but also goes to the saints to find comfort and support.[192]

In the desert of ongoing temptations, lingering illness, and other sudden or prolonged negative events where God's hand and will are veiled, the fallen powers seek to leverage the hiddenness of God to create an anger or indifference toward God in light of what is often seen as God's own apparent anger, absence, or indifference. The Christian turns in love to his neighbor and can work no work of love that can solve the problem. Physically, one can only bring some ease of burden, or simply be present. But one can also pray with the person and on their behalf. The small gestures of help and empathy exemplify solidarity with the neighbor in need, but intercessory prayer with the neighbor embodies the reality of a situation beyond human control but not beyond God. For the Christian in need, the solidarity enacted through intercessory prayer not only shows that the praying person values the welfare of the one who suffers, but God uses it also to bring quiet comfort and peace and to lead the person into further trust in God's promises, even when they do not seem evident. It is the place where Job's friends could have met Job in his suffering and helped him find his rest in the promises of God rather than rankle him with accusation and heresy. In the end, it was Job's faithful intercession by which God brought his friends closer to himself (Job 42:7–9).

For the non-Christian, the use of prayer by the helper may seem off-putting, but combined with the other efforts of mercy and hospitality where possible, God uses intercessory prayer to point the sufferer to the truth that there is a direction and greater purpose and hope to life than this world and its brokenness.

192. From Luther's treatise *Comfort When Facing Grave Temptations*, discussed in Sánchez, *Sculptor Spirit*, 103–5.

The fallen powers seek to disrupt all of the work of God behind his masks by causing those in need to despair in their need despite helps or to ignore God's hand in the help received. The fallen powers work on those in need but also work to stymie the compulsion of the Christian into action for the neighbor. There are two ways the fallen powers seek to prevent these actions: first, to hide God's mask by refusing to act. The fallen powers encourage the person to hide Christian identity and balk at action out of fear of rejection or persecution and reprisal due to faith in Christ. In this scenario, the person becomes a "hidden mask" that refuses action under which God can act. The second barrier is to become a "false mask." This occurs when the Christian sees the need of the other and is tempted by the fallen powers to abandon God's ways to reach a desired end. When the Christian adopts the tempting, but ungodly, methods, even for a perceived noble purpose, the person becomes a false mask. Ignoring or setting aside the law of God that guides and shapes Christian love, the Christian acts in whatever way seems expedient for a quick end to the situation, or to minimize damage, or for other reasons that the fallen powers argue in favor of. The Christian feels compelled to act in a manner inconsistent with their regenerate identity, convinced that it is the only way to manage a situation. God can still bring good from this, indeed, he promises to do so, but the person is no longer working as a mask of God. Instead the person is being confused by the fallen powers. The Spirit then uses his sword to call the Christian back into the cycle of repentance and forgiveness, reminded of his identity in Christ, so that he can be sent back out for service to his neighbor.

Reflections on the Antifragile Approach

In these brief glimpses at some of the masks of God in light of spiritual warfare, the one acting is strengthened in the midst of adversity because he is enacting life in the Spirit on behalf of his neighbor. The neighbor is being worked upon by God behind the scenes either to strengthen faith in himself or to draw the unbeliever toward redemption with examples of his love.

The above section on the sword and the masks of God focuses on God's actions in and through the Christian to the point that, at first, glance, it might appear that the Christian has no recourse before the fallen powers but to cling for life to Jesus. This is true. But that clinging to Jesus brings with it a great power and privilege wherein the Christian is God's instrument by which the devil is driven back as the Christian uses God's word and as the Christian acts in love for the neighbor. The Christian prayer is powerful as it is working because the Christian is in Christ. The Christian can use the word to make the devil flee because that word is Christ whose power it is to repel the devil. Because God chooses to work mediately rather than immediately, the antifragile approach to spiritual warfare recognizes the active, daily work of the Christian in the face of the fallen powers yet maintains the balance of recognizing how that work is really being accomplished.

This chapter has outlined the foundations of an antifragile approach to spiritual warfare. The social and pneumatic approaches began with an anthropocentric, "from below," look at human evil and problems to develop a doctrine of spiritual warfare. The antifragile approach began with an examination of Christ's reign and how the fallen powers fit into that reign. The fallen powers do not lie outside Christ's power and authority but do rail against it in reaction to his work of regenerating persons.

The three fallen powers are fairly familiar in Christian tradition, the sinful nature, the fallen world, and the fallen angels. However, a closer look at their narratives showed that their primary purpose was more than just defying God's will but to cause persons to reject Christ and his salvation and authority. The sinful, unregenerate nature rails against Christ's authority by trying to subdue the regenerate, imputed identity in Christ. The fallen world, defined as collectives of sinners of any size and strata of society, were also noted as collectively denying Christ's reign in assertion of the collective's own authority. That authority not only runs into issues with Christ's authority but also with any other collective that appears to be in competition with itself. While the first two powers are familiar to Lutherans from their confessional documents, the fallen angels are historically more opaque. This section provided a narrative of the fallen angels in which they were shown to deny Christ's reign out of hatred for God. The work of the fallen angels is to destroy as many persons as possible simply because God loves them, in order to hurt God. This spite is directed, then, at humanity in general but particularly at Christians and the church.

These fallen powers work in tandem with one another, making it often difficult to parse out which fallen powers are at work in any given moment. Nevertheless, some assertions were made that while the devils work to destroy, it is primarily the actions of persons which enact and concretize evils in the world. In this acknowledgement, the fallen powers are held in balance because the supernatural source is recognized and treated seriously, but is not made into a scapegoat to be blamed for human evil. Yet, human evil can be traced to often be more than a sum of the actions of sinful persons. The fallen powers work in tandem because of the common goal to refuse to acknowledge the authority of Christ, but while the first two fallen powers do so to assert their own authority in lieu of Christ, the third encourages that rebellion for the purpose of the damnation of persons.

The final section to examine the antifragile approach examined God's activity against which the fallen powers rail. The main motifs used to describe this work are the sword of the Spirit and the masks of God. The sword of the Spirit was shown to be the word of God and prayer by which the Holy Spirit works in the Christian life and in the world. By that sword, the Spirit brings persons into faith in Jesus with transformation by a regenerate nature in Christ's salvific work. He then engages the Christian in the ongoing cycle of repentance and forgiveness, acknowledging the sinful nature but also recognizing that God has redefined the Christian's identity through forgiveness and reconciliation with the person on account of Christ. The fallen powers seek to disrupt that cycle.

The section also explored the Spirit's sword in action via the proclamatory nature of the word of God as Christians speak God's truth to one another, model the cycle of repentance and forgiveness with one another, and speak God's truth into the world. It also emphasized the formal aspect of the Spirit's sword acting via the divine service and the sacraments.

At every one of these points, the fallen powers attempt to discourage, distract, and destroy faith in Christ and the Christian life. Yet, despite temptation, persecution, heresy, and the other ways the fallen powers bring the *Anfechtungen* to the Christian life, it was shown that the Holy Spirit causes these efforts to backfire, encouraging the Christian to meet these issues with a return to Jesus and his salvation and hope in his promises. The faith of the Christian is actually deepened and the person's identity in Christ is made more real to the Christian despite the efforts to subdue faith.

The final section explored the masks of God, which is the enactment of the regenerate identity toward the neighbor. The scope of being a mask of God was recognized as in its exclusivity for Christians as well as its encompassing of vocation and general Christian love. The mask of God was shown to be God working behind the scenes on the worker to deepen faith and Christian identity via the enactment of Christian life. It was also shown as working on the receiver of the Christian love, verifying God's love for them and deepening their connection to who God has made them. For the non-Christian receiver, the love shown by the Christian is used by God as a platform to reveal his own love for the person and to draw them into a position to hear the word of God and be in relation with persons of faith that they may also be redeemed. Three examples, of mercy and hospitality, social justice, and intercessory prayer, were briefly examined in light of the masks of God. In all three cases, a more robust account of spiritual warfare was outlined than could be proposed by the other approaches to spiritual warfare.

Looking back at the entire scope of the antifragile approach, God's actions stand out starkly against the stratagems of the fallen powers. The fallen powers are immense and daunting; one only has to look at the world, at the wholesale rejection of God's love among so many persons, at the destruction wrought by so many collectives, from small groups all the way to nations, to see the power they have to not only draw persons from Christ but also to inflict horrors into the world. Yet, Christians should not be daunted because the one who makes the Christian right with his blood shed on the cross is also the one who reigns and who sends his Spirit to act for his people and in the world. Indeed, as Luther composed, "Though devils all the world should fill, all eager to devour us, we tremble not, we fear no ill, they shall not overpower us . . . and take they our life, goods, fame, child, and wife, let these all be gone, our victory has been won; the kingdom ours remaineth."[193] Indeed, not only does the kingdom remain to God's people, but the more the fallen powers rail, the more the Christian identifies with the only sure thing—that God is true to his promises.

---

193. *LSB* 656:3–4.

7

Further Implications of an Antifragile Approach to Spiritual Warfare

A Short Summary of the Foregoing

The church and culture are confused regarding the character and nature of spiritual warfare. As noted in chapter 1, very few persons who have written on the subject of spiritual warfare have defined the term about which they write. There, I defined spiritual warfare as "the powers of the fallen creation railing against the reign of Christ." The fallen powers of creation mentioned were the sinful nature, the sinful world, and the fallen angels. These were described as working in tandem to try to defy God's will as it is carried out in Christ's reign.

Moreover, in our Western culture, an understanding of the supernatural in general, and of spiritual warfare in particular, is a big mess. There is a wide array of approaches and concepts of spiritual warfare, particularly concerning the nature of the fallen angels.[1] The overall perspective in Western culture is an amalgamation of folklore, paganism, Christian tradition, and entertainment media concepts. For the Western church, the boundaries were slightly narrower than in the wider culture but the attempts to address the subject of the supernatural and evil powers still varied widely.

Within Christendom, there are four main approaches to spiritual warfare. The dismissive approach was noted for its complete rejection of

---

1. A person's sinful nature and the sinful world are not normally put in connection with the fallen angels. In this way, the secular culture resembles the bifurcated approach.

any supernatural fallen power. Though it had little to offer on the subject of spiritual warfare, it also laid the foundation for the social approach to the topic.

The social approach was examined based on one of its more influential voices, Walter Wink. Like the dismissive approach, Wink rejected personal supernatural forces, including fallen angels. Instead of rejecting those scriptural references completely, though, he wrestled with them symbolically to find out what was being said about the nature of evil in the world. Wink concluded references to supernatural powers in Scripture are really symbolic myth statements addressing the reality of powers in social institutions. The culture of these institutions and the resulting manner in which they exert their power is angelic or demonic depending on if it helped or hindered the greater good of those in their purview. Wink called oppressive social systems "Domination Systems" and charged the church to expose the demonic aspects of such systems to shame them into turning their culture and action to benevolence.

Wink's conclusions created a system wherein God is apathetic toward evil and his reign is contingent upon human action. In this view, God does not address oppressive systems or act himself against evil and sin. Instead, the ideal man, the anthropological myth Jesus, is inspiration, a model for the church exemplifying how to call out oppressive systems and how to be charitable with any power obtained. This approach is inadequate. God as agent is minimized in favor of an anthropocentric view of persons acting for the liberation of others from oppressive systems. For Wink, God's rule is contingent on the Christian's ability to influence temporal social justice. Prayer is a way to ask God for help, but that help is mysterious and abstruse, and relatively of little importance. Jesus has been relegated to myth and Scripture has been reduced to a handbook for humanistic liberation theology. However, Wink's recognition of the pervasiveness of evil in social structures is impossible to ignore.

A third approach to spiritual warfare is the pneumatic view exemplified by C. Peter Wagner. In his view, the supernatural world is very much alive with personal beings, angels loyal to God or demons opposed to him. In Wagner's view, Jesus rules in heaven, but only rules those places where the truth of the gospel has free course to be shared. Jesus turned the tide of the battle between God and Satan, but the war continues. Any place that is not overtly Christian or completely open to Christian mission is under the domain of the devil and not of Jesus. For Wagner, the job of the church is to act as the army of God set to retake the world from Satan and his demonic forces. The manner in which the church is to carry out this mission is to wrest lands from the powers of evil by enacting Strategic-Level Spiritual Warfare (SLSW) against the ruling demonic powers.

SLSW involves four intertwined steps. The first is spiritual mapping of the given area to gain insight into its history of evils, along with any related supernatural information also given by the Holy Spirit. The second step is identificational repentance, praying for forgiveness on behalf of the persons of the area due to current and past sins done there. Third, these steps are combined with *rhema* from God concerning the demonic entities and God's directives for combat against them. Finally, these three are also combined with prayerwalking, in which the Christian wanders the area in question, praying for the persons there and against the spiritual bondage over the place. If the Christians or Christian groups enacting SLSW are both earnest in their work and pure before God, they will have success and that area will be taken for God.

Wagner's conclusions, like Wink, created a system in which God is apathetic toward evil and his power is contingent on human action, though in a different manner than Wink's conclusions. For Wagner, God does not address these demonic power structures or act himself against evil and sin because of divine legal constraints. Instead, the pure Christian is called upon to wrestle spiritually with demonic strongholds. This pneumatic approach of Wagner is also rejected. God as agent is minimized in favor of an anthropocentric view of the pious Christian's efforts at SLSW. The boundaries of Christ's reign are contingent upon the Christian's effectiveness. Wagner rightly recognizes the reality of the fallen angels and the call for intercessory prayer, but where Wink highlighted the concrete temporal needs of the neighbor, Wagner largely ignores those needs to focus almost exclusively on the spiritual forces of the fallen angels.

The final traditional view examined was the bifurcated approach, which is the view of most mainline denominations. It has the advantage over Wink in that it typically holds to a higher view of Scripture and to the reality of the supernatural beings while, unlike Wagner, also having something to say about the plight of persons in a sinful world. But this approach separates, or at best, severely limits, the points of contact understood between the natural and supernatural realms. Typically, the fallen angels are relegated to works of temptation into sin, to the occult, and to possession. All other aspects of life are largely treated as separate from their influence. Sinful persons and the sinful world are the main antagonists in this approach, largely separated from any influence of the fallen angels. As long as the Christian keeps strong during temptation, he is largely exempt from dealing with the devil.

The bifurcated approach is inadequate because it does not have a cohesive understanding of the connection of the fallen powers or a full narrative of their state and purpose. It has something to say about social ills but does not link them to supernatural influence. The work of the demons is relegated to tiny portions of human life. Like treating the symptoms of a disease without correcting the source, it points out places which might be problematic with the fallen powers in a person's life but does not address why those places exist or how to address them systemically, or even intimate that these issues might be connected.

While this is generally the perspective of the Lutheran church today, three contemporary, non-North American, Lutheran voices were noted who had something more to say about spiritual warfare concepts. Wingren wrote about the devil's work to confuse the vocations of civil and church governments for the purpose of defying God's will. Kleinig wrote about the centrality of God's word and prayer for a receptive life in which the person receives all help from God. Sánchez wrote about the Spirit's interaction with Jesus during the Savior's life and ministry. In addition, his depiction of the continuity of God's work from Jesus' ministry to his enthronement at his ascension is helpful for presenting a picture of how God reigns and acts today.

Sánchez also pointed out in his other works how God is not apathetic but active in the narrative concerning the fallen powers. He points out that God is completely sovereign over his creation. Though evil emerges in the world, God is not the author of it, but is able to use it in an unseen way to maintain oversight of his people in a providential way. Sánchez outlines how God uses Christians as his instruments through which he desires to act to bring his love upon the neighbor. For Sánchez, the sinful nature is the place where vocational confusion takes place, which the devil promotes in a person's life. This is a different way to speak about temptation, as enacted vocational confusion, that connects Sánchez with Wingren's concept of vocational confusion in the governments of the earthly kingdom.

The final chapter brought all of these themes together into a new approach to spiritual warfare, the antifragile approach. Working from a theocentric, "from above," beginning, it showed that the fallen powers are actually fighting in reaction against God's continued redemptive work in the world. The Holy Spirit uses the word of God to shape, enact, and deepen Christian faith in God's promises and an understanding of identity as God's child in Christ. The Christian also is compelled to act in love for the neighbor, behind which God brings true good into the world. Despite all the work of the fallen powers against God's efforts, God is able to turn their efforts into moments wherein Christians end up in a stronger position of faith and identity than before while also continuing to be instruments for God's love in the world in the myriad of ways God's creative love manifests itself.

When one takes a step back from the contemplation of the details of the antifragile approach, one can see that spiritual warfare is not an esoteric part of theology, to be put into the corner of the theological shelf, taken out to display when cultural trends show an interest. Spiritual warfare is endemic to the world and the Christian life. It permeates the Christian experience of identity in Christ and relations with the neighbor because those are places where the fallen powers are also acting in defiance of Christ. Spiritual warfare can be considered a lens through which to look at the redemptive acts of God by way of his enemies, highlighting the parts of the Christian life they explicitly target.

Building Higher on the Foundations

The subtitle of this book speaks of "building" a new account of spiritual warfare because the implications of the antifragile apporach go beyond the contemplative limits of this work. To conclude, I propose three areas where the antifragile approach to spiritual warfare can be of aid for further contemplation and dialogue: Pastoral care with regard to exorcism, concepts of ethics, and in theological discussion with fellow Christians around the globe.

Exorcism

The rite of exorcism has been sensationalized in many movies over the years, as shown in chapter 2. The surface concept of the pastor or priest confronting demonic forces in a test of wills over the soul of a person can make for a compelling, though inaccurate, narrative. The policy of control that Roman Catholicism exercises concerning the discernment of a possession, the need for an exorcism, and having a properly trained exorcist ready to perform the rite has been well documented. Persons in the framework of the pneumatic approach are trained to see demons in every problem and they argue for any person's ability to exorcise on a personal level, though as Wagner noted, it takes more pious persons to take on demons of higher rank and power. In light of the antifragile approach's view of the fallen powers, and the demons in particular, what kinds of guidelines can be considered for this particular act of pastoral care?

As noted in chapters 5 and 6, demonic possession is a biblical reality. The demon takes over a person in such a manner that the demon can speak through the person and have some degree of bodily manipulation. But they cannot just take over anyone at will. Paul tells us that the Christian is "sealed with the promised Holy Spirit" (Eph 1:13), and where the Spirit is dwelling a demon would not also dwell.[2]

If the goal of the demonic forces is to prevent faith in Jesus or remove faith in him, then there is a strategy behind the event of possession, which is to either keep the possessed person from Jesus or to use them as a tool to hinder those around them from becoming or remaining Christian. A possessed person is not a Christian, properly speaking. The person could be baptized and may have been Christian at some point in life, but is not if the demons have purchase in them. Most credible accounts I have read or encountered of demonic harassment or possession revolve around persons who are not Christian having troubles and it is a friend or family member who brings the issue to a church or a pastor.[3]

Discernment of a possession is an entire topic in itself, as noted in the second chapter. Here, I want to focus not on how to determine possession or on the rubrics of a rite of exorcism but to spend a moment to discuss what is going on in an exorcism. In Luke's account, when Jesus sailed to the Gerasenes, he got off the boat and, in this case, the possessed person came to Jesus. As consistent with the antifragile view, the demons within spoke about Jesus to damage the onlookers' view of Jesus before begging to go into the pigs. Jesus, by his own authority, demands the demons to depart and they do, killing the pigs. For the implications of the antifragile view, this is where the event becomes intriguing, because

---

2. This is specifically concerning possession. Demons tempting, haunting, and harassing Christians is still a reality outside of this particular issue.

3. As one example, most stories in Bennet's book *I Am Not Afraid* speak of, at best, a Christian/ancestor worship combination, and often just the indigenous religion before conversion, among those who emerge from cases of possession into the Christian faith.

the onlookers flee and get more persons from town who "came to Jesus and found the man from whom the demons had gone, sitting at the feet of Jesus, clothed and in his right mind" (Luke 8:35). The first observation is that the person was back to his normal physiological and mental state. Reading on, Luke also records, "the man from whom the demons had gone begged that he might be with him, but Jesus sent him away, saying, 'Return to your home, and declare how much God has done for you.' And he went away, proclaiming throughout the whole city how much Jesus had done for him" (Luke 8:38–39). The second observation is the faith that is created and shaped by the event in the former demoniac. The man wants to continue to be with Jesus but Jesus tells him instead "to be a disciple—and evangelist—in his own home area,"[4] and the man does exactly this.

What is to be learned here? For the social approach, the whole thing is a metaphor for Roman oppression and social scapegoats, as noted in chapter 3. For the pneumatic approach, the exorcism portion is the important part so that one can note how Jesus operated and copy his moves. But for the antifragile approach, the important parts are the beginning and the end. Jesus went to a gentile location across the Sea of Galilee. The man is not labeled as a Jew, so is most likely a gentile and an unbeliever who has, through some course of his life, ended up in this situation. Jesus brings his authority and presence to bear on the situation. The man is freed of the demonic bondage but, more importantly, he is brought into faith in Jesus. He is not only physiologically and mentally healed, but we find that he is now spiritually alive also with faith in Jesus, and goes on to enact his new, gifted identity.

The difficulty with exorcism is not the exorcism but the perspective on it. The battle is not between the exorcist and the demonic forces for the soul of the person, or to exorcise a territory in order to claim it again for God. God does not need the pastor to drive away demons; he is almighty and sovereign. Rather, the exorcist is a mask of God in a particular way—he is there to bring the presence of Christ's authority and power to bear for the sake of the possessed neighbor. He brings the sword of the Spirit, *oratio* and *meditatio*, into the midst of the person's *tentatio*. This is a different view of exorcism than the typical viewpoints. The challenge with exorcism is exposed at this point as an issue of faith. The person did not have faith in Jesus, or would not need exorcism. Like a person who

---

4. Just, *Luke 1:1—9:50*, 365.

keeps going back to an abuser, there is a relationship established between a fallen angel and a person such that possession happens in the first place. The final goal of an exorcism is not really to get rid of the demon(s), that is the beginning and an incidental product. The goal is faith and redemption for the one who is possessed. If the person refuses to let the Holy Spirit fill the "house swept clean" with faith in Jesus, then when the demon comes back, it will be even more entrenched than before.

For a non-Western example, consider the *Fifohazana* movement of the Malagasy Lutheran Church, which has a large arm of exorcism conducted by elders of the church called *mpiandry*.[5] One issue this movement faces is that persons who are possessed or have been possessed have been under the mistaken notion that it is the spirits of their ancestors coming over them to tell them how to gain the blessings of the family spirits, with the result that the houses of the dead were more lavish than those of the living.[6] The persons who are interacting with being possessed do not believe the entities are demons, but ancestors who care. The challenge the exorcist faces in this situation is helping persons realize the reality that faith cannot be an amalgamation of Jesus and ancestor worship. Demonic problems will remain for those who still keep an anchor in their animistic roots.[7]

The success of the exorcism, as exorcism in the moment, is fleeting. The demon has been sent away for a time. It is the witness to Christ's authority to save which the exorcism brings, the sword of the Spirit enacted, God's action and presence in the act that are really at the heart of the event. However, if the person from whom a demon is exorcised ends up rejecting the gospel pronounced to them and which acted for them, it is not that the exorcism, or the exorcist, failed. Rather, it is the fallen powers striving to keep persons away from Jesus, continually at work even in the face of such a moment of God's action in their life, bearing their influence upon their, perhaps willing, victims. This view of the process of the exorcistic activity contributes to ideas of rubrics for exorcisms and the post-exorcistic counseling for the person and others who are affected by their state.

---

5. For a discussion of this arm of the Malagasy Lutheran Church from its own perspective, see Austnaberg, *Shepherds and Demons*.

6. Bennett, *I Am Not Afraid*, 40.

7. Bennett, *I Am Not Afraid*, 21–25.

Ethics

Because one part of the antifragile approach is about the nature of a world that is fallen, and the other is about interaction in Christian love with the neighbor, aspects of ethical concerns could be considered in light of the antifragile approach to spiritual warfare. The approach gives a different perspective on concepts of neighbor and issues of human dignity and care.

Vocational integrity of state, church, and home, as well as the Decalogue's boundaries created for Christian love to be enacted, "the law of Christ,"[8] can be considered in light of the fallen powers and their work to confuse, deny, and thwart acts of Christian love under which God might work. Ethics suddenly matter simply because my neighbor matters and because of my calling to serve them as part of my enacted identity in Christ in contrast to the deceit of the fallen powers.

Moreover, there is a drive for mechanisms for ethics privately and in the public square to consider the nature and purpose of the fallen powers in the contemplation of a view of ethics. For example, what kinds of checks and considerations would corporate entities need in place to maintain a right position toward its neighbors, including those who are employed, those who are recipients of its work, those in the community of the company, and the natural world in which the edifices of the corporation are situated? From the viewpoint of spiritual warfare, the recognition that the company is comprised of sinners should foster an assumption of a need for prevention of power abuse to be put in place as part of its business ethic.

Or, as another example, incarceration practices which would be framed to see inmates as persons whom God loves, not just as criminals, and the implications of that dynamic upon the purpose of incarceration itself. What is an ethic that stares at unrepentant evil and still bears the "law of Christ" toward that person?

On a broader level, if the fallen powers are recognized in tandem and an antifragile view of the neighbor is used, what are the ethical and theological implications of war in light of God's redemptive goals for the neighbor? These questions press against the discussion of just war as well as pacifism to look at the question not from a position of God's tolerance or intolerance of violence but from a position of every human as a person for whom Christ died and who he desires to redeem yet acknowledging

---

8. See Heckel, *Lex Charitatis*, 84–93.

the reality of the fallen powers that refuse to acknowledge his authority and reign. What concepts of warfare and violence can be construed in this framework? Is it possible to have a warfare methodology that does not give in to the fallen powers on every side? The antifragile approach allows for a new lens through which to ponder Christian ethics.

Ecumenism

The majority of Christians now live south of the equator.[9] In the postcolonial cultures of the Global South, Christianity has taken different directions and been forced to contend with different issues than those predominant in the West. The result was a disparity and a disjointedness regarding the supernatural and the demonic for which missionaries like Wagner were unprepared.[10] Two of the points of departure are a worldview in which the demonic is a reality and the prevalent issues of social justice framed in Global South concepts of liberation theology. The antifragile approach offers a bridge concerning both of these issues.

Not only does the antifragile approach acknowledge the existence of the fallen angels, but it manages to maintain their ever-present reality while still subsuming them to Christ. Additionally, because the fallen powers work in tandem, it allows for room of expression regarding the origin of problems of evil in the perspective of different cultures, allowing for changes in emphasis on different fallen powers without alienating the other powers that might receive the main focus on the same issue among other cultures.

For example, among the Malagasy who participate in the practice of being possessed by ancestors, one of the purposes is for gaining blessings of prosperity from them. A Western mindset would focus on the sinful nature, because that is the most familiar fallen power in Western eyes, and downplay the demonic aspect by commenting that the people should not give in to a selfishness or greed that seeks mysterious help and secrets from the unseen. But that would both insult the people and insult their understanding of the ancestors. The Malagasy Lutheran Church rightly emphasizes the same cultural points as its people, the demonic influence

---

9. Jenkins, *Next Christendom*, 2–3.

10. A similar experience is recounted by A. Scott Moreau in his first encounter with possession while teaching in Swaziland. Moreau, *Contextualizing the Faith*, 187–88.

embedded in the culture, and then over time those who become a part of Christ's family learn new ways to approach their temporal needs. The antifragile view of the fallen powers allows for this cultural flexibility.

The antifragile approach also confirms the dignity of every Christian in every land. The Christian identity is based on the imputation of it by the Spirit on account of Christ. Every Christian is also a regenerated person whom God loves. Technology, education, cultural differences, community experience, all of the factors that become barriers to human care or consideration among Christians have no place or value in the antifragile approach, except to show the unlimited creativity of God, that amongst all the variety of cultures and situations he continues to make a people for himself and increase our faith and wisdom despite all of the efforts of the fallen powers.

One of the main questions this book asked was, "What is a Confessional Lutheran approach to spiritual warfare?" The antifragile approach to spiritual warfare connects the positive parts of the previous approaches to spiritual warfare and creates a more comprehensive view of that warfare, taking the reality of the fallen angels, temporal injustice, and the struggles of the sinful nature and putting them all together into a cohesive narrative of life in the Holy Spirit as a regenerate child of God.

The approach recognizes Christ's reign and, in light of it, has two parts, an examination of the fallen powers and their rage against Christ's reign and God's part, wherein the Holy Spirit acts upon the Christian through the various forms of God's word and compels Christian acts under which he brings true good to the neighbor. As the Spirit uses this sword and mask in the Christian life, he shapes and deepens the Christian's identity in Christ by turning the person constantly toward Christ in the word of God and prayer and by compelling the Christian to enact that identity in love toward the neighbor. In turn, the neighbor is helped with temporal needs but also pointed to the greater reality of redemption in Christ. As the fallen powers react to these works of God, they seek to separate the person from God's word and from enacting the Christian identity in love toward the neighbor, but life in the Spirit is such that those efforts are used by the Spirit to deepen faith in God's promises and to increase self-identification in those promises. The Spirit turns the Christian back to the word of God and Christ and, renewed and strengthened in his love and forgiveness, is sent back to the world with that same love and forgiveness for the world.

In the face of the strength of the fallen powers, the antifragile approach gives hope because while it does not shy away from the power of those forces, it keeps a proper perspective on them compared to the reign of Christ. As the beneficiaries of that reign, we have the daily reminder that the sum of our sins, the damage the world around us does to us, the harassment and ploys of the devil and his forces, none of these things define us. Christ does, and because we are, in his eyes, the righteous children of God, then that is how reality is defined. As John says, "See what kind of love the Father has given to us that we should be *called* the children of God—and so we *are*" (1 John 3:1).

Bibliography

Adler, Margot. *Drawing Down the Moon: Witches, Druids, Goddess-Worshippers, and Other Pagans in America Today*. Rev. ed., Boston: Beacon, 1986.
Alon, Nahi, and Haim Omer. *The Psychology of Demonization: Promoting Acceptance and Reducing Conflict*. Mahwah, NJ: Erlbaum, 2006.
Althaus, Paul. *The Theology of Martin Luther*. Translated by Robert C. Schultz. Philadelphia: Fortress, 1966.
Alves, Elizabeth. *Becoming a Prayer Warrior: A Guide to Effective and Powerful Prayer*. Ventura, CA: Regal, 1998.
Amorth, Gabriele. *An Exorcist: More Stories*. Translated by Nicoletta V. MacKenzie. San Francisco: Ignatius, 2002.
———. *An Exorcist Tells His Story*. Translated by Nicoletta V. MacKenzie. San Francisco: Ignatius, 1999.
Arnold, Clinton E. *3 Crucial Questions about Spiritual Warfare*. Grand Rapids: Baker, 1997.
———. *Ephesians: Power and Magic: The Concept of Power in Ephesians in Light of Its Historical Setting*. Cambridge: Cambridge University Press, 1989.
Arthur, Kay. *Lord, Is It Warfare? Teach Me to Stand*. Sisters, OR: Multnomah, 1991.
Aulén, Gustav. *Christus Victor: An Historical Study of the Three Main Types of the Idea of Atonement*. Translated by A. G. Herbert. London: SPCK, 1931.
Austnaberg, Hans. *Shepherds and Demons: A Study of Exorcism as Practised and Understood by Shepherds in the Malagasy Lutheran Church* New York: Peter Lang, 2008.
Baglio, Matt. *The Rite: The Making of a Modern Exorcist*. New York: Doubleday, 2009.
Barnhouse, Donald Grey. *The Invisible War: The Panorama of the Continuing Conflict Between Good and Evil*. Grand Rapids: Zondervan, 1965.
Barry, Alyson M. "A Quantitative Analysis of Reports of Dissociative Trance Experiences in the United States." PhD diss., Seattle Pacific University, 2012.
Barth, Karl. *Church Dogmatics*. Vol. 3, *The Doctrine of Creation, Part 3*. Translated by G. W. Bromiley and R. J. Ehrlich. Edinburgh: T. & T. Clark, 1961.
Basham, Don. *Deliver Us From Evil: The Story of a Man Who Dared to Explore the Censored Fourth of Christ's Ministry*. Old Tappan, NJ: Spire, 1972.
Becker, Michael. "Anmerkungen zur Dämonologie in den Patriarchentestamenten." In *Dualismus, Dämonologie und diabolische Figuren*, edited by Jörg Frey and Enno Edzard Popkes, 169–85. Tübingen: Mohr Siebeck, 2018.

Beeke, Joel. *Striving Against Satan: Knowing the Enemy—His Weakness, His Strategy, His Defeat*. Wales, UK: Bryntirion, 2006.

Beekmann, Sharon. *Enticed By the Light: The Terrifying Story of One Woman's Encounter with the New Age*. Eugene, OR: Resource, 1997.

Beilby, James K., and Paul Rhodes Eddy, eds. *Understanding Spiritual Warfare*. Grand Rapids: Baker, 2012.

Bell, Richard H. *Deliver Us From Evil: Interpreting the Redemption from the Power of Satan in New Testament Theology*. Tübingen: Mohr Siebeck, 2007.

Bennett, Robert H. *Afraid: Demon Possession and Spiritual Warfare in America*. St. Louis: Concordia, 2016.

———. *I Am Not Afraid: Demon Possession and Spiritual Warfare: True Accounts from the Lutheran Church of Madagascar*. St. Louis: Concordia, 2013.

Berkhof, Hendrickus. *Christ and the Powers*. Translated by John Howard Yoder. Scottsdale, PA: Herald, 1962.

Blatty, William Peter, dir. *The Exorcist III*. Los Angeles: Morgan Creek Entertainment, 1990.

Boff, Leonardo, and Clodovis Boff. *Introducing Liberation Theology*. Translated by Paul Burns. Maryknoll, NY: Orbis, 1987.

Bosker, Bianca. "Why Is Witchcraft on the Rise?" *The Atlantic*, March 2020. https://www.theatlantic.com/magazine/archive/2020/03/witchcraft-juliet-diaz/605518/.

Boyd, Gregory A. *God at War: The Bible and Spiritual Conflict*. Downers Grove, IL: InterVarsity, 1997.

———. "Response to David Powlison." In *Understanding Spiritual Warfare*, by James K. Beilby and Paul Rhodes Eddy, 117–22. Grand Rapids: Baker, 2012.

———. *Satan and the Problem of Evil: Constructing a Trinitarian Warfare Theodicy*. Downers Grove, IL: InterVarsity, 2001.

Brennan, J. H. *Whisperers: The Secret History of the Spirit World*. New York: Overlook Duckworth, 2013.

Brighton, Louis A. *Revelation*. Concordia Commentary. St. Louis: Concordia, 1999.

Brown, Derek R. *The God of This Age*. Tübingen: Mohr Siebeck, 2015.

Browning, Tod, dir. *Dracula*. Universal City, CA: Universal Pictures, 1931.

Bruce, F. F. *The Epistle to the Hebrews*. Grand Rapids: Eerdmans, 1964.

Bultmann, Rudolf. "The New Testament and Mythology." In *Kerygma and Myth: A Theological Debate*, edited by H. Werner Bartsch, 1–44. London: SPCK, 1953.

Burreson, Kent J. "The Saving Flood: The Medieval Origins, Historical Development, and Theological Import of the Sixteenth Century Lutheran Baptismal Rites." PhD diss., University of Notre Dame, 2002.

Byrne, Rhonda. *Hero*. New York: Atria, 2013.

———. *The Magic*. New York: Atria, 2010.

———. *The Power*. New York: Atria, 2009.

———. *The Secret*. New York: Atria, 2006.

Capra, Frank, dir. *It's a Wonderful Life*. New York: RKO Pictures, 1946.

Caro, Ernesto María. "The Importance and Urgency of Deliverance and Exorcism in the Priestly Ministry." Paper presented at a meeting of the Congress of the International Association of Exorcists, n/p, July 13, 2009

Carpenter, John, dir. *Big Trouble in Little China*. 1986. Blu-ray. Los Angeles: 20th Century Fox, 2007.

———. *Vampires*. Culver City, CA: Columbia Pictures, 1998.

Catechism of the Catholic Church. 2nd ed. Vatican City: Vatican, 1997.
Cerone, Daniel, and David S. Goyer, creators. *Constantine.* Burbank, CA: Warner Bros., 2014–15.
Clegg, Brian. *Extra Sensory: The Science and Pseudoscience of Telepathy and Other Powers of the Mind.* New York: St. Martin's, 2013.
Cole, Philip. *The Myth of Evil: Demonizing the Enemy.* Westport, CT: Praeger, 2006.
Coleman, Landon Matthew. "Principalities & Powers: A Historical and Biblical Study with Strategic Application in North American Churches." PhD diss., Southern Baptist Theological Seminary, 2010.
Commission on Theology and Church Relations. *The Charismatic Movement and Lutheran Theology.* St. Louis: The Lutheran Church—Missouri Synod, 1972.
———. *A Comparative Study of Varying Contemporary Approaches to Biblical Interpretation.* St. Louis: The Lutheran Church—Missouri Synod, 1973.
———. *Gospel and Scripture: Interrelationship of Material & Formal Principles in Lutheran Theology.* St. Louis: The Lutheran Church—Missouri Synod, 1972.
———. *Guiding Principles for the Use of a Statement of Scriptural and Confessional Principles.* St. Louis: The Lutheran Church—Missouri Synod, 1974.
———. *The Inspiration of Scripture.* St. Louis: The Lutheran Church—Missouri Synod, 1975.
———. *The Lutheran Church and the Charismatic Movement: Guidelines for Congregations and Pastors.* St. Louis: The Lutheran Church—Missouri Synod, 1977.
———. *A Lutheran Stance Toward Biblical Studies.* St. Louis: The Lutheran Church—Missouri Synod, 1966.
———. *Report on Dissent from a Statement of Scriptural and Confessional Principles.* St. Louis: The Lutheran Church—Missouri Synod, 1974.
———. *Seven Theses on Reformation Hermeneutics.* St. Louis: The Lutheran Church—Missouri Synod, 1969.
———. *Spiritual Gifts.* St. Louis: The Lutheran Church—Missouri Synod, 1994.
Committee on Worship of The Lutheran Church—Missouri Synod. *Lutheran Service Book.* St. Louis: Concordia, 2006.
Conway, Daniel. *Demonology and Devil-Lore.* New York: Holt, 1879.
Cook, Robert. "Devils and Manticores: Plundering Jung for a Plausible Demonology." In *The Unseen World: Christian Reflections on Angels, Demons, and the Heavenly Realm,* edited by Anthony N. S. Lane, 165–84. Grand Rapids: Baker, 1996.
Cornell, John, dir. *Almost an Angel.* Los Angeles: Paramount, 1990.
Cox, Harvey. *Fire from Heaven: The Rise of Pentecostal Spirituality and the Reshaping of Religion in the Twenty-first Century.* 1995. Reprint, Cambridge, MA: Da Capo, 2001.
Cruz, Joan Carroll. *Angels and Devils.* Rockford, IL: TAN, 1999.
Cuneo, Michael W. *American Exorcism: Expelling Demons from the Land of Plenty.* New York: Broadway, 2001.
Cunningham, Scott. *Wicca: A Guide for the Solitary Practitioner.* Woodbury, MN: Llewellyn, 1988.
Dawn, Marva J. *Powers, Weakness, and the Tabernacling of God.* Grand Rapids: Eerdmans, 2001.
Dawson, John. *Healing America's Wounds.* Grand Rapids: Baker, 1994.

De La Torre, Miguel, and Albert Hernández. *The Quest for the Historical Satan.* Minneapolis: Fortress, 2011.

DePalatis, Ray S. "An Explanation of Different Responses to a Deliverance Ministry Procedure: Possession Trance and Dissociation in a Protestant Christian Expulsion Ritual Setting" PhD diss., Capella University, 2006.

Derrickson, Scott, dir. *The Exorcism of Emily Rose.* Beverly Hills, CA: Lakeshore Entertainment, 2005.

Deterding, Paul E. *Colossians.* Concordia Commentary. St. Louis: Concordia, 2003.

Diaz, Juliet. *Witchery: Embrace the Witch Within.* Carlsbad, CA: Hay House, 2019.

Doyle, Arthur Conan. *The New Revelation.* New York: Doran, 1918.

———. *The Vital Message.* New York: Doran, 1919.

Durst, David M. "Fighting the Good Fight: Missional Use of Militant Language." PhD diss., Asbury Theological Seminary, 2010.

Eisner, Breck, dir. *The Last Witch Hunter.* Santa Monica, CA: Summit Entertainment, 2015.

Fagerberg, Holsten. *A New Look at the Lutheran Confessions: 1529–1537.* Translated by Gene J. Lund. St. Louis: Concordia, 1972.

Fearnow, Benjamin. "Number of Witches Rises Dramatically across U.S. as Millennials Reject Christianity." *Newsweek,* November 18, 2018. https://www.newsweek.com/witchcraft-wiccans-mysticism-astrology-witches-millennials-pagans-religion-1221019.

Fernando, Keith. *The Message of Spiritual Warfare: The Lord Is a Warrior! The Lord Is His Name.* Downers Grove, IL: InterVarsity, 2016.

———. "Screwtape Revisited: Demonology Western, African, and Biblical." In *The Unseen World: Christian Reflections on Angels, Demons, and the Heavenly Realm,* edited by Anthony N. S. Lane, 103–32. Grand Rapids: Baker, 1996.

Finlay, Anthony. *Demons! The Devil, Possession, and Exorcism.* London: Blandford, 1999.

Forde, Gerhard O. *Theology Is for Proclamation.* Minneapolis: Fortress, 1990.

Frei, Hans W. *The Eclipse of the Biblical Narrative: A Study in Eighteenth and Nineteenth Century Hermeneutics.* New Haven, CT: Yale University Press, 1974.

Friedkin, William, dir. *The Exorcist.* Burbank, CA: Warner Bros., 1973.

Geivett, Douglas, and Holly Pivec. *A New Apostolic Reformation? A Biblical Response to a Worldwide Movement.* Wooster, OH: Weaver, 2014.

Gibbs, Jeffrey A. *Matthew 1:1—11:1.* Concordia Commentary. St. Louis: Concordia, 2006.

———. *Matthew 21:1—28:20.* Concordia Commentary. St. Louis: Concordia, 2018.

Graebner, Theodore. *Spiritism: A Study of Its Phenomena and Religious Teachings.* St. Louis: Concordia, 1919.

Graf, Arturo. *The Story of the Devil.* 1889. Reprint, New York: MacMillan, 1931.

Gutiérrez, Gustavo. *The Theology of Liberation: History, Politics, and Salvation.* Translated and edited by Caridad Inda and John Eagleson. Rev. ed. Maryknoll, NY: Orbis, 1988.

Hackford, Taylor, dir. *The Devil's Advocate.* Hollywood: Regency Pictures, 1997.

Häfstrom, Mikael, dir. *The Rite.* Burbank, CA: New Line Cinema, 2011.

Hardy, Corin, dir. *The Nun.* Burbank, CA: Warner Bros., 2018.

Harris, Sam. *The End of Faith: Religion, Terror, and the Future of Reason.* New York: Norton, 2005.

Hawthorne, Gerald F. *The Presence and the Power: The Significance of the Holy Spirit in the Life and Ministry of Jesus*. Dallas, TX: Word, 1991.

Heckel, Johannes. *Lex Charitatis: A Juristic Disquisition on Law in the Theology of Martin Luther*. Translated by Gottfried G. Krodel. Grand Rapids: Eerdmans, 2010.

Hermann, Robert J. "What You Don't Know about Spiritual Warfare Can Hurt You." Talk recorded March 7, 2014. St. Charles, MO: St. Joseph Radio. CD-Rom. 2014.

Heston, Frasier, dir. *Needful Things*. Beverly Hills, CA: Castle Rock, 1993.

Hiebert, Paul. "Spiritual Warfare and Worldviews." *Global Missiology: Featured Articles, Special Issue*, January 2004. http://globalmissiology.org/images/stories/hiebert/hiebert_spiritual_warfare_and_worldviews.pdf.

Horsley, Richard A. "Jesus as Exorcist and Healer." The 2007–2008 Edward G. Weltin Lecture in Early Christianity, Washington University, St. Louis, February 18, 2008.

Hyams, Peter, dir. *End of Days*. Universal City, CA: Universal Pictures, 1999.

Isaacs, T. Craig. "The Possessive States Disorder: The Differentiation of Involuntary Spirit-Possession from Present Diagnostic Categories." PhD diss., The California School of Professional Psychology, 1985.

Jacobs, Cindy. *Possessing the Gates of the Enemy: A Training Manual for Militant Intercession*. Tarrytown, NY: Chosen, 1991.

Jenkins, Philip. *The New Faces of Christianity: Believing the Bible in the Global South*. New York: Oxford University Press, 2006.

———. *The Next Christendom: The Coming of Global Christianity*. New York: Oxford University Press, 2002.

John Paul II, Pope. *Catechesis on the Angels*. General Audience. August 13, 1986. http://w2.vatican.va/content/john-paul-ii/it/audiences/1986/documents/hf_jp-ii_aud_19860813.html

Just, Arthur A., Jr. *Heaven on Earth: The Gifts of Christ in the Divine Service*. St. Louis: Concordia, 2008.

———. *Luke 1:1—9:50*. Concordia Commentary St. Louis: Concordia, 1996.

———. *Luke 9:51—24:53*. Concordia Commentary. St. Louis: Concordia, 1997.

Klaus, Kenneth Richard. *Exorcism: A Viable Rite for the Twentieth Century Church*. MDiv Report. Unpublished, 1974.

Kleinig, John W. *Grace Upon Grace: Spirituality for Today*. St. Louis: Concordia, 2008.

———. "Oratio, Meditatio, Tentatio: What Makes a Theologian?" *Concordia Theological Quarterly* 66.3 (2002) 255–67.

Kreeft, Peter. *Angels (and Demons): What Do We Really Know about Them?* San Francisco: Ignatius, 1995.

Kolb, Robert. *The Christian Faith*. St. Louis: Concordia, 1993.

Kolb, Robert, and Charles P. Arand. *The Genius of Martin Luther's Theology: A Wittenberg Way of Thinking for the Contemporary Church*. Grand Rapids: Baker Academic, 2008.

Kolb, Robert, and Timothy J. Wengert, eds. *The Book of Concord: The Confessions of the Evangelical Lutheran Church*. Minneapolis: Fortress, 2000.

Kraftchick, Steven J., et al., eds. *Biblical Theology, Problems and Perspectives: Essays in Honor of J. Christiaan Beker*. Nashville: Abingdon, 1995.

Landon, Michael, creator. *Highway to Heaven*. Agoura Hills, CA: Michael Landon Productions, 1984–89.

Lane, Anthony N. S., ed. *The Unseen World: Christian Reflections on Angels, Demons, and the Heavenly Realm*. Grand Rapids: Baker, 1996.

Larson, Bob. *Larson's Book of Spiritual Warfare*. Nashville: Thomas Nelson, 1996.

Lausanne Movement. "Statement on Spiritual Warfare (1993)." Lausanne Movement. https://www.lausanne.org /content/statement/statement-on-spiritual-warfare-1993.

Lawless, Chuck, and John Franklin. *Spiritual Warfare: Biblical Truth for Victory*. Nashville: Lifeway, 2007.

Lawrence, Francis, dir. *Constantine*. Burbank, CA: Warner Bros., 2005.

Leonetti, John R, dir. *Annabelle*. Burbank, CA: Warner Bros., 2014.

Lewis, C. S. *Mere Christianity*. Rev. ed. New York: HarperCollins, 1952.

———. *The Screwtape Letters*. Rev. ed. New York: MacMillan, 1982.

Lindsell, Harold. *The World, the Flesh, and the Devil*. Washington, DC: Canon, 1973.

Lodge, Oliver. *Raymond, or Life and Death*. New York: George H. Doran, 1916.

Lovett, C. S. *Dealing with the Devil*. Baldwin Park, CA: Personal Christianity, 1967.

Luther, Martin. *Luthers Werke: Kritische Gesamtausgabe*. Vol. 32. Weimar: H. Böhlau, 1906.

———. *Luther's Works: American Edition*. Edited by Jaroslav Pelikan and Helmut T. Lehman. 56 vols. St. Louis: Concordia, 1955–86.

MacMullen, Ramsay. *Christianizing the Roman Empire A.D. 100–400*. New Haven: Yale University Press, 1984.

MacNutt, Francis. *Deliverance from Evil Spirits: A Practical Manual*. Grand Rapids: Chosen, 1995.

Marquardt, Kurt E. *Anatomy of an Explosion*. Fort Wayne, IN: Concordia Theological Seminary Press, 1988.

Masius, John, creator. *Touched by an Angel*. New York: CBS Television, 1994–2003.

Mayes, Benjamin T. G. "Luther on Vocation and Baptism: A Correction to Charismatic and Situational Ways of Discerning God's Call." *Concordia Theological Quarterly* 82.1–2 (2018) 45–64.

McCallum, Dennis. *Satan and His Kingdom: What the Bible Really Says and How It Matters to You*. Minneapolis: Bethany, 2009.

McCarter, P. K. *II Samuel*. Garden City, NY: Doubleday, 1985.

McCulley, Darrell Arthur. *The House Swept Clean: A Biblically Balanced Pattern for the Diagnosis, Exorcism, and Pastoral Care of the Victims of Demonic Possession*. Self-published, 2002.

McGavran, Donald. *Understanding Church Growth*. Grand Rapids: Eerdmans, 1969.

Miles, Jack. "The Myth of the Suppressing Church: A Comment on Walter Wink's *The Human Being*." *Cross Currents* 53.2 (2003) 293.

Miner, Steve, dir. *Warlock*. Inglewood, CA: New World Pictures, 1991.

Montgomery, John Warwick. *Principalities and Powers: A New Look at the World of the Occult*. Minneapolis: Dimension, 1975.

Moore, David W. "Three in Four Americans Believe in the Paranormal." *Gallup*, June 16, 2005. http://www.gallup.com/poll/16915/Three-Four-Americans-Believe-Paranormal.aspx

Moreau, A. Scott. *Contextualizing the Faith: A Holistic Approach*. Grand Rapids: Baker Academic, 2018.

Moreau, A. Scott, et al., eds. *Deliver Us From Evil: An Uneasy Frontier in Christian Mission*. Monrovia, CA: World Vision, 2002.

Mueller, Timothy P., ed. *Our God, Our Help in Ages Past: 150 Years of Documents, Pictures, and Other Tokens of God's Blessings upon St. John's Lutheran Congregation New Minden, Illinois*. Nashville, IL: John's Lutheran Church of New Minden, 1996.

Murphy, Ed. *The Handbook of Spiritual Warfare*. Nashville: Nelson, 1985.
Nafzger, Samuel H., ed. *Confessing the Gospel: A Lutheran Approach to Systematic Theology*. Vol. 1. St. Louis: Concordia, 2017.
Neufeld, Thomas R. Yoder. *Killing Enmity: Violence and the New Testament*. Grand Rapids: Baker Academic, 2011.
Oberman, Heiko. *Luther: Man Between God and the Devil*. New Haven, CT: Yale University Press, 1989.
Oliva, James, dir. *Justice League Dark*. Burbank, CA: Warner Bros. Animation, 2017.
Orr, John. *English Deism: Its Roots and its Fruits*. Grand Rapids: Eerdmans, 1934.
Otis, George, Jr. *The Last of the Giants*. Tarrytown, NY: Chosen, 1991.
Owen, Richard. "Chief Exorcist Father Gabriele Amorth Says Devil Is in the Vatican." *The Times*, March 11, 2010. https://www.thetimes.co.uk/article/chief-exorcist-father-gabriele-amorth-says-devil-is-in-the-vatican-x3hs22jz7gc.
Page, Sydney H. T. *Powers of Evil: A Biblical Study of Satan and Demons*. Grand Rapids: Baker, 1995.
Peck, M. Scott. *Glimpses of the Devil: A Psychologist's Personal Accounts of Possession, Exorcism, and Redemption*. New York: Free, 2005.
———. *The People of the Lie: The Hope for Healing Human Evil*. New York: Simon & Schuster, 1983.
Penn-Lewis, Jesse, and Evan Roberts. *War on the Saints*. 1912. Reprint, Dorset, England: Overcomer Literature Trust, 1988.
Pieper, Francis. *Christian Dogmatics*, Vol. 1. St. Louis: Concordia, 1950.
———. *Christian Dogmatics*, Vol. 2. St. Louis: Concordia, 1951.
———. *Christian Dogmatics*, Vol. 3. St. Louis: Concordia, 1953.
Powlison, David. *Power Encounters: Reclaiming Spiritual Warfare*. Grand Rapids: Baker, 1995.
———. "Response to Walter Wink." In *Understanding Spiritual Warfare*, by James K. Beilby and Paul Rhodes Eddy, 72–77. Grand Rapids: Baker, 2012.
Prince, Derek. *Spiritual Warfare*. Fort Lauderdale, FL: Derek Prince Ministries, 1987.
Raabe, Paul A. "Christ's Ascension and Session." *Concordia Journal* 36.4 (2019) 67–76.
Ramsey, Arthur M. *Christianity and the Supernatural*. London: Athelone, 1963.
Ristau, Harold. *My First Exorcism: What the Devil Taught a Lutheran Pastor about Counter-Cultural Spirituality*. Eugene, OR: Resource, 2016.
Robinson, Jennifer. "The Devil and the Demographic Details." *Gallup*, February 25, 2003. http://www.gallup.com/poll/7858/Devil-Demographic-Details.aspx.
Rodewyk, Adolf. *Possessed by Satan: The Church's Teaching on the Devil, Possession, and Exorcism*. Translated by Martin Ebon. Garden City, NY: Doubleday, 1975.
Rosin, Robert. "Bringing Forth Fruit: Luther on Social Welfare." In *A Cup of Cold Water: A Look at Biblical Charity*, edited by Robert Rosin and Charles P. Arand, 131–32. St, Louis: Concordia Seminary Publications, 1996.
Rosin, Robert, and Charles A. Arand, eds. *A Cup of Cold Water: A Look at Biblical Charity*. St. Louis: Concordia Seminary Publications, 1996.
Russell, Jeffrey Burton. *The Devil: Perceptions of Evil from Antiquity to Primitive Christianity*. Ithaca, NY: Cornell University Press, 1977.
———. *Lucifer: The Devil in the Middle Ages*. Ithaca, NY: Cornell University Press, 1984.
———. *Mephistopheles: The Devil in the Modern World*. Ithaca, NY: Cornell University Press, 1986.

———. *The Prince of Darkness: Radical Evil and the Power of Good in History*. Ithaca, NY: Cornell University Press, 1988.

———. *Satan: The Early Christian Tradition*. Ithaca, NY: Cornell University Press, 1981.

Sánchez M., Leopoldo A. "The Church is the House of Abraham: Reflections on Martin Luther's Teaching on Hospitality Toward Exiles." *Concordia Journal* 44.1 (2018) 23–39.

———. "Hispanic Is Not What You Think: Reimagining Hispanic Identity, Implications for an Increasingly Global Church." *Concordia Journal* 42.3 (2016) 223–35.

———. "The Human Face of Justice: Reclaiming the Neighbor in Law, Vocation, and Justice Talk." *Concordia Journal* 39.2 (2013) 117–32.

———. *Pneumatología: El Espíritu Santo y la espiritualidad de la iglesia*. St. Louis: Concordia, 2005.

———. *Receiver, Bearer, and Giver of God's Spirit: Jesus' Life in the Spirit as a Lens for Theology and Life*. Eugene, OR: Pickwick, 2015.

———. *Sculptor Spirit: Models of Sanctification from Spirit Christology*. Downers Grove, IL: InterVarsity, 2019.

———. *Teología de la Santificación: La espiritualidad del cristiano*. St. Louis: Concordia, 2013.

Sandberg, David F., dir. *Annabelle: Creation*. Burbank, CA: Warner Bros., 2017.

Schlier, Heinrich. *Principalities and Powers in the New Testament*. New York: Herder & Herder, 1961.

Schweitzer, Albert. *The Quest of the Historical Jesus*. Translated by W. Montgomery. 1906. Reprint, New York: MacMillan, 1968.

Scott, Walter. *Demonology and Witchcraft: Letters Addressed to J. G. Lockhart, Esq.* 2nd ed. 1830. Reprint, New York: Bell, 1970.

Scupoli, Lorenzo. *Unseen Warfare: The Spiritual Combat and Path to Paradise*. Edited by Nicodemus of the Holy Mountain. Revised by Theophan the Recluse. Translated by E. Kadloubovsky and G. E. H. Palmer. Rev. ed. Crestwood, NY: St. Vladimir's Seminary Press, 1987.

Silberling, Brad, dir. *City of Angels*. Burbank, CA: Warner Bros., 1993.

"Speak No Evil: Witchcraft's Popularity on the Rise in Hudson Valley." *News 12 Westchester*, August 28, 2017. http://westchester.news12.com/story/36227191/speak-no-evil-witchcrafts-popularity-on-the-rise-in-hudson-valley.

Squires, Nick. "Surge in Satanism Sparks Rise in Demand for Exorcists, Says Catholic Church." *The Telegraph*, March 30, 2011. https://www.telegraph.co.uk/news/religion/8416104/Surge-in-Satanism-sparks-rise-in-demand-for-exorcists-says-Catholic-Church.html.

Stamm, Daniel. *The Last Exorcism*. StudioCanal, 2010.

Starhawk. *The Spiral Dance: A Rebirth of the Ancient Religion of the Great Goddess, 20th Anniversary Edition*. New York: HarperCollins, 1999.

Stein, James D. *The Paranormal Equation*. New York: New Page, 2012.

Stoeckhardt, Georg. *Commentary on St. Paul's Letter to the Ephesians*. St. Louis: Concordia, 1952.

Strauss, D. F. *The Life of Jesus Critically Examined*. 1846. Reprint, London: SCM, 1973.

Stricker, Christopher. "Jesus and the Demoniacs." In *The Social Setting of Jesus and the Gospels*, edited by Wolfgang Stigman et al., 117–33. Minneapolis, MN: Fortress, 2002.

Bibliography

Taleb, Nicolas Nassim. *Antifragile: Things that Gain from Disorder*. New York: Random House, 2012.

———. *The Bed of Procrustes: Philosophical and Practical Aphorisms*. New York: Random House, 2010.

———. *The Black Swan: The Impact of the Highly Improbable*. 2nd ed. New York: Random House, 2010.

———. *Fooled by Randomness: The Hidden Role of Chance in Life and in the Markets*. 2nd ed. New York: Random House, 2004.

Targ, Russell. *The Reality of ESP: A Physicist's Proof of Psychic Abilities*. New York: Quest, 2012.

Thielman, Frank. *Ephesians*. Grand Rapids: Baker Academic, 2010.

Tolle, Eckhart. *A New Earth: Awakening to Your Life's Purpose*. New York: Penguin, 2008.

———. *The Power of Now: A Guide to Spiritual Enlightenment*. Novato, CA: New World Library, 1999.

Toso, Perry. "Luther's Theology of the Cross in Preaching and as Spiritual Warfare." In *A Reader in Pastoral Theology: Articles from Logia: A Journal of Lutheran Theology*, 77–87. Fort Wayne, IN: Concordia Theological Seminary Press, 2002.

Traegler, Rob, dir. *The Dead Files*. Season 4, episode 2, "The Beast." Aired March 15, 2013, on The Travel Channel.

Twelftree, Graham H. *In the Name of Jesus: Exorcism Among the Early Christians*. Grand Rapids: Baker Academic, 2007.

Unger, Merrill F. *Biblical Demonology: A Study of the Spiritual Forces Behind the Present World Unrest*. Wheaton: Van Kampen, 1952.

Wagner, C. Peter. *Breaking Spiritual Strongholds in Your City*. 1993. Reprint, Shippensburg, PA: Destiny Image, 2015. Kindle ed.

———. *Confronting the Powers: How the New Testament Church Experienced the Power of Strategic-Level Spiritual Warfare*. Ventura, CA: Regal, 1996.

———. *Frontiers in Mission Strategy*. Chicago: Moody, 1971.

———. *Latin American Theology: Radical or Evangelical?* Grand Rapids: Eerdmans, 1970.

———. *Leading Your Church to Growth*. Ventura: Regal, 1984.

———. *Prayer Shield: How to Intercede for Pastors, Christian Leaders and Others on the Spiritual Frontlines*. Ventura: Regal, 1992.

———. *Praying with Power: How to Pray Effectively and Hear Clearly from God*. Ventura: Regal, 1997.

———. *Spiritual Power and Church Growth: Lessons from the Amazing Growth of Pentecostal Churches in Latin America*. Rev. ed. 1973. Reprint, Altamonte Springs, FL: Strang Communications, 1986.

———. *Strategies for Church Growth*. Ventura: Regal, 1987.

———. *The Third Wave of the Holy Spirit: Encountering the Powers of Signs and Wonders*. Ann Arbor: Vine, 1988.

———. *Warfare Prayer: How to Seek God's Power and Protection in the Battle to Build His Kingdom*. Ventura: Regal, 1992.

———. *Your Spiritual Gifts Can Help Your Church Grow*. Ventura: Regal, 1979.

Wagner, C. Peter, and Rebecca Greenwood. "The Strategic-Level Deliverance Model." In *Understanding Spiritual Warfare*, by James K. Beilby and Paul Rhodes Eddy, 173–98. Grand Rapids: Baker, 2012.

Wagner, Mark. "Overcoming the Demonic Distortions of 'Cultural Themes' as a Means for Increasing the Effectiveness of Evangelistic Missions." PhD diss., Southwestern Baptist Theological Seminary, 1998.

Walther, C. F. W. *Law and Gospel: How to Read and Apply the Bible*. Translated by Christian C. Tiews. St. Louis: Concordia, 2010.

———. *Pastoral Theology*. Translated by Christian C. Tiews. St. Louis: Concordia, 2017.

Wan, James, dir. *The Conjuring*. Burbank, CA: New Line Cinema, 2013.

———. *The Conjuring 2*. Burbank, CA: New Line Cinema, 2016.

Wenders, Wim, dir. *Wings of Desire*. Basis–Film–Verlieh, 1987.

Williams, Daniel Day. *The Demonic and the Divine*. Edited by Stacy A. Evans. Minneapolis: Fortress, 1990.

Winger, Thomas M. *Ephesians*. St. Louis: Concordia, 2015.

Wingren, Gustav. *The Flight from Creation*. Minneapolis: Augsburg, 1971.

———. *The Living Word: A Theological Study of Preaching and the Church*. Eugene, OR: Wipf & Stock, 1960.

———. *Luther on Vocation*. Translated by Carl C. Rasmussen. 1957. Reprint, Evansville, IN: Ballast, 1994.

Wink, Walter. *The Bible in Human Transformation: Toward a New Paradigm for Biblical Study*. Philadelphia: Fortress, 1973.

———. "Biblical Theology and Social Ethics." In *Biblical Theology, Problems and Perspectives: Essays in Honor of J. Christiaan Beker*, edited by Steven J. Kraftchick et al., 264. Nashville: Abingdon, 1995.

———. *Engaging the Powers: Discernment and Resistance in a World of Domination*. Minneapolis: Fortress, 1992.

———. *The Human Being: Jesus and the Enigma of the Son of the Man*. Minneapolis: Fortress, 2002.

———. *Jesus and Nonviolence: A Third Way*. Minneapolis: Fortress, 2003.

———. *Naming the Powers: The Language of Power in the New Testament*. Philadelphia: Fortress, 1984.

———. *The Powers That Be: Theology for a New Millennium*. New York: Galilee Doubleday, 1999.

———. *Unmasking the Powers: The Invisible Forces that Determine Human Existence*. Philadelphia: Fortress, 1986.

———. *Violence and Nonviolence in South Africa*. Philadelphia: New Society, 1987.

———. *When the Powers Fall: Reconciliation in the Healing of Nations*. Philadelphia: Fortress, 1998.

Winker, Eldon K. *The New Age Is Lying to You*. St. Louis: Concordia, 1994.

Wright, N. T. *Jesus and the Victory of God*. Minneapolis: Fortress, 1996.

Yellin, Deena. "'We're in the Middle of a Witch Moment': Hip Witchcraft is on the Rise in the US." *USA Today*, October 28, 2021. https://www.usatoday.com/story/news/nation/2021/10/28/celtic-festival-samhain-2021-celebration-wicca-witches/6182226001/.

Yong, Amos. *In the Days of Caesar: Pentecostalism and Political Theology*. Grand Rapids: Eerdmans, 2010.

Zimmerman, Paul. *A Seminary in Crisis*. St. Louis: Concordia, 2007.

www.ingramcontent.com/pod-product-compliance
Lightning Source LLC
Chambersburg PA
CBHW070318230426
43663CB00011B/2176